The Hermeneı
Ecophilosopł

MW01295300

Chad A. Haag
Uchakkada, India
2019

Table of Contents

Dedicated to Michael Ruppert (1951-2014)

"When the energy information bubble bursts and the truth is finally known, it may be too late for our entire species to do anything about it. That will be the 'bubble' that kills all of us." — Michael Ruppert, *Confronting Collapse*

"At present all we can say is that no True Believer will make a safe recruit to the revolution unless his commitment is exclusively to the destruction of technology" — Ted Kaczynski, *Industrial Society and Its Future*

Part I
Beyond Environmentalism

"The longing for the woods, the mysterious compassion, the ineffable sense of forsakenness — it is all Faustian and only Faustian. Every one of us knows it." — Oswald Spengler, *Decline of the West*

"The question is not how many can possibly survive within the system, but what kind of existence is possible for those who do survive." — Frank Herbert, *The Ecology of Dune*

"Occasionally there is a glimmer of hope, a small improvement in a natural area [such as] a moderate decrease in emissions, a legislative step towards conservation, a new area being protected, some conference at Rio. We immediately try not to remind ourselves that in the meanwhile annihilation is marching on elsewhere. We do our best not to notice that in the end, some of these environmentalist actions are only a sanctimonious masquerade and scam." — Pentti Linkola, *Can Life Prevail?*

Chapter One
Ideological Ethnic Cleansing:
Leftist Pseudo-Environmentalism and the Ecovillage Fallacy

All You Need is Love?

"Ecology" is arguably the single most widely-abused term of our era. Ironically, it has become nearly impossible to rationally comprehend the term ecology, let alone utilize it as a source for serious change, just as the Earth is entering a phase in which it has become more important than ever before to recognize ecological crises as such. Ongoing resource depletion, environmental destruction, mass extinction, agricultural disruption, and technological overshoot literally threaten the very possibility of complex life on the planet; yet bizarrely, these crimes against Nature are being carried out by the same politically correct corporate, academic, and governmental forces which somehow claim to be filled with self-identifying "environmentalists." Paradoxically, these figures have made ecological awareness impossible precisely through excessively referencing it.

George Orwell speculated in *1984* that the system of Newspeak could cause heretical words like "honour," "justice," and "morality" to disappear from language, but it could accomplish this lexical destruction without ever needing to ban the terms outright; it would be far more efficient to just absorb them into a blanket term which would rob them of their existence precisely by providing an illusory front for their preservation. The speaking subject would then be fooled into causing the old term to vanish exactly by using the new term which seemed to contain it, though the new term was indeed the only option available in this totalitarian dystopia:

> [I]n the case of the word *free*, words which had once borne a heretical meaning were sometimes to be retained simply for the sake of convenience, but only with the undesirable

meaning purged out of them. Countless other words such as *honor, justice, morality, internationalism, democracy, science,* and *religion* had simply ceased to exist. A few blanket words covered them, and in covering them, abolished them. All words grouping themselves around the concepts of liberty and equality, for instance, were contained in the single word *crimethink,* while all words grouping themselves round the concepts of objectivity and rationalism were contained in the single word *oldthink.* Greater precision would have been dangerous.[1]

It is no exaggeration to say that "environmentalism" has devolved to the status of an Orwellian Newspeak blanket term which has blotted out genuine ecological awareness simply through providing what appears to be the only possible outlet to express it. Just as Newspeak ruled out linguistic precision for its dangers to the System, we find ourselves incapable of gaining greater precision than whatever the vague notion of "environmentalist love for the Earth" can supply.

The time has come to abandon the term "environmentalism." All too often, the term merely conjures images of elitist hypocrisy, evidenced by Democrat Party politicians and Hollywood celebrities who find that their own mansions and private jets should be exempt from the demands that everyone else cut their carbon footprint. Even their "selfless acts of sacrifice" for the cause can hardly be taken seriously, since all too often they bear an embarrassing, unacknowledged energy subsidy from the same fossil fuels they condemn. In October, 2019, Jane Fonda made the headlines when she was arrested during a climate change protest in Washington, D.C. What was left out of the media's hagiographical accounts of her "environmentalist martyrdom" was the fact that she had flown in all the way from California, basically just to have an arrest photo-op. One can only assume that in addition to the promise of sympathetic coverage in the news, a desire for all of the complementary likes and shares on social media plays a major role

---

[1] George Orwell, *1984* (New York: Signet, 1977), p. 304.

in motivating publicity stunts of this kind. The author is old enough to remember when MTV used to count down the most expensive music videos of all time; it would be interesting in our era to rank the most expensive "likes" of all time by measuring how much fossil fuel energy was wasted just to get some reactions on Facebook and mentions on cable news before the story was inevitably forgotten just a few days later.

Environmentalism's deterioration into just another politically correct token to be publicly flashed in elites' virtue signalling rituals has allowed it to be incorporated into the most absurd of contexts. Many SUV's, for example, come equipped with a little green icon which will light up when the user is driving with the greatest fuel efficiency; this light holds the laughable title of the "eco-friendly indicator." Few seem to realize that the very term "eco-friendly SUV" is a contradiction embodied in a physical medium. This is far from the only example of such stupidity, nor is it even the worst one. Data centres' gargantuan energy requirements are almost never discussed by the technophile bootlickers in the state-controlled media, but one exception occurred when a major company opened data centres near the North Pole in the upper region of Finland, to unanimous applause among the global intelligentsia. As it was situated in a naturally cold location, we were assured that slightly less energy would be required for cooling purposes. Never mind that data centres (even ones located in cold places) require truckloads of new hardware materials to be delivered on a constant basis, all of which bear enormous energy costs and entail severe environmental damage in their own right. In a 2015 *Archdruid Report* post titled "The Death of the Internet: A Pre-Mortem," John Michael Greer noted that people who have actually worked at such places will describe having to unload "pallet after pallet of brand new hard drives and other components, to replace those that will burn out the same day," as well as describing "power bills that could easily cover the electricity costs of a small city." [2] One must be reminded that the total energy cost to run these operations would remain extravagantly high even if one were to go

---

[2] John Michael Greer, "The Death of the Internet: A Pre-Mortem", in *Archdruid Report*, Vol. 9 (Chicago: Founders House, 2018), p. 129.

for the "eco-friendly option" near the North Pole. In fact, the very term "eco-friendly option" is at this point little more than a marketing gimmick which allows wealthy customers to offset their sins against the environment by buying enough indulgences from the Priesthood of Progress to restore a clean balance sheet in the public eye. Needless to say, if the "eco-friendly option" is an overpriced luxury item designed with an eye for the shopping tastes of the well to do, even the ability to pretend to care about the environment is restricted to the very same elites who damage it the most.

Even if elitist hypocrisy were not a problem, however, the term "environmentalist" is intrinsically lacking in usefulness simply on grounds of clarity. In fact, the author shall argue over the course of the present chapter that "environmentalism" does not even mean only one thing; rather, it is an ad hoc label for many different counter sense objects, all which are unintelligible outside of a historical and ecological context in which fossil fuels are burned at breakneck rates. In addition, environmentalism's dependence upon ideologies of social and political progress merely demonstrates that it is indigenous to the era of fossil fuels. The grand irony is that environmentalism cannot challenge the ecological problem of fossil fuel-based pollution because, in a very real sense, environmentalism simply *is* fossil fuels, viewed through the epistemological standard of a set of self-contradictory counter sense objects (rather than as a purified energy source). Paradoxically, environmentalism can only exist if the same pollution it claims to challenge does as well.

An additional problem with the term is that it implies that only leftists are allowed to express concern (however empty or hypocritical) over the ecological consequences of Modern Industrialism. However, there are very significant examples of thinkers who embody such concerns yet simultaneously lack any ideological common ground with leftists. The present work shall discuss the most important of these figures, including Pentti Linkola, Ted Kaczynski, John Michael Greer, David Icke, Michael Ruppert, Varg Vikernes, and John Zerzan. In fact, it is precisely because they reject the stranglehold of dogmatic leftist politics that they are freed up to contemplate ecological problems with the proper level of seriousness rather than take the easy way out by arguing in favour of electing more Democrat Party politicians. Anyone who doubts the author's scepticism towards the effectiveness of liberal political rule should simply consider whether having decades of uninterrupted Democrat Party control has made Flint, Michigan into an ecological utopia or precisely into the kind of environmental nightmare which liberal politicians pretend to be deeply invested in preventing, as Flint is ground zero for one of the worst water pollution crises in the United States, as well as countless other economic and sociological problems. San Francisco, Portland, and Los Angeles offer similarly ghastly reminders of how cities which actually achieve the fantasy of unrestricted leftist political domination quickly become faeces-splattered, needle-ridden, garbage-strewn, rat-infested cesspools which even Third World nations would feel insulted to be compared to. It is quite literally the case that medieval diseases like the bubonic plague and typhus are quietly making a comeback within the most progressive cities in the West.

Anti-left ecological thinkers remain ignored within mainstream environmentalist circles primarily because their perspectives would require leftist environmentalists to do something more difficult than to just "love Nature." Such a shift, however unpopular, is impossible to postpone any longer. Decades of dead ends and false starts have conclusively proved that "all you need is" *not* "love" if you are really serious about addressing our current ecological woes.

Although the term environmentalism has become so universalized as to be meaningless, ecophilosophy remains arguably the most underexplored territory within all of Philosophy. Even the Wikipedia article for the subject is fragmentary and contains only two short subsections and very little information of substance. It is similarly difficult to think of notable figures who are explicitly designated as "ecophilosophers." Arguably, John Zerzan is the most significant of all, yet his work remains relatively little read outside of post-left anarchy and anarcho-primitivist circles. Worse still, recent fads within academia to pay lip service to ecology have largely been restricted to materialists, such as Jane Bennett, whose

12

main interest was to continue the post-modernist assault on human subjectivity in the guise of a reverential stance towards Nature.

This lack of clarity regarding ecophilosophy is only to be expected, as the term "eco" is a transliteration from the Greek word οἶκος but this word has long since lost its usefulness for defining our relation to Nature. Originally, this Greek term was employed in the context of ecology in order to describe a living organism's relation to its environment through the metaphor of a household. In such a context, one was not an isolated individual because, as a member of the extended family, one was bound by relationships to many other people within this shared living space. In addition, it was only very recently that a household came to be seen as a leisure space suited only for eating, sleeping, and watching television. John Michael Greer has repeatedly written on the fact that for the vast majority of human history, the "household economy" was the primary location where most of the food and tangible goods were produced by the same people who would end up using them.[3]

This older view of the "household" as something like a mini-ecosystem or economy is reflected in a Socratic dialogue titled *Oeconomicus* (*Οἰκονομικός*), which provided a thorough exploration of the problems involved with running such an operation in the Ancient World.[4] In this context, a "household" was far more than just a cardboard McMansion which imports all of its food and manufactured products from outside by means of frequent SUV-trips to the mall and grocery store. Rather, the head of the household had to oversee slaves, animals, equipment, agricultural cycles, and even small-scale manufacturing procedures. In fact,

---

[3] One of the more memorable postings on this topic was his two-part series in 2008 titled "Reviving the Household Economy": "The World Outside the Market" and "The Decline and Fall of Home Economics." These can be found in the second volume of the *Archdruid Report*.

[4] Interestingly, this dialogue was not authored by Plato but by another of Socrates' students, Xenophon. It is all too often forgotten that Plato was not the only student of Socrates to have written dialogues. Historians have long suspected, in fact, that Xenophon's accounts of Socrates are more likely to accurately reflect the historical facts. Ironically, this was precisely because his dialogues are "more boring" than Plato's. Needless to say, it is for just this reason that they are far less frequently read.

Jürgen Habermas claimed in his *Structural Transformation of the Public Sphere* that prior to the rise of modern market economics in the seventeenth century, the οἶκος (household) was not merely a metaphorical symbol for the economy: it quite literally *was* the economy.[5] In our era, however, this archaic understanding of the household as a complicated ecosystem with its own productive potential which must be overseen responsibly by someone who has an understanding of how each part within the whole functions has all but completely vanished from our comprehension of the term. For most people today, "running a household" just means finding enough money to pay the mortgage each month.

In fact, these days, a "household" could just as easily refer to an uptown condo in which a middle aged yuppie hosts his teenage daughter from his first marriage every other weekend (no doubt, simply out of obligation) and then takes advantage of his proximity to the "happening night life scene" in the city the rest of the time to live an extended bachelor's lifestyle of cosmopolitan independence. Far from having to constantly live in each other's presence within the same habitat or invest labour into producing food and goods for themselves, "family members" in our era largely exist in a state of distantiated indifference from one another. The only ethical duty required of them is to have some vague sense of "good will" for one another on the very rare occasions that they remember each other at all.

At worst, the mainstream understanding of ecology simply refers to this same sense of "good will" towards the environment. In fact, one's ethical duty as an environmentalist need not go any further than smiling at the plants as one drives a gas-guzzling vehicle down an artificial highway paved through the forest; in the very worst cases, such a person might even sport a bumper sticker warning about Global Warming while doing so. It is no exaggeration to say that the meaningless politically correct gesture of "tolerance" has been extended even to the trees.

Disliked into Non-Existence

---

5 Jürgen Habermas, *The Structural Transformation of the Public Sphere* (Cambridge: MIT Press, 1991), p. 20.

The official "Priesthood of Progress" within the academic industry offers little hope, since the secular clerics of Modern Technology all too often find it satisfactory to just represent the same stereotypical view that ecology is nothing more than an attitude of "good will" towards Nature. This is particularly true within materialist circles, despite the fact that this is one of the most common academic venues in which one might hear lip service paid to "ecology." Jane Bennett's *Vibrant Matter: Towards an Ecology of Things* enjoyed 15 minutes of academic fashionableness for its attempt to join materialist reductivism with environmentalist ethics. Even Slavoj Zizek felt a need to reference it in his 2014 book *Absolute Recoil: Towards a New Foundation of Dialectical Materialism*, due to his recognition that her text offered a competing definition of (pseudo-ecological) materialist philosophy which was becoming trendy on college campuses. This book's success was somewhat surprising, since almost all of the intellectual resources that made up her argument were directly borrowed from Deleuze and Guattari in the first place. For example, she claims herself that the idea for the book came to her when she saw a dead rat mixed in with some garbage in a gutter on a filthy street in Baltimore one day; at that moment, it suddenly dawned on her that this was not at all a lifeless set of inanimate trash, as it would appear to be to the naïve viewer who lacks fluency in Postmodernist Critical Theory. Rather, even *this* was a Deleuzian "assemblage" no less vibrant than the humans such as herself who could no longer claim to be uniquely endowed with agency over against an exterior world filled with dead "stuff."

Zizek aptly responded to Bennett's argument by showing that it does not at all devalue human agency to the status of just one more example of vibrant matter among all others, as she herself would claim. Rather, she simply "reinscrib[es] subjective agency [back] into natural reality as its immanent agential principle."[6] Zizek noted that Jane Bennett embodies the same paradox as Tolkien's *Lord of the Rings,* that of a pagan universe without the pagan gods:

---

[6] Slavoj Zizek, *Absolute Recoil* (London: Verso, 2014), p. 18.

15

If, then, New Materialism can still be considered a variant of materialism, it is materialist [only] in the sense in which Tolkien's Middle-earth is materialist: as an enchanted world full of magical forces, good and evil spirits etc., but strangely *without gods*—there are no transcendent divine entities in Tolkien's universe, all magic is immanent to matter, as a spiritual power that dwells in our terrestrial world.[7]

Zizek goes on to note, however, that Bennett's pseudo-mystical insight that "all matter is magically endowed with agency" has far more to do with the New Age theory of "a deeper spiritual interconnection and unity of the universe" than any materialist stance, let alone any genuinely ecological one. This is because she fails to recognise that to engage with a truly "inhuman Other" would not at all feel like a harmonious reunion with a long lost friend; rather, this would be an "extremely traumatic" encounter without so much as the possibility of a common language of intersubjective communication to mediate it.[8]

Yet it would be incorrect even to say that Bennett's error was to over-anthropomorphize Nature by restoring an artificial channel of communicative solidarity with a dead rat and a pile of trash. Rather, for Zizek even the encounter with the *human* Other, if properly understood, is inherently traumatic. In his 2010 book *Living in the End Times,* he addressed the then-current debates over banning the Islamic Burqa from public spaces in France by noting that, above all, the Burqa challenges standard models which posit the face of the Other as the foundation of the ethical relation. The most important of these, of course, was Levinas's theory that the human face establishes the base from which the "unconditional ethical call emanates."[9] Zizek warns that Levinas's overemphasis on the human face misses the point that the face is itself the real mask which covers over the traumatic proximity of the neighbour, a

[7] Ibid.
[8] Ibid.
[9] Slavoj Zizek, *Living in the End Times* (London: Verso, 2011), p. 2.

neighbour who ultimately holds the status of a "Neighbour-Thing" rather than an alter ego:

> [T]he face is the ultimate mask that conceals the horror of the Neighbour-Thing: the face is [precisely what] makes the Neighbour *le semblable*, a fellow-man with whom we can identify and empathize.[10]

According to Zizek, it is only when we pull back the curtain of the digestible human face that we can reveal the neighbour in its terrifying alterity; contrary to Levinas, it is only if the Other *loses* his or her face that we can identify the Other as the pathological stain which resists any totalizing representation on our own part.

We might go further even than Zizek himself was willing to go and claim that Bennett's reduction of all of Nature to an intersubjective harmony is the ultimate act of covering over the Other with a presentable human face. This is doubly problematic, since for Zizek, this act of "face-ization" would provide a poor description even for our relations with other humans, let alone the shadowy realm of inhuman matter which Bennett claims to be uniquely interested in "encountering ecologically." One could hardly imagine a more unstable foundation upon which to ground the ecological ethics of the future.

In fact, Bennett's combination of ethics and ecology amounts to literal more than a vague sense that one should have "good feelings" towards the environment, simply out of the realization that it is composed of "vibrant matter" which is worthy of reverence. This is a predictable outcome of the trajectory of campus politics, since this attitude is fully consistent with the essence of leftist political engagement in general. It is laughable, for example, that we live in an era in which even those who literally consider "radical political engagement" to be "their job" will rarely find any need to engage in action beyond publicly exuding good feelings towards the trending sympathetic figure or group *du jour* and publicly exuding bad feelings towards the latest figure

---

[10] Ibid.

unfortunate enough to find himself or herself on the wrong end of a social media lynch mob. It is deeply troubling to consider how much effort is devoted on a daily basis to tracking down the social media accounts of such people in order to bombard them with hate, as though sending anonymous death threats to strangers simply because they were accused of the thoughtcrime of politically incorrect speech has literally become one's "ethical duty."

Graduate students who realize they must maintain public profiles as "political activists" if they are to have any hope of competing on a bloated academic "job market" embody this principle perfectly. It is ironic that the next generation of "professional intellectuals" largely consider maintaining a steady stream of Twitter and Facebook postings in favour of electing Democrat Party politicians to be some sign that they are deeply invested in *radical political change*. This is even more humorous when such people live in blue states where Democrats win every election anyway. Ironically, however, virtually all of these posts that go into a "hard day's labour" are themselves likely to just be *retweets* from other established social justice pages with millions of followers. Apparently, thinking up enough original content to fill the 150 characters allocated to a single tweet is too much work, even for someone who literally claims to be a "professional thinker."

This is just one example of how an unspoken symbiotic relationship has been established between the social justice pages and their millions of ordinary followers. The page holds up its end of the deal by providing raw material for others to share and therefore provides them with the means to get a nice little dopamine rush to their brains from getting likes, without having to be bothered with actually thinking of anything original to say. In return, the page will get millions of followers and the benefits of getting to make a living from social media presence, a virtual case of "I'll scratch your back if you scratch mine."

This social media virtue signalling is not entirely unworthy of examination for our purposes, however. The Refugee Crisis of 2015 demonstrated a certain inverse relation between the amount of virtual "good will" one was willing to dispense towards a group and the likelihood that he or she would ever actually encounter them; no doubt, this was driven by an aversion to the idea of ever having to do something more concrete than "express feelings of solidarity" with some anonymous, comfortably distant Other across the globe. It bears mentioning, of course, that the refugee crisis was driven by the horrific civil war in Syria which was itself the result of Hillary Clinton's "brilliant tenure" as Secretary of State under a liberal Democrat president. The fact that most of the people who publicly obsessed over refugees in 2015 used their same social media accounts to relentlessly promote Hillary Clinton in 2016, just one year later, demonstrates that Orwellian doublethink is rarely even recognized as such anymore.

It is absurd, for example, that upper-income liberals at Ivy League universities and major corporations who leapt at every opportunity to share social media postings in favour of refugees migrating into Europe, Canada, and the United States could somehow pretend that their own communities were not *already* flooded with refugees who had been driven to destitution precisely as a result of these same elites' business activities. The widespread epidemic of homelessness and vehicular habitation in the United States is precisely a domestic "refugee crisis" resulting from the massive displacement of working-class families out of their traditional rural occupation as farmers and their more recent urban occupations as factory workers.

Yet the same leftist college students and salaried professionals who claim that stereotyping refugees is the greatest of all sins will often see no contradiction in gleefully sharing caricatures which portray the working class refugees in their own communities as "ignorant, toothless, inbred hillbillies" in order to relieve the well-to-do of any sense that the income inequality in their own nation, from which they personally benefit, might be problematic on ethical grounds. Rather, this systematic dehumanization of the not-currently-fashionable Other simply normalizes this economic injustice as a perverse form of justice, since the ignorant masses would seem to have gotten "exactly what they deserve."

One leftist social media page with hundreds of thousands of followers exemplified this trend nicely when it reacted to Trump's threat for tougher restrictions on H-1B visas with a meme that presented an image of a well-educated foreign employee who could fulfil a technical function within the corporate economy and then contrasted it with a stereotypical image of an uneducated middle aged flyover state "redneck," complete with a sagging beer belly, a red baseball cap, visible stubble, an ill-fitting T-shirt, an exaggerated grin displaying an incomplete set of teeth, and a shotgun in hand. The meme sneeringly asked why any sane person would prefer to keep the former out but allow the latter to stay. Needless to say, the primary reaction by its "tolerant" social media followers was the laughter icon.

Of course, what they were really asking is why poor people who don't fill some technical engineering function within the corporate economy should be allowed to remain in their own country. It is chillingly easy to imagine that these same social justice leftists who claim to "fight for allowing marginalized indigenous peoples to stay in their homelands" might someday propose that all the poor citizens with non-technical jobs should be banished from their communities in order to allow foreign-born engineers and their families to take over living in their houses. In many metropolitan areas in the United States, gentrification driven by absurdly-overinflated real state bubbles has effectively already accomplished something very close to this sort of mass displacement, only by covert means. In typical Orwellian fashion, everyone is equal under the Social Justice Movement, but some people are more equal than others, especially if they can fulfil some role in directly facilitating the Techno-Industrial System's growth. Of course, this expansion of the beast of Modern Technology is quite literally just a euphemism for more ecological destruction, since the two absolutely cannot be separated. It is supremely ironic, therefore that the same social justice leftists who claim to be environmentalists "deeply concerned about climate change" would basically argue that a new caste system should be created, in which people's worth is literally measured by how much ecological damage they inflict, since the very same engineering feats which supposedly evidence some people's "higher intrinsic value" cannot honestly be described any other way.

In addition, the fact that both images were literally cartoons dispels any claim that class prejudice does not play a role in this subtle demand that "people of lesser worth" should kindly give up their homes in order to make room for people with "better jobs." On one hand, a photograph of a real, non-staged event will capture numerous contingencies which the photographer merely reports objectively but did not consciously choose. A cartoon illustration, on the other hand, literally has no accidental features. Every detail had to be deliberately drawn by an artist with a very clear motivation behind choosing which stereotypical details to include. Jordan Peterson is fond of reminding his readers that every single detail in the extant myths from the Ancient World is significant, because anything which did not serve a role within the story would have long since disappeared over the centuries of oral tradition.[11] Similarly, it's quite clear that the beer belly, T-shirt, baseball cap, stubble, lack of teeth, and shotgun are all just dog whistles for one very simple attribute: poverty.

It would be intellectually dishonest to claim that the purpose of this meme was merely to argue that *all* Americans should make room for visa holders sponsored by major corporations, because there was clearly no intention to question whether lawyers, dentists, tenured professors, or electrical engineers should be allowed to stay or not. Yet the only reason why it would seem completely unreasonable to uproot such people from their careers, their zip codes, and their children's school districts is that they lie comfortably enough within a higher income bracket to escape the sweeping generalizations so casually applied to the "ignorant masses." We have almost reached the point where professional "radical political theorists" whose favourite motifs include "class struggle" and "postcolonial Othering" will see no problem in exiling tens of millions of Others from their own countries, for no reason except that they are poor.

---

[11] Peterson, Jordan, 12 Rules for Life (New Delhi: Allen Lane, 2018), p. 34.

21

Amazingly, these social justice leftists were the same people who generated such explosive demand for social media postings on Syrian refugees that much of the material ended up having to be fabricated outright to meet this market for self-interested virtue signalling. Some of the most famous images that circulated on social media in 2015 actually turned out to be images which were neither from Syria nor from the year 2015. More recently, when the 2019 Amazon Rainforest fires in Brazil briefly became a fashionable topic of concern for liberal celebrities, some notable names were caught sharing viral images of forest fires which were actually taken *decades ago* in countries that were not Brazil; we can only assume that the temptation to get millions of likes from one's followers will always be strong enough to justify outright dishonest behaviour.

We have literally reached the point, in other words, at which social media likes have become the most addictive drug on Earth, something for which even billionaires and celebrities will engage in shameful or embarrassing behaviour just to get another hit. Yet the social media "like" is the ultimate paradoxical counter sense object, since there is literally no tangible thing there at all, only a set of pixels which light up on a screen at the command of an impersonal algorithm executed from a remote data centre owned by a self-interested corporation. The social media like's character is so artificial, in fact, that in many cases there actually is "nobody" on the other side of it at all. An icon which pixelates at the request of a machine's command is something which can quite literally be purchased on demand, as troll farms will supply the illusion of millions of devoted followers, even for the most despised entities in the world, in exchange for a fee. Recently, it was claimed that one major social media platform had quite literally accomplished the impossible, as they boasted having 12 billion accounts on a planet with just 7 billion people.

Whistle-blowers from the social media industry have revealed that significant financial resources were invested into finding ways to hijack the human body's internal biological functions in order to enact a chemical addiction that would use the body's own resources against it. Each social media like was found to release some *six chemicals* in the body, generating a lifelong addiction among the global population without ever having to ship a single tangible good over international borders. In his 1994 classic *Robots' Rebellion*, David Icke once warned:

> They're after your mind. If they can control the way you think and feel they can control your behaviour and hijack your individuality. They can take you over.[12]

It is no exaggeration to say that we have quite literally reached the point where they *can* "control the way you feel" by manipulating your body's internal chemistry to serve a technical function to advance corporate interests.

Mainstream leftist environmentalism fails to enact any genuine ecological relation to Nature because environmentalism is simply one more example of what might be called the "Like Button Fallacy." The Like Button Fallacy is the delusion that major world problems can be changed simply through gathering enough "likes." It is no coincidence that the "professional political activists" today literally consider getting likes, comments, and shares to be their job, even if many of these must be purchased fraudulently from troll farms.

The Like Button Fallacy was illustrated quite nicely by a well-known meme which circulated in early 2017. In it, a doctor in a Third World nation stands over a boy on an operating table but finds that he is unable to start the procedure until he gets enough likes from the audience. He holds up a bucket of "thumbs ups" and begs the audience to please contribute to saving the boy's life. This meme is doubly ironic, of course, since it itself circulated on social media and one's first reaction on seeing it was to click share in order to vicariously generate more likes for oneself in the process, a virtual case of Zizek's phrase "I know very well [that this behaviour is exactly what this meme is mocking] but [I'll do it myself anyway] . . ."[13]

---

[12] David Icke, *Robots' Rebellion: The Story of the Spiritual Renaissance* (Bath, Gateway: 1994), p. 320.
[13] Slavoj Zizek, *The Fragile Absolute* (London: Verso, 2000), p. 6.

Likewise, it is incorrect to say that environmentalism is all about "loving Nature," as the usual definition would have it. It is far closer to the truth to say that Environmentalism is all about "liking Nature." We have reached the point where Man's entire ecological responsibility towards the Earth has devolved to a meaningless gesture of liking environmentalist social media pages and sharing their posts, no doubt in order to get some likes for oneself in the process.

The tragic irony of this situation is that few things are quite as detrimental to the environment as these very same social media likes, since the energy and hardware requirements to sustain a worldwide 24/7 circus of liking, sharing, and commenting bears an unspeakably-vast ecological cost. One of the most fiercely-suppressed facts of our era is that even an activity as seemingly harmless as regularly using email generates as much carbon dioxide pollution as driving a car. John Michael Greer himself has repeatedly warned that the internet is arguably the single most energy-expensive piece of infrastructure ever constructed in human history.[14] Therefore, "liking Nature" is quite literally a physical contradiction, since this liking only hastens its destruction.

This Fight He Cannot Win

In at least one definition of the term, the essence of environmentalism overlaps perfectly with the essence of the social media like. In fact, both are species of the same counter sense object, exemplified by a panel of buttons allowing a user to arbitrarily vote up or vote down any content at will from a safe distance of solipsistic abstraction. Environmentalism is simply the belief that one's only ethical responsibility towards the planet is to publicly like the right things and publicly dislike the wrong things, though of course these lists themselves are far from objective. It is an open secret that they simply reduplicate the biases of 21st Century social justice leftists whose thought process is often indistinguishable from the very same ecologically-destructive

---

[14] John Michael Greer, "The Death of the Internet: A Pre-Mortem", in *Archdruid Report*, Vol. 9 (Chicago: Founders House, 2018), p. 127.

industrial practices based upon fossil fuels and Modern Technology which they might otherwise claim to reject. In fact, leftist environmentalists are quite literally forced to "like" things which directly contradict ecological principles, simply in order to maintain good standing within their political circles.

It is one's ethical duty as a mainstream liberal environmentalist, for example, to like investing government funds into failing companies for so-called Clean Energy sources, despite the fact that these companies are literally incapable of conducting their operations in the absence of fossil fuels. It is wrong to call solar panels an energy source at all, since the total amount of fossil fuel energy required to build a functioning solar panel is about equal to the total amount of energy it will yield before needing to be repaired or replaced, a process which will itself require more fossil fuels. Ironically enough, it is precisely on *ecological grounds* that solar panels are proven to be failures, yet it remains an unquestionable dogma among leftist environmentalists that supporting Clean Energy is an ecologically-sound response to the problem of fossil fuel pollution. Clearly, in any case in which political ideology must compete with ecological principles, the political ideology will be favoured.

We might even argue for the following rule of thumb: the most reliable indicator that someone is actually serious about the planet's impending ecological crises (and not merely pretending to be in order to gain social media likes, career advancement, or positive media coverage) is precisely his or her willingness to contradict the politically correct sensibilities of the academic intelligentsia, media, and political establishment; above any other factor, *shock value* is the most consistent common denominator to separate the wheat from the chaff on this issue. Contrary to expectation, Ted Kaczynski's monumental writings continue to be dismissed as the "paranoid, incoherent ramblings of a madman" primarily for their intrinsic shock value in questioning Modern Technology and leftist politics, and only secondarily out of one's supposedly "ethical refusal to air the views of a convicted murderer."

Pentti Linkola has similarly gained notoriety for his unusual willingness to openly contradict the politically correct ideology of the European intelligentsia by revealing that it is impossible to justify currently-fashionable views promoting unrestricted immigration on ecological grounds alone. Although it is fashionable to argue that any discussion of immigration is actually just a discussion on race in disguise, there are serious ecological problems with overpopulation which will hold true regardless of what "race" happens to inhabit a country with a fixed ecological capacity to feed its own citizens. For example, it is already the case that some 80% of food consumed in the United Kingdom must be imported from other nations;[15] this statistic should not surprise anyone who has noticed that this is a relatively small nation which has long since overstepped its intrinsic population capacity. The response of radical social justice leftists, of course, has been to double down on this same trend by viciously arguing for even more human bodies to be allowed onto a lifeboat which has definitively broken the fire code.

Few have the guts to admit that there is an all too human motivation behind shifting the discussion to race and "xenophobia." Such discussions are intrinsically easy to carry out, since the *only* thing required of the participants is to go around the room and take turns proudly proclaiming that they themselves are not racist and then harshly condemn anyone who is. It is not at all clear, however, what to do with an island which cannot feed its own population and will not be able to rely on importing food from abroad after access to fossil fuels declines. When this occurs, transportation costs will rise to prohibitively high levels; this alone would be enough to drive the poorest consumers out of the marketplace for good. Worse still, agricultural yields will intrinsically drop, arguably to famine-inducing levels, as one will no longer be able to rely on fossil fuel-based pesticides, fertilizers, and machines to cheat one's way to artificially large grain surpluses. It will not even be a matter of simply switching back to traditional methods after this occurs, since

---

[15] Jim Edwards, "Say goodbye to tea and carrots: 80% of British food is imported so there will be food shortages if there's a no-deal Brexit, HSBC tells clients," *Business Insider*, 1-5-2019.

the long-term damage inflicted by modern industrial agriculture will be so severe that much of the United States' breadbasket will devolve to a North American equivalent of the Sahara in the near future. Anyone who has travelled through Western Kansas in recent years will know that any patches of land not directly irrigated by the agricultural industry are already basically desert. For the moment, we are still temporarily cheating Nature by generating a vast artificial oasis, yet even this has only been possible through ruthlessly drawing down the non-renewing Ogallala Aquifer. Worse still, these precious water reserves were largely squandered just to provide empty calories for the soda pop and fast food industries.

Ironically, calls for unrestricted immigration might very well be nothing more than calls for all ethnic and religious groups to starve equally within a tragically-mismanaged situation. Few things are quite as democratic as famine, which tends not to discriminate on grounds of race or religion if it is founded on strictly ecological grounds.

The Ecovillage Fallacy

Without doubt, the ultimate example of how politically correct leftist ideology will always be favoured in a competition with ecological reality is to be found in the hippie ecovillage. It is especially crucial to address this topic within Peak Oil circles, since this is one of the most common responses to an impending collapse of the global industrial economy, as John Michael Greer has had to devote numerous *Archdruid Report* posts to this topic alone.[16] Even the author himself was involved in plans to launch an ecovillage in Oregon in the year 2011 and hopes to warn the reader not to repeat the mistakes which he has himself made.

---

[16] Greer's January, 2015 post "The Mariner's Rule" is one of his more memorable pieces exposing the uncomfortable fact that ecovillages and doomstead projects in general tend to function more as a "comforting daydream" than a serious plan to survive the difficult post-oil future.
John Michael Greer, "The Mariner's Rule," in *The Archdruid Report*, Vol. 9 (Chicago: Founders House, 2018), p. 21.

An ecovillage can be defined as a hypothetical human settlement which is built from the ground up, preferably on some idyllic tract of virginal forest land, by people who had outright abandoned the suburbs or city to instead focus on constructing a perfect community with an eye towards ecological sustainability. Typically, this will include plans for cob houses (constructed from mud and straw) surrounded by acres of permaculture gardens. Although these factors may sound appealing on purely theoretical grounds, the uncomfortable truth is that all too often these physical factors are merely a means to an end to the project of constructing a utopia which reflects the makers' vision for ideological perfection; needless to say, the kind of "ideological perfection" sought is all too often one rooted in leftist political biases. These prejudices are far more beholden to the historically anomalous situation of fossil fuel industrialism and Modern Technology than its adherents will ever admit.

It must be mentioned at the outset that ecovillages are prohibitively expensive. Greer has claimed that the price tag to construct a liveable human settlement of this kind is at least in the seven-figure range, if not much higher. In fact, in the year 2007 he noted that although countless hypothetical projects had been proposed, the number which had actually ever been constructed could be counted with the toes on one foot. Even if such a place could be constructed, it would have to be funded by someone with considerable wealth. Needless to say, the class prejudices of the affluent would literally be hard-wired into the project just to get it launched.

The unadulterated ecovillage in the woods is actually something of a fiction which is nearly impossible to locate in reality. Far more often, what one will actually find if one tries to visit a functioning "ecovillage" is just a half-serious project set up on a few acres of land (or perhaps much less) located near enough to some major city to allow the owner to keep commuting by private car to his or her high-paying job which provides the raw funds needed to keep the operation running. Due to real estate inflation, "ecovillages" (in the increasingly loose sense of that term) are clearly only available to the well to do and will therefore reflect their class prejudices even in the guise of "disinterested ecological activism."

Leftists' Selective Hearing for Others' Suffering

As a result, ecovillages are far more often a front operation for leftist political activism than a human settlement with any serious long-term viability on ecological grounds. By its very definition, leftist political activism, especially from the Social Justice Movement, is incapable of seriously challenging the System. This is because "social justice leftism" is merely a euphemism for the following psychological traits which Ted Kaczynski identified in *Industrial Society and Its Future*: leftism is just oversocialization, or the tendency to do exactly what society demands even while claiming to rebel against it; and feelings of inferiority, or the projection of one's own weakness into acts of hostility which are supposedly motivated by currently-trending political issues but are really just an excuse to vent one's own self-hate in a publicly acceptable form.[17]

In a certain sense, oversocialization and feelings of inferiority are both just euphemisms for Modern Technology. Oversocialization is simply the absolute conformity to the System which Modern Technology is already hard-wired to demand from its subjects, while feelings of inferiority are just negative energies which are generated by this loss of freedom yet, precisely because of oversocialization, cannot be expressed spontaneously but must instead be channelled into an "acceptable outlet" which the System had already approved beforehand.

For example, it is peculiar that any action by the U.S. Border Patrol, however legitimate it might be, is immediately deemed "fascist" and any facility run by them labelled a "concentration camp,"[18] while far worse abuses of undocumented migrants go unnoticed if they lie outside this pre-approved channel of criticism.

---

[17] Ted Kaczynski, *Industrial Society and Its Future*, in *Technological Slavery* (Scottsdale: Fitch & Madison, 2019), para. 9.
[18] Nicholas Wu, "AOC defends claim that migrant detention centers are 'concentration camps'." USA Today, 18, June, 2019.

In October, 2019, over 300 Indians were deported from Mexico back to Delhi after spending months trapped in an illegal camp and living under horrific conditions. They had wasted considerable money paying agents to smuggle them into the United States but found upon arriving in Mexico that they had been swindled. They were forced to live in crowded tin shacks, eating nothing except rice and pest-infested red beans. Of course, if the same thing had been done by the U.S. Border Patrol rather than by fraudsters in Mexico, the Social Justice Movement would literally be calling for blood to be spilled in retaliation. It is peculiar that this suffering has largely gone ignored within the Social Justice Movement, simply because the agent of this oppression was not one of the pre-approved targets of criticism. Leftists tend to have selective hearing for the suffering of oppressed peoples if they are not currently trending on the Social Justice Stock Market. One might be at a loss for words if one tries to recall the last time he or she heard a major social justice activist mention the violent persecution of Sikhs, Christians, and Hindus in Kashmir and Pakistan, concerns which are apparently far less important than campaigning for transgender bathrooms in retail shopping centres[19] or "heroically" fighting to stop paying customers from the "crime" of enjoying a chicken sandwich at Chick-fil-A on their own time by forcing the sole outlet in the U.K. to shut down after just one week of business.[20]

Far from providing an outlet for any victim to spontaneously express his or her oppression in a public medium, the Social Justice Movement actively silences any suffering which does not fit one of the pre-approved channels which had been generated by the System itself. These channels, in turn, are only established because they directly advance some purely technical interest of the System. Virtually no one has the guts to acknowledge that the real reason the System actively mandates its oversocialized subjects to demonize any restrictions on immigration by the U.S. Border Patrol but ignore far worse abuses if they occur anywhere else is that open borders

---

[19] Hadley Malcom, "More than 700,000 pledge to boycott Target over transgender bathroom policy." USA Today, 25, April, 2016.
[20] Brittany Shamas, "Days after opening its first U.K. restaurant, Chick-fil-A announces the location will close." Washington Post, 20, October, 2019.

advance the technical functioning of the System in the U.S. through providing cheap labour for corporations and driving down wages for all workers across the board. In turn, the lower classes of the population, including the immigrants themselves, will become more desperate, more impoverished, and more terrified of violating any of the System's demands, lest they be thrown to the lions of homelessness or prison, fates which many of them will inevitably fail to escape even despite their best efforts to remain good citizens. Social justice leftists merely reiterate the demands which the System itself had already created yet for that very reason they just worsen everyone's suffering by accelerating its underlying conditions.

Social justice leftists are therefore literally human embodiments of the essence of Modern Technology. On ecological grounds, this means that it is logically impossible for them to challenge the true source of the ongoing environmental destruction, for that would require them to break out of the two features which define their identity. If the reader is sceptical of this claim, he or she should merely consider why social justice warriors have managed to invent dozens upon dozens of bizarre intersectional categories of oppression and yet remain completely uninterested in providing even *one* formal category of representation for suffering generated by Modern Technology. This is doubly ironic, since this is the ultimate source of everyone's suffering in our current situation. Ted Kaczynski's unpublished text "Ship of Fools" explained this through an allegorical narrative of a ship that had one day deviated from its normal course and sailed northward into dangerous conditions.[21] Everyone on the ship could subjectively feel that something was wrong, yet rather than acknowledge that it was a change in ecological conditions that caused this suffering, each subject was seduced into focusing upon the personal grievances of his or her own specific identity category. For example, even on this ship, a feminist laments that the gender wage gap actively inhibits her progress. A homosexual claims discrimination on the basis of sexual orientation. An immigrant claims the System is rigged

---

[21] Ted Kaczynski, "Ship of Fools" (unpublished manuscript).

against undocumented workers, while a native claims the same for indigenous peoples. What they all miss is the simple fact that even if reforms are granted for each of their specific categories, these will easily be negated by the overall decline in conditions on the ship as a whole as it sails into progressively colder and more dangerous waters. One might argue that ecological suffering is the one type which cannot be represented on the ship. Social justice leftist ecovillages similarly fail to acknowledge the one kind of suffering which would actually make a difference if it were eliminated.

Tolerance: Banning Families?

Ecovillages' lack of seriousness and commitment to dogmatic leftist ideology are easily observable just by examining the demographical characteristics of the people who keep the operation running while the owner who claims to be deeply concerned about fossil fuel-based climate change is busy at his or her corporate office job in some major city located an hour's drive away. The workers are almost exclusively made up of 18-22-year-old kids who simply found volunteering for one summer between college semesters to be a more appealing way to pass the season than working a burger flipping job in the college town or moving back in with their parents. In addition, this experience of self-righteous "environmental activism" would be an appealing factor to add to one's resumé when seeking a high-paying job (a.k.a., a job within the System) after graduation. The ecovillage is therefore more like a summer camp for wealthy young people to "hang out" than any long-term human settlement which would actually embody self-sufficiency or ecological responsibility. Needless to say, virtually all of these temporary volunteers will simply go back to the same urban or suburban lifestyles after the summer season is over but still pride themselves on having been virtuous enough to commit a few months of their lives to "saving the planet" by growing half-organic tomatoes in some high-income yuppie's back yard.

It is troubling, however, that this situation of a small group of college age kids camping outside a wealthy person's house for one summer before returning to college is often misrecognized as a manifestation of the "ideal human community." Sometimes, it is even viciously promoted as the way that all humans should be forced to live. The author himself recalls his own involvement in certain discussions over plans for a proposed ecovillage in 2011. Regarding the topic of family, one member of the group was adamant in denouncing the family as one of the main obstacles standing in the way of his utopian fantasy for the ideal human settlement. After all, leftist ideology tells us that the family is a primitive, outdated, sexist, heteronormative, and patriarchal relic of the pre-modern past and must be done away with. The ecovillage, therefore, would be a utopian space only if families were banned, especially those consisting of a monogamous heterosexual married couple raising their own children autonomously.

It is curious, however, that someone who claimed to be committed to abandoning fossil fuel-based pollution and capitalist consumerism would fail to see the irony that his calls to systematically dismantle the human family are themselves merely a luxury of fossil fuels and capitalist consumerism. The idea that family is obsolete simply betrays the economic privilege of whichever self-righteous progressive thinker mouths such a claim.

Anyone who has lived in India (as the author does) can testify to the very different attitudes which people hold on the extended family in so-called Third World nations. In fact, from the author's own experience, it is exceedingly rare to find anyone living alone in such nations, since even the elderly will often be housed by their younger family members rather than be shipped to overpriced "care facilities." While homelessness is rampant in the United States, it is almost unheard of in the author's own locality in India, since few families there have the indecency to let one of their own sleep on the street if there is room in the house available.

Nor is this situation unique to India. In his 2008 classic *Reinventing Collapse: The Soviet Experience and American Prospects,* Dmitry Orlov wrote extensively on the crucial role which the extended family played in reducing the traumatic impact of the Soviet Union's collapse in Russia by providing a parachute against decline which most Americans will not have at their disposal when disaster strikes in their own nation.[22] Orlov's experience living outside the United States proved valuable for challenging certain American consumerist dogmas which seem impossible to question. The American consumerist belief that one must always opt for overpriced "professional" services rather than seek family help is peculiar, since it actually forces one to pay way too much money for an experience which is both less efficient in terms of resources and more unsatisfying in its results. It is more wasteful both financially and in terms of energy to cook food for one person who lives alone than to cook meals for large groups of people sharing the same space; coincidentally, this tends to leave fewer people unfed overall as well. In addition, services which Western "professionals" charge exorbitant rates for can be gotten for free with a much higher quality from family members. For example, one could pay over $1,500 per month for day care, a mere euphemism for a crowded space in which over 30 toddlers scream all day for the attention of one indifferent worker (also, a place in which the likelihood of suffering sexual abuse is uncomfortably high); or one could just have a grandparent who actually likes the child provide much better care for free. Similarly, one could pay over $7,000 per month for a nursing home, a mere euphemism for a crowded building that stinks of urine, in which someone's grandparent will sit in his or her faeces-filled adult diaper in front of a television set until a poorly-paid, overworked CNA finally reaches this room on her cleaning route;[23] or one could just provide much better care to one's own aging relatives for free. This list certainly does go on much longer, but the reader should already be able to see the irony that the Western ideal of a financially-independent perpetual bachelor or bachelorette with no need for a family is anything but an ecologically-minded rejection of capitalist consumerism. One could hardly imagine a more blatant example of a luxury founded on abundant fossil fuels and very sophisticated Modern Technology. This attitude is not only extremely expensive

---

[22] Orlov, Dmitry, *Reinventing Collapse: The Soviet Experience and American Prospects*, (Gabriola Island: New Society Publishers, 2011).
[23] The author's own experience working in various nursing homes in the United States before moving to India has provided more than enough empirical evidence to confirm that this is indeed an accurate description.

in terms of energy and money (and therefore, restricted to a very particular socioeconomic class), it is also just plain *bad* at meeting human needs anyway. It is therefore even more bizarre to hear leftist ecovillage planners claim that it provides the ideal model for a post-consumerist and post-fossil fuel living arrangement.

Further, it is patently absurd to claim that a handful of college kids who live together for a mere three months before flying back to their home countries have "figured out" once and for all the ideal human living arrangement, since this is the ultimate example of a shallow relationship which can hardly survive a single growing season before being forgotten forever. Further, anyone who has actually visited such a place knows that petty conflicts are far from rare. The social relations in such places tend to have much more in common with the infighting on "reality shows" like *Jersey Shore* and *Big Brother* than the utopian fantasies one might naively expect.

Jordan Peterson was abruptly launched into intellectual celebrity status by having the courage to venture into supremely politically incorrect territory; without doubt, one of his boldest feats lay in questioning whether the divorce laws which were so casually loosened in recent decades in the name of "feminist liberation" might have accidentally disrupted a delicate social system which had evolved over a very long period of time and which, for all its admitted flaws, proved durable enough to function for millennia before it was so casually abandoned. Above all, easy access to divorce effectively dismantled the last remnant of the traditional family in the West. In his 2018 *12 Rules for Life*, Peterson noted:

> In many households, in recent decades, the traditional household division of labour has been demolished, not least in the name of liberation and freedom. That demolition, however, has not left so much glorious lack of restriction in its wake as chaos, conflict and indeterminacy. The escape from tyranny is often followed not by Paradise, but by a sojourn in the desert, aimless, confused, and deprived. Furthermore, in the absence of agreed-upon tradition (and

the constraints . . . it imposes) there exist only three difficult options: slavery, tyranny, or negotiation.[24]

One could go a step further even than Peterson is willing to go and argue that there is a fourth option: collapse, followed by death. In that case even tyranny ceases to exist as an option, for all had found themselves to be losers. This seems by far to be the most realistic long-term result of allowing the hippie ecovillage to achieve their fantasy of becoming the only social unit allowed to exist. Famine, fuelled by incompetence, tends not to discriminate on the basis of political ideology if it is founded on strictly ecological foundations.

Although this is almost never explicitly stated, the real reason why the family has come to be devalued in the eyes of leftist ecovillage social justice warriors is that it is incompatible with the essence of a familiar counter sense object: the social media like button. It is quite literally the case that one does not get to choose which family one is born into, since it is only by happenstance that one is born into a particular family and not another and this occurs when one is in an infantile state that predates rational decision-making. One is born into a family one did not choose, composed of people one very well may not like; on the contrary, one always does get to choose one's friends, quite literally on the basis of "liking" them. It only requires a short logical leap to universalize this desire to dictate one's living situation with a figurative "like button" into the "ideal living situation" which all people must be forced to join. The mere historical fact that the family was the default human institution for countless millennia makes no difference, apparently, if it has been devalued by progress (a mere euphemism for fossil fuels and Modern Technology).

In reality, the ideal of a "group of friends living together just cuz they like each other" simply reflects the very same consumerist attitude which these hippies claim to rebel against; this is doubly ironic, since the "courageous rebellion against global capitalism" is precisely the defining motivation for joining such a community in

---

[24] Peterson, Jordan, *12 Rules for Life* (New Delhi: Allen Lane, 2018), p. 271-2.

the first place. Worse still, there is a very troubling sense in which this proposal for "like button communities" simply amounts to a politically correct dog whistle for calls to literally abandon those who are "disliked" to starvation. If the leftist ecovillage ever does manage to achieve its intended goal of replacing the industrial agricultural industry to provide the food supply for the whole world, this would simply allow them to distribute food to those who are "liked" and shut out those who are "disliked." Because the ecovillage is primarily founded on ideological grounds, this would result in a politically-motivated genocide that would leave the Earth with a smaller, more politically correct population. By insisting that social justice leftists should seize control of the food supply and distribute goods only to the members who have been deemed sufficiently ideologically pure to live on site with the other cult members, they are quite literally calling for an ideological ethnic cleansing.

Suburbs in the Forest

In some cases, however, even being a leftist will not be sufficient to escape the fate of being "disliked" into death by famine (all in the name of tolerance, of course). There are some pseudo-ecovillages based upon the ideology of extreme feminism and open only to the subset of women who hate men vehemently enough to be deemed worthy of survival in the coming Amazonian utopia. This is arguably the most laughable case of political ideology being favoured over ecological reality of all, since they fail to see the irony that ridding the Earth of men will also rid the Earth of women (even the "right kind") and of people in general in the long run. This simply demonstrates that social justice leftist environmentalism is indistinguishable from the essence of the social media like button, in which a disconnected subject is free to arbitrarily like and dislike contents at will, however irrational or ecologically destructive the results might be. This attitude of selfish detachment is the purified antithesis to any genuine ecological awareness.

In fact, in his ecological encyclical *Laudato Si*, Pope Francis openly cited this irresponsible, solipsistic "internet communication" as a symptom of the technological destruction of genuine community. It is all too easy to overlook that this attitude risks negating the fundamental social presupposition of ecology by causing us all to "un-learn" how to care about someone or something else:

> Real relationships with others, with all the challenges they entail, now tend to be replaced by a type of internet communication which enables us to choose or eliminate relationships at whim, thus giving rise to a new type of contrived emotion which has more to do with devices and displays than with other people and with nature. Today's media do enable us to communicate and to share our knowledge and affections. Yet at times they also shield us from direct contact with the pain, the fears and the joys of others and the complexity of their personal experiences.[25]

One might go a step further than Pope Francis and argue that social media companies' tendency to turn us all into conscienceless trolls is systematically destroying our ability to feel empathy, not only for our fellow humans but even for the Earth itself. Pope Francis rightly warns that this is not merely a matter of abstract emoting with no real-life consequences. This technological deterioration of empathy directly inhibits elites located in urban First World bureaucracies from "feeling the pain" they inflict on poor citizens in distant lands, even as they pay lip service to whichever version of "green rhetoric" happens to be currently fashionable among Western liberal elites:

> [M]any professionals, opinion makers, communications media and centres of power, being located in affluent urban areas, are far removed from the poor, with little direct contact with their problems. They live and reason from the comfortable position of a high level of development and a quality of life well beyond the reach of the majority of the

---

[25] Pope Francis, *Laudato Si*, p. 33.

world's population. This lack of physical contact and encounter, encouraged at times by the disintegration of our cities, can lead to a numbing of conscience and to tendentious analyses which neglect parts of reality. At times this attitude [even] exists side by side with a "green" rhetoric. Today, however, we have to realize that a true ecological approach always becomes a social approach; it must integrate questions of justice in debates on the environment, so as to hear both the cry of the earth and the cry of the poor.[26]

It is therefore all the more ironic that this anti-ecological attitude of anonymous, purposeless liking and disliking, combined with empty lip service to "going green," has come to define the very term "environmentalism" through the ecovillage movement.

Admittedly, extreme feminist ecovillages are far from the norm. However, there is another bias which is indeed present in virtually all of the pseudo-ecovillages which the author has seen. Although virtually *no one* (with the notable exception of John Michael Greer) has the guts to acknowledge this fact, ecovillages are basically just suburbs in the forest; in the worst cases, they are just suburbs inside suburbs. In a May, 2008 *Archdruid Report* post titled "Preparing for What Future?" Greer listed ecovillages as one of the most common knee-jerk responses which Americans tend to fall back upon on the rare occasions that they are forced to contemplate the demise of industrialism. Ecovillages are a peculiar solution to demise of industrialism, since virtually all of the half-serious plans to build them amount to little more than a fantasy that one can preserve suburban living (the very worst industrial living arrangement, by the way) in an era after the suburbs had vanished:

> Second [in this list] are those who talk about building ecovillages in the countryside, to provide a post-apocalyptic version of suburban living to today's smart investors . . . [What the ecovillage fantasy has in common with the other

---

26 Ibid., p. 35.

options on the list is that] each of them is [merely] something which many people in today's American middle class [already] want to do anyway.[27]

As Greer noted, it is ridiculous to claim that moving to a suburb in the forest is a radical innovation, since this merely demonstrates middle class Americans' *refusal* to give up the luxuries of industrialism, even in an era where they must resort to outright absurdity to try to cling to them for just a little longer.

It bears mentioning that the construction of suburbs was one of the greatest ecological crimes of human history, in addition to being the "single greatest misinvestment of resources" ever to occur, as James Howard Kunstler is fond of saying.[28] This is because a suburb is basically just an artificially-engineered community in which a vast amount of fossil fuel energy is wasted for one purpose alone: to maintain class segregation through locating the well-to-do a comfortable physical distance away from the poor. Although it is somewhat fashionable to criticize suburban "white flight" from so-called "inner city" urban areas (something which Michelle Obama recently denounced, even as she and her husband live in a fifteen million dollar Martha's Vineyard estate), one should bear in mind that maintaining distance from the rural poor was an equally powerful motivating force behind suburban segregation.

Needless to say, this arrangement would be impossible to maintain without Modern Technology and abundant fossil fuels, since the SUV's required for 140-mile round trip daily commutes are only one of countless examples of how rampant energy waste is devoted to merely shielding the well-to-do from having to see any person with a slightly lower income.

The suburb, like the social media like button, is a counter sense object which would be inconceivable outside the Soma of fossil fuels. It is all the more ironic to find angry calls to "do

---

[27] John Michael Greer, "Preparing for What Future?", in *Archdruid Report*, Vol. 2. (Chicago: Founders House, 2017), p. 84.

[28] Kunstler, James Howard. *Too Much Magic: Wishful Thinking, Technology, and the Fate of the Nation* (New York: Grove Press, 2012).

something about climate change" spring up in the very same suburbs which are literally hard-wired to accelerate it. The author recalls from his own experience that his most liberal professor at university would routinely use class time to rant about global warming and would harshly condemn the Republican Party for failing to "do anything about" it; of course, this same professor saw no ecological problem in her own decision to drive over two hours per day to commute from an affluent suburb located in another county just to avoid living in a "boring" town with a poor population. It is chilling to think that even people who consciously know the scientific reasons why such a daily commute would devastate the environment will still find that asking them to live in a slightly less wealthy town with a lamer nightlife scene is simply "too much to demand of them." Suburbs are arguably the most selfish invention of recent times, in that even those educated on impending ecological catastrophes will still willingly contribute to them just in order to have access to slightly-better dining and shopping options or to avoid being surrounded by low income neighbours who work blue collar jobs.

Regarding the ideal of "suburbs in the forest" (ecovillages), it should be emphasized that there are extremely serious doubts regarding these pseudo-ecovillages' long-term viability as agricultural centres, even for the "lucky few" who are deemed sufficiently ideologically pure to be allowed a ration card within the cult. In all likelihood, handing over the responsibility to feed the entire world to a handful of college-age potheads will simply result in famine for *everyone*, regardless of political doctrine.

It is absurd to imagine that a handful of suburban teenagers who have likely never so much as held a shovel before flying across the world to volunteer at an ecovillage could somehow claim that they know more about farming than the countless generations of agrarian peasants who preceded them thousands of years into the past but likely held religious or political views which would be considered objectionable on a college campus today. One might argue that in their obsession with perfect linguistic ideological conformity, many of them forgot along the way that incompetence will lead to crop failures regardless of whether one knows the correct number of genders or the current sequence of letters following "LGBTQ." Poorly-tended plants or livestock will not happen to care about one's views on gay marriage or "white privilege" if their basic survival needs fail to be met. Once again, ecological principles will always be neglected in favour of political ideology.

It is ironic that a project whose very definition is built around "self-sufficiency" is, in almost all cases, anything but that. On the contrary, due to their unspeakable connection to salary class privilege, leftist ecovillages tend to demonstrate a troubling dependence upon the same unsustainable energy sources (in the form of fossil fuels) and the same ecologically-destructive infrastructure (in the form of Modern Technology) as any other arrangement of our era. It might even be argued that leftist ecovillages are even *more* dependent upon these factors, and even more wasteful in their relation towards them.

For an example of ecovillages' reliance on fossil fuels, one might consider the unspeakable fact that volunteering on ecovillages is all too often treated as nothing more than an excuse to kill three birds with one stone, since international tourism, recreational marijuana use, and social justice political activism are three of the favourite surrogate activities[29] amongst the privileged youth today anyway. It is hard to imagine how flying from California to New Zealand for one season just to "hang out" and smoke a ton of pot around the campfire with other wealthy kids could somehow pass as a "selfless act of labour to save the Earth,"

---

[29] In *Industrial Society and Its Future*, Ted Kaczynski defined a surrogate activity as an artificial way for the subject to go through the Power Process in order to satisfy trivial goals. In the absence of Modern Technology, there would be little need for surrogate activities, since the subject would already need to go through the Power Process just to get enough food and water to survive. Under Modern Technology, however, all of the serious opportunities had vanished but the subject's need to go through the Power Process would remain but would be channeled into harmless activities such as collecting stamps or cheering for a football team. Kaczyński notes that leftist political activism is just one more surrogate activity.
Ted Kaczynski, *Industrial Society and Its Future* (Scottsdale: Fitch & Madison, 2019), para. 39.

as though growing a few baskets of overpriced half-organic lettuce could even begin to offset the gargantuan carbon footprint required to fly halfway across the globe for a few months before flying all the way back. Worse still, the "Local Food Movement" all too often simply serves as another form of class segregation by providing wealthy customers with an opportunity to publicly demonstrate their virtue by paying higher food prices than the genuinely-struggling masses who will find it difficult to stay adequately fed at any price. Once again, the eco-friendly option is little more than a modern secular form of indulgences which allow the rich to pay off their sins against the environment with cold hard cash.

The Philosophy of Ana Kasparian

There is an unspoken rule that the kind of "ecological awareness" that characterizes the Environmentalist Movement presupposes a perspective rooted in a very particular socioeconomic class. The other classes are not portrayed as neutral to the goals of environmentalist activism but are portrayed as "active obstructers" ruining the Earth, either out of ignorance (in the case of the poor) or out of greed (in the case of the superrich). Likewise, the duty to save the Earth from both clearly falls on one social class alone.

This claim that salary class professionals must take up the burden to save the Earth all too often merely serves as a politically correct excuse to promote classist bullying. For example, the recent extinction protests in the United Kingdom have tended to be led by activists who claim to be willing to resort to "extreme measures" to disrupt the flow of daily life in order to force the System to wake up and solve global warming for them. In this sense, they basically brand themselves as a leftist equivalent of Linkola's green police, a revolutionary force willing to suspend human biases in order to directly force "the will of Nature" to speak in the public venue. It is comical, however, to claim to embody the will of Nature while overwhelmingly targeting working class labourers, such as blocking butchers and meat packers from getting to their jobs, while giving giant social media companies a free pass. In fact, one might argue that gaining public approval through posturing on social media platforms is the true, unspoken purpose for staging these farces in the first place. Nothing says "solidarity with Mother Nature" quite as succinctly as fighting viciously to put manual labourers with relatively low incomes out of work for good, while leaping at the opportunity to immediately share selfies of the event on social media platforms whose contributions to global warming through carbon dioxide pollution and energy-intensive hardware manufacturing procedures are far ghastlier than anything a simple sausage maker could dream of doing on his own. Anyone who was truly consistent in his or her attempts to stop pollution and greenhouse gas emissions would have to block engineers from getting to their office jobs just as enthusiastically as he or she campaigned to shut down coal mining operations. Of course, such an act is basically unthinkable, even to those who claim to cite none other than *the fear of human extinction itself* as the motivating force behind their protests. Are we really to believe, though, that Mother Nature has a preference for excusing ecologically-destructive behaviour if it is done by corporate professionals who have "good jobs," as though the Earth itself holds the same class prejudices as the media and academic intelligentsia?

The Young Turks similarly portray themselves as a courageous renegade news agency, one filled with "independent voices" who have the guts to speak the truth while the talking heads on cable television news will only represent the privileged class of billionaires. It is ironic, however, that TYT would claim to challenge the dominant ideology of the culture when their rambling, angry, profanity-ridden segments are unintelligible outside one very specific class perspective, one which the System is already hard-wired to privilege over all the others.

It is all too easy to interpret Ana Kasparian's articles for RawStory as reinforcements of the same privilege which the salary class already enjoys, in the guise of a "radical challenge to the status quo." In an article titled "The Economist Can't Figure Out Why Millennials Aren't Buying Diamonds," Kasparian rallies against the economic injustice which caused diamond sales to drop among millennials. Above all, she spends the article insisting that millennials deserve sympathy from their parents' generation since they are the victims of unfavorable economic conditions which inhibit their success, despite the fact that they did everything they were supposed to do:

> Before I get the obligatory comments about how we're all lazy assholes who mistakenly majored in nonsense, keep this in mind: we're the most educated generation with the largest percentage of people either with a degree or currently enrolled in college. We're not all studying women's studies or Greek mythology either. There's been a trend of lawyers graduating from prestigious law schools, passing the bar, and not finding any work. Americans specializing in STEM jobs are getting replaced by cheaper foreign employees with H-1B visas. Then there's the constant outsourcing of jobs to countries like India and China. All these economic issues are forcing my peers to hold off on everything from moving out of their parent's home to having children. This is not a sob story, but rather the real explanation for why we don't give a shit about how many carats of carbon we can embellish our fingers with.[30]

It is ironic that the very same factors cited in this article as excuses for why educated professionals among the millennial generation "don't give a shit about how many carats of carbon we can embellish our fingers with" would be considered objectionable if applied to any other social class. For example, if a wage class worker were to cite immigration as a factor which has impacted him or her negatively, this would immediately be deemed racist, yet Kasparian literally cites exactly the same factor as a crisis when applied to "Americans [who] specializ[ed] in STEM jobs" but are "replac[ed] by cheaper foreign employees with H-1B visas." In addition, if a wage class worker voiced opposition to the "constant outsourcing of jobs to countries like India and China," this person would be seen as casting the blame for his or her own personal

---

[30] Ana Kasparian, "The Economist Can't Figure Out Why Millennials Aren't Buying Diamonds," RawStory, https://www.rawstory.com/2016/07/the-economist-cant-figure-out-why-millennials-arent-buying-diamonds/

failures onto developing economies and "darker skinned Others." Yet this is exactly what Kasparian cites as a legitimate excuse when applied to educated salary class professionals seeking the high-paying jobs they would seem to deserve.

This tendency to uniquely shield the salary class from criticism is inherent not only in her commentary on economic issues but even provides the standpoint for her passing references to environmental concerns. One can observe this in her response to a ridiculous statistic claiming that the minimal cost to raise one child in the United States is over $300,000 (college *not* included):

> But to have a better understanding of the current fertility trend in full context, consider that the U.S. Department of Agriculture found that the average family will spend close to $304,500 on a kid from the moment he or she is born to when the child turns 18. That means that a middle-class family will pay $17,000 a year for one child, and it doesn't even include private school or a college education.[31]

Kasparian's 2016 RawStory article "The Real Reason We're Not Having Kids," from which this quote originated, does not challenge this intrinsically questionable figure. Although it is passed off as "objective fact," it is not difficult to smell the grotesque class prejudices on the part of the "disinterested experts" who made it up out of whole cloth. In fact, one of the great mysteries of World History is how human reproduction was able to continue uninterrupted for hundreds of thousands of years before the contemporary era, since until very recently, *absolutely no one* on the Earth possessed the kind of wealth which this ridiculous statistic claims is the bare minimum required to bear a child.

Admittedly, Kasparian does not celebrate this fact but instead cites it as the ultimate example of the economic disenfranchisement weighing down upon millennials, since even reproduction has suddenly become unaffordable to those who find themselves unable to pay similarly overpriced college tuition rates:

[31] Ana Kasparian, "The real reasons we're not having kids", RawStory, https://www.rawstory.com/2016/08/the-real-reason-were-not-having-kids/

Income inequality has made having kids, much like getting a quality college education, a rich person's privilege.[32]

The most bizarre thing about this article, however, is that she relates this issue to the environmental problem of climate change, yet still completely misses the properly ecological point anyway. She even explicitly mentions fossil fuels while remaining blind to the fact that it is only in a world structured around fossil fuel consumption that such preposterous figures could pass as credible. That is to say, she fails to realize that fossil fuels' influence in enabling distorted ways of thinking to pass as sane is precisely the ecological problem at hand. In the absence of any hermeneutical understanding of Limitation, though, fossil fuels merely serve as one more opportunity to voice lip service to "going green":

> Maybe this isn't a common thought that goes through one's mind when considering children, but I think about the ramifications of climate change, and how the extreme weather conditions will only get worse as we keep drilling for oil and fracking for natural gas. Do I want to bring a little human into that mix?[33]

Rather than question fossil fuels' somatic relation to irrational expectations of infinite growth, she simply uses them as an excuse to fantasize about eco-apocalypse. It is not at all clear, though, how seriously the reader should take these predictions of environmental doom. After reading them, the typical reader certainly wouldn't be inspired to implement personal changes as modest as, say, cutting down on the number of miles one commutes to work or on casual flights across the North American continent, let alone cancelling his or her smartphone or adopting "outdated' technologies. At best, this appeal to Eco-Armageddon just seems to fit in with a general nihilistic sense that "life under modern conditions sucks anyway, so why bother forcing another person to live under them?" This is

---

[32] Ibid.
[33] Ibid.

much more a testament to the pervasive suffering under Modern Technology than an expectation for what will actually happen in the near future, yet one completely misses the point if one does not see that the solution is to reduce one's reliance on technological gimmicks rather than seek even greater access to them.

The most troubling feature of her article, in fact, is that it cedes far too much ground to the upper income elites who crafted this bogus stat in order to implicitly demand that no one less wealthy than they are should be allowed to reproduce. However, it is precisely on *ecological grounds* that this statement's absurdity should be most visible. To argue that of all the humans currently inhabiting the Earth, only the *very most wasteful* in terms of energy, water, food, technology, and financial resources should be allowed to exist is to phrase the problem completely backwards. To comply with a class-based genocide which effectively rids the Earth of all of its Third World slum dwellers and rural villagers, people whose carbon footprint and total resource waste are negligible in comparison with First World suburbanites, is to miss the point entirely. Once again, however, in a competition between political ideology and ecological reality, it is all too clear which one will win.

Worse still, even a nominally vast sum of money is nothing without the fossil fuels it merely symbolizes indirectly. Without petroleum, natural gas, and coal, this $300,000 "ticket of admission to not be genocided out of existence" would be utterly meaningless. The high standard of living denoted by this arbitrary sum of cash is quite literally just a euphemism for the mountains of fossil fuel energy which must be burned in order to make any of the effects of using it into a reality. Michael Ruppert stated the problem concisely in his 2009 classic *Confronting Collapse:*

> [Most of the political solutions favoured today involve throwing money at the problems. It is all too easy to forget that m]oney has no value without energy to back it up. Problems can be solved by throwing energy at them. But what kinds of energies? [Any attempt to provide the same

results as fossil fuels through some alternative energy hoax will prove inefficient.][34]

Despite its overt emphasis on money, what this eugenicist policy really states is just that humans cannot exist or reproduce without a huge amount of fossil fuels. While it is uncomfortably likely that human extinction very well might coincide with these energy sources' disappearance, this is not at all what these class-based ethnic cleansers who drafted this number up out of whole cloth had in mind. Sometimes, though, history has a nasty sense of humour.

The one solution to our ecological crises which no one except politically incorrect heretics like Pentti Linkola, Ted Kaczynski, John Michael Greer, and Michael Ruppert will contemplate is a reduction in fossil fuel-based economic consumption and a reduction in technological gadgetry, however slight. To part ways with euphemism, the solution is for everyone to get just a little poorer and for everyone to use fewer machines. Kasparian, however, at least in this article, appears not to provide an exception to the nearly-universal aversion to this hard reality. In fact, she explicitly claims that the solution is "higher wages" and more company-sponsored benefits; in other words, she just demands more fossil fuel-based wealth:

> If the federal government is so concerned with why people are deciding against having kids, maybe they should consider how little support and protection the middle class gets when it comes to being parents. Paid leave would be a good start and increasing wages would also help.[35]

It is difficult to imagine how exactly one single baby could bear a price tag of over quarter of a million dollars, since all over the world people who live on one dollar per day somehow raise children on unimaginably modest funds, but one could only imagine

---

[34] Ruppert, Michael C.. *Confronting Collapse* . Chelsea Green Publishing. Kindle Edition.
[35] Ana Kasparian, "The real reasons we're not having kids", RawStory, https://www.rawstory.com/2016/08/the-real-reason-were-not-having-kids/

that much of the total bill which the "disinterested experts" cite as dogmatic fact is to be wasted on technological gimmicks. Ironically, these technological gimmicks are actually outright harmful to the child's physical and psychological health. The irony is that if one followed through with this mandate, one would literally restrict the very right to exist to a set of humans whose psychological and physical health are hard-wired to continually deteriorate under the weight of Modern Technology. It is overwhelmingly politically incorrect to acknowledge, but this class-based ethnic cleansing would literally transform the extant human race into a weak, helpless, and decrepit species in which the very possibility of strength and greatness will eventually vanish altogether.

Although Pentti Linkola has called for a drastic reduction in the global human population as a necessary safeguard to prevent ecological collapse, a perceptive reader will quickly realize that this hypothetical genocide that saves the Earth only for the top ten percent income earners in the United States would accomplish the *exact opposite* of any serious solution to overpopulation. This is because it would effectively remove the last few humans who know how to use hand tools, grow food with traditional methods, or survive with little or no fossil fuels. In turn, it would replace them with a universally-passivized class of techno-idlers whose very existence is a euphemism for massive fossil fuel consumption, as many of them have a personal carbon footprint outpacing entire villages in the Third World. Due to their growing reliance on technological gadgets, most of them will eventually prove incapable of even feeding themselves without pushing a button which will prompt a robot to raise a spoon into their mouths so that their eyes can remain permanently fixed on screens displaying electronic entertainment; the reader very well might be sceptical of this prediction, but anyone who has visited a public restaurant in recent days and observed the diners' activity with their smartphones during meals will realize that we are not far from this point even today. Needless to say, one day the robots will simply refuse to follow through with their feeding duties, proving that this arrangement had provided the technical foundations to make human extinction a shockingly easy task to pull off.

Of course, the author does not mean to suggest that Kasparian finds the extravagantly high cost of living in the United States to be agreeable, nor that she consciously promotes any of the ghastly conclusions the author has just cited, especially human extinction; however, whatever her intentions might be, she still ends up missing the ecological point of the problem, since one of the only solutions she cites is to demand "higher pay for the middle class." It seems not to cross her mind to suggest instead that people simply reduce their consumption by saying "no" to the overpriced, unnecessary junk which is pushed upon them by corporations which are clearly acting in order to advance their own financial self-interests alone. This ecological mismatch is all the more troubling, of course, precisely because she considers herself to be an environmentalist.

The author's appeal to a drop in consumption (along with production and waste) should not be thought of as merely ideological, for Michael Ruppert demonstrated in his 2009 classic *Confronting Collapse* that a drop in all economic activity is necessitated not by political forces, which are more or less open to human manipulation, but by nothing short of the Laws of Physics and of Thermodynamics:

> An American president . . . cannot materialize hamburgers while locked inside a vault of public expectations or change the laws of physics and thermodynamics just because people demand it. A "let them eat cake" approach will not solve anything. A bloody revolution started just after those infuriating words were allegedly spoken by Marie Antoinette . . . After answering all these questions [regarding proposed alternative energies], you will see— from a scientific perspective, rather than an emotional one— that there are no effective replacements (or combination of replacements) for what hydrocarbon energy provides today. This leaves the president with the decision of supporting those choices that have the best chance of allowing the nation to function until a new, greatly slimmed-down energy and economic regime can evolve and, most importantly, be

51

put in place; one that will inevitably require greatly reduced production, consumption and waste across the board.[36]

One of the great ironies of the situation is that the most certain way to generate enthusiasm and funding within the scientific community these days is to promise, somehow, to overturn the Laws of Thermodynamics, since defying them would be the only thing that could prevent humans from seeing their standard of living drop as access to fossil fuel reserves continues to decline. To quote Michael Ruppert once again:

> No one seemed to grasp the fact that money cannot be decoupled from energy. For without energy and what it produces (e.g. food), money is valueless. You cannot eat a $100 bill, nor can you put one in your gas tank and expect to get any benefit from it. Fiat currency is any currency that is created merely by a directive to print it—a fiat. Energy, however, which is essential to give money value, cannot be created out of thin air. Presidential candidates and presidents cannot issue a directive creating more energy. The First Law of Thermodynamics overrules them. Energy can neither be created nor destroyed. The Second Law of Thermodynamics locks them into a dilemma they cannot escape from: energy only converts in one direction, from useable to unusable, and some of the useful energy is always lost in the transaction—entropy. Things always break down into smaller and not larger units.[37]

Needless to say, any solution which involves allowing the American salary class (people who enjoy a higher standard of living than Ancient and Medieval emperors) to become slightly poorer will be fought against to the death; the fact that this fight will literally be a battle against the Laws of Physics will likely require this statement to be interpreted literally rather than figuratively.

---

[36] Ruppert, Michael C.. *Confronting Collapse* . Chelsea Green Publishing. Kindle Edition.
[37] Ibid.

It is peculiar for social justice leftists to suggest that the Environmentalist Movement is primarily the educated salary class's struggle against both the ignorant, climate-denying masses and the greedy, corrupt One Percent, since it is precisely the American salary class who are responsible for the bulk of our ecological crises in the first place. Few who have not personally lived in Third World nations have any grasp of the gargantuan energy cost required for Western suburbanites to fund their 150-mile daily commutes, frequent international flights, and to keep cardboard McMansions with little to no insulation heated in the winter and cooled in the summer. Although it is far more fashionable to publicly condemn the super-rich, it is intellectually dishonest to claim that a tiny handful of billionaires are uniquely responsible for all the pollution in the world, since even the most irresponsible CEO's energy waste is still easily dwarfed by the millions upon millions of clueless suburbanites whose carbon footprint cumulatively add up to a sum far exceeding anything the nefarious One Percent could hope to accomplish. This is just another example of the way that in a competition between political ideology and ecological reality, the politically correct image will be favoured even in the face of blatant absurdity.

Above all, the idea that the educated salary class is uniquely qualified to speak for the Environmentalist Movement is simply one more example of the unspeakable privilege which this class already holds in all other aspects of our current historical situation. It is bizarre for Ana Kasparian to claim that the "struggling middle class" are uniquely disenfranchised under the present conditions, given that the System arguably is tilted even more into their favour than that of the One Percent. John Michael Greer has repeatedly noted that the scandal of homelessness in the United States, for example, is simply the result of favouring real estate bubbles which boost the net worth of salary class homeowners but effectively make it impossible to keep a roof over one's head even if one devotes every day of one's life to labouring at three part-time minimum wage jobs.

For an all too real example, in 2014 it was reported in the news that a woman from Portugal immigrated to New York City but found she had to work some four jobs at coffee shops and fast food restaurants in order to try to cobble together a living. Despite being very good at her jobs and being well liked among her customers, the prohibitively high cost of living in New York made it clear that something as basic as housing is a privilege only to be reserved for salaried employees in the usury industry. She was forced to live in her car, trying to steal a few hours of sleep here and there between shifts at her multiple jobs. One day, it proved too much even for the strongest of spirits. She was found dead in her car while trying to get a little more rest before the next gruelling day of minimum wage work.[38]

On the rare occasions that real estate bubbles are discussed at all, the media gets the problem exactly backwards: rather than recognize the immorally high housing prices as an injustice which is literally killing people, the media instead sounds the alarm of crisis every time the slightest drop in real estate values occurs. Clearly, mass homelessness among the poor, even leading to death in many cases, is not nearly as important as seeing the home owner class lose a little bit of nominal wealth, as though a class of people who literally have more material comforts than Augustus Caesar had in Ancient Rome would be uniquely oppressed among all the peoples in history if they were to see their net worth fall by just a modest amount, a drop which would likely leave their overall standard of living completely unchanged.

Behind the media's façade of politically correct calls towards egalitarianism lies a shockingly misanthropic indifference towards letting the "ignorant masses" go without even the most basic of services if they do not happen to have one of the so-called "good jobs" which the media happens to respect. One should bear in mind that lacking access to housing generates a series of other detrimental side effects as well, since those who do not have a

[38] David Moye, "Maria Fernandes, Who Worked 4 Jobs, Dies While Napping In Car", HuffPost, 28 August, 2014.

kitchen will be forced to subsist off the unhealthy processed foods available at fast food restaurants, convenience stores, and truck stops; an entire generation of low income Americans are literally being condemned to the inevitable fate of developing long term health problems, including diabetes and heart diseases, simply in order to keep the salary class's real estate values from slightly dropping.

One of the greatest ironies of the situation, of course, is that even if one does manage to ascend the ladder of economic inequality to climb into one of the higher income brackets in which something as basic as bearing a child or having a kitchen is allowed by Big Brother, the only thing one will gain from performing such a leap is the ability to finally join the chorus whose oppression under the One Percent is the only type of economic injustice which is allowed formal representation by the media. Even the right to be oppressed economically is reserved for those with six figure salaries, rising home values in suburban cul-de-sacs, company-sponsored retirement plans, and children attending out of state universities.

One might be reminded of the idiotic news articles which consist of interviewing millionaires in Silicon Valley who assure the readers that they too are "poor" (or rather, not as rich as they think they deserve to be) by the standards of an area filled with billionaires. Needless to say, such articles did not provide a space for truck stop janitors or hotel housekeepers to comment, since even the "right to lament one's poverty" had suddenly been reserved for millionaires.

One should keep in mind that having a roof over one's head and a space in which to cook food are amenities to which even Third World slum dwellers and rural villagers still have access; in the United States, however, these have literally come to be seen as privileges reserved for student loan usurers, petroleum engineers, and stock brokers. However, the idea that having an opinion on ecology should similarly be reserved only for this class is *outright preposterous*, since the so-called "good jobs" are almost always located within the same corporate and government entities which are directly responsible for generating these ecological messes in the first place.

The "struggling middle class" is itself arguably the single most ecologically-destructive entity on the planet today, but to criticize it in public is literally unimaginable for those who realize all too clearly that this would amount to the worst of Orwellian thought crimes. Needless to say, no other class enjoys this immunity from criticism. It is not at all unacceptable to publicly mock the "ignorant masses" from the working class and suggest that they are virtually   all "racist misogynist homophobes," nor is it politically incorrect to publicly castigate the One Percent for its greed and corruption. Even when members of these classes are allowed to speak in official media broadcasts, it is an unspoken rule that they must devote some time towards lecturing their own class about its shortcomings or to publicly apologize for the wrongs their peers have committed. However, to even suggest the modest demand that the American salary class should slightly cut their consumption and standard of living is as heretical as publicly proclaiming in Medieval Europe that Jesus Christ was not the son of God. This simply confirms once again that the politically correct ideology will always take precedence over ecological reality.

Cable TV's Revenge

Nor are the privileged within our society content to seize control over housing, home-cooked meals, or the right to speak on Climate Change. We are beginning to hear thinly-veiled calls for the salary class to hold a monopoly over the right to speak in all venues, even including YouTube and other social media platforms. The decision to ban Alex Jones, David Icke, Varg Vikernes, and Paul Joseph Watson from various social media platforms should not at all mislead one to think that this censorship will be reserved only for the highest-profile controversial figures who have millions of followers. Rather, plans are already underway to remove the technical condition for *anyone* outside a particular standpoint to speak on social media. This should not at all be mistaken for a ban on conservative speech, since David Icke could hardly be considered a neo-con capitalist Republican, let alone a member of the Religious Right. Rather, those with views which genuinely contradict any established political or economic viewpoint are quickly running out of platforms willing to host their content.

On June 8, 2019, *The New York Times* generated controversy by publishing an outright idiotic article as front page news called "The Making of a YouTube Radical." The article centred on telling the story of a troubled young white man from the "remote flyover state" of West Virginia who "fell through the cracks of the System" when he dropped out of college and was forced to move back in with family. As the story goes, lacking direction in life provided by the System (a not-so-subtle infomercial promoting the college industry and therefore the student loan scam) he struggled to find meaning and turned to filling this personal vacuum by consuming hours upon hours of YouTube videos. The article suggests that the YouTube algorithm was masterfully-designed to suck the user in by leading the viewer from one video to another, generating a sequence of interlinked flashes of entertainment which were so engrossing that one would find it effectively impossible to "get out" after being sucked in. Unfortunately, this created a perverse incentive for the algorithm to redirect the user to videos with "objectionable political content," simply because numerical considerations had taken precedence over ideological ones. The end result, we are told, is that one will wake up one day and suddenly find that one had unwittingly transformed into a "racist" behind one's own back, simply through absorbing videos by "dangerous radicals" which the company had failed to properly moderate. It is quite humorous to note, however, that it was apparently not even worth the media's time to double check who these radicals were, since *The New York Times* featured an image of none other than far left social justice activist Cenk Uygur of the Young Turks in the collage of "racist far right vloggers" which the young man had in his watch history.

This sensationalist deployment of the R-Word ("racism") is, of course, just a politically correct dog whistle to signal a somewhat different message to the audience: the era of allowing "the ignorant masses" to produce content which could potentially go viral and accidentally land any Average Joe into celebrity vlogger status should come to an end. Above all, the article might be interpreted as a subtle call for YouTube to go the way of cable television: that is, to become a paid service in which a high monthly bill would be justified by the "guarantee of quality" stemming from the fact that only "professionals" would be allowed to produce content. The irony, of course, is that subscriptions to cable television have radically declined in recent years precisely because the entertainment offered for free by "amateur" vloggers on YouTube was so much better than the "professional" services offered on television for nearly $100 per month, most of which was shockingly lacking in originality and which demonstrated a work ethic of in-your-face laziness. It would be comical, for example, to claim that the same business model that gave the world *Keeping Up with the Kardashians* should provide the standard for "high quality entertainment," let alone "intellectually stimulating material." One might perhaps argue that the *only* advantage which cable news networks and Hollywood studios hold over amateur vloggers is access to superior technology. This is therefore simply a call to hand the prize over to the people with the most expensive machines, as though technological superiority was misrecognized as a measure of intellectual competence or creative genius.

Arguably, the real point of the article is simply to promote class interests in the guise of disinterested ethical concern over "hate speech." The idea that YouTube should just become a paid service which airs "professional content" produced from major studios with a high operating budget is no different in essence from the idea that social media should ban links that did not originate from major newspapers as examples of "fake news," or that thinking itself should be restricted to a privilege of tenured professors at R1 universities.

Anyone with even a basic familiarity with the sorry state of academic publishing will realize that forcibly banning non-professors from doing an activity as basic as *thinking* is preposterous on the objective grounds of quality alone. It is strange to claim that "hard core" academic monographs which often fail to generate enough enthusiasm for even one person to rate or review them on Amazon even decades after their release should be the only form of intellectual activity allowed, when even a cheap grocery store romance novel will generate multiple reviews in the two months before its unsold copies are pulped by store employees to make room for the next month's releases.

Even more laughable is the claim that doctoral dissertations represent the highest standard of intellectual rigor in the world. All too often, even the PhD candidate's advisor will never read this document word for word. Ironically, this remains the case even after technical solutions were implemented to maximize dissertations' potential readership. In earlier eras when a doctoral dissertation was a single hardcover book stored in the student's alma mater's vast archives, it was understandably difficult to access this single copy located in a faraway state, even on the once-in-a-lifetime chance that someone cared enough to seek it out in the first place. Only the most dedicated reader would go through the trouble of scheduling to borrow the single copy through the interlibrary loan system; almost always, such a reader would only even know of this dissertation's existence if his or her very favourite professor were the author. For the unfortunate masses of PhD's who had to find work outside the academy (including the 3,500 janitors with doctorate degrees in the U.S.), this was not even an option.

Today, however, none of these technological hurdles remain in place. In fact, at this point there is no hardcover copy to access through interlibrary loan because there is no hardcover copy in the first place. A doctoral dissertation has literally just devolved to a euphemism for a 200-page pdf. Despite the fact that these are instantly available from anywhere in the world and can be downloaded for free from the university's website, it is quite literally the case that you can't even give them away, because the audience effectively doesn't exist. Many academic careerists are aware of this open secret and gleefully abuse this system in order to pump out poorly-researched, quickly-written pseudo-scholarship (simply in order to fulfil a requirement on the path to getting a job) with the *hope* that no one will ever actually read the document in its entirety.

The author recalls reading one doctoral dissertation, nominally written on the topic of Phenomenology, which provides a good example of this unspeakable fact. Anyone who has studied Phenomenology, even on a casual level, will know that it is a very rigorous science which began as an attempt to provide an alternative theoretical framework to resolve problems with the foundations of logic and mathematics.[39] Anyone who has actually read Husserl's *Ideas* or *Logical Investigations*, for example, will know that one of his main interests was to unearth a universal science which could suspend Euclid's axiomatic requirement for "fundamental constructs" by instead positing a pathway of access for eidetic structures[40] and purified essences[41] to manifest themselves directly within consciousness itself.[42] Arguably, Husserl's main interest lay in his ambition to establish eidetic certainties without any need for some extrinsic axiomatic system to provide the origin for their justification on a merely symbolic level,[43] a concern evident even as early as his distinction between "authentically representable multiplicities" (i.e., 3, 5) and impossible mathematical objects (i.e., square root of -1) in his 1891 text *Philosophy of Arithmetic*.[44]

In the absence of the kind of outright fraudulent grade inflation rampant today on American college campuses, even writing a good *undergraduate* paper on the topic would require one to have some understanding of Euclidian Geometry, Peano Arithmetic, Psychologism, and Fregean Logicism, since these were the concerns which Husserl was actually interested in while writing his works. The author of the present text was shocked to find that the standards of academic writing have dropped so low today that it is possible to pass the defence for a doctoral dissertation on the topic yet ignore these problems altogether. It very well might be the

---

[39] Edmund Husserl, *Prolegomena to Pure Logic,* In *Logical Investigations,* Vol. 1, Trans. J. N. Findlay (London: Routledge, 1970).

[40] Edmund Husserl, *Ideas* (Eastford: Martino Fine Books, 2017), p. 206.

[41] Ibid., p. 207.

[42] Ibid., p. 197.

[43] Ibid., p. 210.

[44] Edmund Husserl, *The Philosophy of Arithmetic* (Dordrecht: Kluwer Academic Publishers, 2003), p. 16.

case that this PhD recipient had done the hard work of learning about these topics but left them out simply because they were "too boring" to include in a document which was mostly about leftist political issues of the early 21st Century anyway. It is peculiar, at any rate, to claim that one has "written a doctoral dissertation on Phenomenology" while focusing on crass, politicized articles from the early 21st Century online news media, since Husserl himself obviously did not care in the least about any of the viral headlines circulating among social justice warrior Twitter accounts today. Of course, there is very little reason to believe that the recipient had any knowledge that these real problems of Phenomenology exist in the first place. In fact, this so-called "doctoral dissertation on Phenomenology" contained not even one single reference to any of Edmund Husserl's works. One could compare this to writing a dissertation on Psychoanalysis without feeling the need to read even one text by Freud, though the author does not doubt that such a project has been done.

Even the treatment of other literature within the field was cursory at best. The document literally opened by rattling off a list of recent translations of key texts within the genre as proof that enthusiasm for the field was not dead. One cannot help but suspect that listing out names of translations stemmed only from the desperate need to have *something* to say about a group of texts this person found at the library but did not understand because the subject matter was intrinsically difficult. Somehow, we have literally reached the point where the world's official experts on Phenomenology need not even know what this word means, since the system of institutionalized fraud within the academic industry has become so entrenched that few would even imagine that a real reader might ever be on the other side to catch such abuses.

If only one thing can be certain about these academic publications, it is that they are not changing the world. The irony is that the "professionals" consistently prove themselves to be much worse at precisely the same set of skills they believe the rest of the population should be forcibly barred from practicing. It would be impossible to arrive at the decision to restrict the production of intellectual content to college professors and graduate students alone simply from objectively viewing the material they produce, which is all too often both abysmal in quality and too boring to read in the first place. This view can only be justified through a very subtle but dominating class prejudice. It simply makes sense to someone working for a major newspaper or television network to argue that anyone outside his or her own circle of "professional journalists" should be forcibly banned from social media sites as "fake news," yet this is simply a euphemism for saying that earning a salary from a major corporate entity is the sole standard to distinguish the "real thing" from a fraudulent imitation. The same logic provides the true explanation behind the claim that academic monographs which tend to collect dust on university library shelves far more often than enthusiasm among readers should be the only form of intellectual writing allowed; in this case as well, earning a salary from a major university is the only distinction between the so-called professional and amateur.

This attitude is, however, a historical anomaly which is inconceivable outside fossil fuels and Modern Technology. It is all too often forgotten that Immanuel Kant was the first major philosopher who was also a college professor in the modern sense of the term. The historical norm, in fact, was for the very best philosophy to be done by people who did not earn a pay check from a university but rather worked out of a genuine interest in the subject. Descartes, for example, was a musketeer who wrote his best work during retirement. John Locke was a physician, Baruch Spinoza was a lens-maker, and George Berkeley was a clergyman. One might argue that it was only because fossil fuels interfered on ecological grounds that this arrangement came to be tilted in favour of the academic hierarchy which was briefly dominant but is quickly fading out of existence as university administrators allow tenured academic positions to die with the same human barnacles which filled them for decades before but couldn't easily be gotten rid of. Replacing these "professional researchers" with armies of underpaid adjuncts will effectively end the trend that began with Kant, since an adjunct living in her car and driving among four different counties on a daily basis just to try to cobble together less than a minimum wage income will neither have the time nor the institutional support to produce the academic monographs which will quietly go extinct as a genre.

Yet extending the idea that only salaried professionals should be allowed to speak to the realm of ecological awareness has proven the most counter-productive of all. The negative effects of restricting this discourse to the class of "professional thinkers" are not merely hypothetical, as we already have abundant evidence of the sorry state "ecological awareness" has devolved to when left to a handful of cable news networks and university professors. Almost exclusively, in such cases the sole concern is which mystery clean energy source will allow the privileged classes of the West to continue living a lifestyle which is historically unprecedented, ecologically unsustainable, intrinsically wasteful, and just plain unsatisfying anyway. Claiming that someday soon a group of "brilliant scientists" will discover this Fountain of Youth which will allow them to keep using Modern Technology without ever having to face the ecological consequences of doing just that reveals that their only true interest lies in finding a magical "pollution free machine" which performs all the wonders of fossil fuel-based technology, but with all the nasty environmental side effects removed. The fact that it will *never* be discovered does not matter as much as one might expect, for it serves their true purpose just as well when left in a purely hypothetical state: it will allow an unsustainable ecological arrangement to continue under the promise that "very smart people are working on it." These "very smart people" are, of course, simply another term for a group of professionals receiving their pay checks from major corporate, academic, and government entities, institutions which will surely influence their thinking to favour the status quo even in their supposed acts of rebellion against it. In addition, their socioeconomic position within the salary class will have long since accustomed them to dependence upon all of the energy-wasting luxuries and material comforts which are only possible due to fossil fuels; they very well may ask that everyone else give up their suburban McMansion, SUV, and international vacations to Europe; but the majority of them would never dream of letting go of such things in their own lives. They might find that such things will be "pried from their cold, dead hands" after all, but by the very same environmental disasters they were overpaid to pretend to find solutions for but decided for ideological reasons to make inevitable.

The very term "environmentalism" has therefore come to be seen as nothing more than a euphemism for elitist hypocrisy. Many people who are legitimately horrified at the current trajectory of industrialism will be reluctant to call themselves "environmentalists" because the term ironically enough would negate what they intend to express precisely by providing the most literal expression for ecological concern. In classic Orwellian fashion, concern for the environment has been made nearly impossible by the term "environmentalism" itself. This term is itself merely an ad hoc label for a sprawling set of many different meanings. The following list summarizes all of the examples considered in this chapter.

The Truth about Environmentalism

On one hand, environmentalism refers to the counter sense object of the mystery clean energy source which holds as much concentrated power as fossil fuels but produces no pollution and is infinitely renewable. The only problem with this is, of course, that it just doesn't happen to exist. Worse still, even the so-called "green energy" gimmicks have grotesque pollution requirements which are suppressed as much out of financial as out of ideological necessity. One of the only people honest enough to admit this fact was Michael Ruppert before his tragic suicide in 2014. The following quotes from his 2009 classic *Confronting Collapse* are worth repeating in full:

> There is no method of generating energy from a source that does not produce some form of waste (pollution). Even wind and solar create waste as a result of the construction of wind turbines and solar cells.[45]

---

[45] Ruppert, Michael C.. *Confronting Collapse* . Chelsea Green Publishing. Kindle Edition.

He went as far as to claim that the very term "clean energy" amounts to nothing more than a marketing campaign to raise capital for projects which are anything but that:

> The term clean coal is a marketing gimmick because the technology does not remove the poisons from either the mining or the combustion—only the exhaust gasses. It has never been implemented commercially. I repeat . . . never in the process of commercial power generation has any so-called clean coal plant produced 1 kWh of electricity.[46]

Environmentalism also refers to the counter sense object of the social media like button which allows a disconnected user to anonymously like and dislike content with no need to justify why and no need to be accountable for the consequences. One might even argue that the social media platforms are hard-wired to breed a spirit of irresponsibility in their users by equipping them with this feature. Many people who were unfortunate enough to find themselves "disliked" on a massive scale by Twitter lynch mobs have noted, in retrospect, that they had never quite understood just how distasteful this behaviour was until they were on the receiving end of it themselves. When caught up in the virtual mosh pit, one never gave a second thought to joining in with cyber-stoning the unfortunates to death; in fact, one leapt at the opportunity to do so precisely because there was something sickly pleasurable about getting an opportunity to act out that way and still claim to hold the moral high ground. One might even argue that one of the unspoken incentives for allowing public acts of stupidity to go viral and generate rage in the first place is that this allows people the chance to act horribly in response without facing any consequences, since it was all justified by whatever politically incorrect thing the Other was foolish enough to say out loud.

Environmentalism also refers to the counter sense object of the leftist ecovillage, a suburb in a forest (or worse, a suburb in a suburb) which claims to reject capitalist consumerism but extends

---

[46] Ibid.

the consumerist attitude of "choosing products" based on personal preference to the supreme act of arbitrary consumerist choice: an act of selecting who gets to survive into the future by only feeding those who are sufficiently "liked" to avoid starvation. The supreme irony is that "social progress" is the main standard to determine who is sufficiently up-to-date to be allowed to exist (i.e., knowing that there are 68 genders, knowing how many letters currently follow after LGBTQIA. . .). Yet this appeal to progress is literally just the deep meme of fossil fuels in disguise. The ecovillage is impossible to imagine outside of the very same industrialist framework it claims to reject, since the most reliable predictor to determine whether someone will know the latest arbitrary number of genders is whether one is already grandfathered into some elite institution in which knowing such information is a requirement to advance one's career. Imposing genocide in the name of political correctness is therefore literally just a call to reserve the Earth for the handful of tenured professors, corporate boardroom drones, and political party insiders whose ticket of admission onto the half-filled lifeboat off the Titanic is based upon socioeconomic class more than any other factor. Needless to say, fossil fuels provide the sole basis for their privileged position within society in the first place and are therefore impossible for them to question at any meaningful level.

Environmentalism also refers to the salary class privilege which reserves the right to comment on ecological crises to a set of talking heads on the state-controlled media or the university industry; in addition, it reserves the right to draft solutions to a set of scientists or engineers, yet these will inevitably be figures whose salaries are beholden to major institutions which will not accept any answer that does not involve more economic growth or more technological automation. To trust the fate of the planet to people who literally cannot challenge fossil fuels because they cannot challenge progress is to surrender any hope for serious change; it very well amount to surrendering the possibility of life on Earth.

Environmentalism is therefore not one single, consistently-defined thing; it is a euphemism for a number of different counter sense objects, all of which are founded upon the Soma of Fossil

Fuels. Environmentalism can never lead one to ecology because it can never lead one to somatic hermeneutics. It is simply ruled out from doing so because it is definitively restricted to the layer of counter sense objects, all of which are far more fragile than one might expect. The only thing that is absolutely certain is that none of these will make any sense in the not so distant future when fossil fuels cease to be the Soma that grounds one's worldview. The following chapters shall explore this problem in far greater detail by shifting emphasis away from a merely negative analysis of environmentalism's shortcomings to a more positive analysis of ecology as somatic hermeneutics, the hermeneutical horizon in which the Soma can appear and be understood as Limitation.

Chapter Two
Ecological Hermeneutics and Linguistification:
Gadamer, Zizek, and the Transcendence of the Linguistic Turn

Somatic Contexts

We are not powerless to offer a better alternative to address the frighteningly-serious ecological problems of our era. The present text shall argue that the term "somatic hermeneutics" should supplant the term "environmentalism" to denote the kind of engagement founded on genuine concern for ecological problems which is currently impossible among mainstream leftist environmentalists. In the author's earlier work *Being and Oil: Volume One: Peak Oil Philosophy and the Ontology of Limitation,* the author borrowed the term Soma (σῶμα) from the Ancient Greek word for a body which really exists in order to refer to the crucial resource which a subject depends upon for survival within a given ecological context. The Soma is herds of megafauna for the hunter gatherer, mobile flocks of sheep or herds of camels for the nomad, large fields of grain for the agrarian peasant, fossil fuels for the industrial citizen, post-industrial ruins for the salvager, and water for the Arrakeen or extreme desert dweller.

Although anthropologists and historians have provided abundant empirical data on different cultures' resource bases, the properly epistemological significance of the Soma has almost never received due attention. Remarkably few thinkers have noticed that the Soma provides the minimal standard of meaning for a finite human subject, since contents from the higher order layers of mythology, system, object, and deep meme are all intelligible only insofar as they minimally correspond to the Soma which provides the deepest layer of meaning for the subject.

Fossil fuels' somatic influence over our thought process can be observed in the following simple example. In our era it is almost universally taken for granted that issuing massive loans with high interest rates to people who have little hope of paying them back is just an ordinary activity. In fact, we have reached the bizarre stage in history where we literally evaluate how "successful" someone is by measuring how deep in debt he or she is. In one memorable episode of *The George Lopez Show*, the title character tried to prove to his wife that he had somehow defied his grade school teachers' low expectations for his future by becoming a successful middle-class careerist. After all, he and his family had a mortgage for an overpriced house in Los Angeles, as well as two car loans and student loans to finance his daughter's education. He couldn't help asking, "Just think, honey, if I wasn't successful would we be this deep in debt?"

It is a supreme irony of history that participating in something which was once considered a damnable offense worthy of capital punishment has suddenly become the very measure for how "normal" a person is. One should be reminded that in the medieval era the penalty for usury was public hanging and that early Christian texts such as the non-canonical *Apocalypse of Peter* warned that usurers will receive the very specific punishment in Hell of being covered up to their knees in filth as a mystical reflection of their crime against humanity, Nature, and God.[47] It is not enough, however, to say that something which was once considered breathtakingly scandalous has lost its former taboo status, as though widespread acceptance of usury were simply a matter of greater tolerance within the social body; rather, usury's irrational expectations of extracting infinite wealth out of borrowers' finite bank accounts has been elevated to the very ontological standard of Being itself.

It is not only student loans which embody the expectation that an infinite profit should be made from a finite investment. Virtually every other object must fit this shape of infinite progress or it will not be understood at all. Machines are every bit as illogical, since the only thing which machines reliably accomplish

---

[47] "And in another place nearby [in Hell], full of filth, they cast men and women up to the knees. These are they who lent money and took usury." Anonymous, *The Apocalypse of Peter*, in *Lost Scriptures: Books that did not Make it into the New Testament* (Oxford: Oxford University Press, 2003), p. 284.

with perfection is burning energy sources out of existence. Citing "technological innovation" as the solution to fossil fuel depletion is literally just an appeal to burn through what little remains of this energy source even faster. Still, this blatant logical absurdity goes unnoticed because the subject living under fossil fuels' somatic influence will take for granted that any object which does not embody the expectation of an infinite return on a finite investment is not even real. Anyone foolhardy enough to challenge the ideology of progress in public can count on being accused of being "out of touch with reality."

This bias is not completely unfounded. Especially in the early years of fossil fuel extraction, it was not unreasonable to get something like a return of 200 units of energy for every unit of energy invested for extraction operations. Of course, the contemporary fracking and tar sand hoaxes have yielded far poorer returns on investment, if they have even done so at all. Still, fossil fuels were the sole somatic foundation for the widespread belief that similar massive surpluses are not only reasonable to expect in fields like energy extraction, but that unrelated social and political venues must be forced to embody them as well.

The following hierarchy of meanings shows how a somatic context (in the case we are considering now, fossil fuels) provide the transcendental conditions of experience for all five layers of consciousness. We shall examine each briefly before proceeding.

First, in the mythological layer, we find the logic of fossil fuels embodied through a compelling narrative event, such as the fantasy of the "universal middle class." What this really means, of course, is just that someday soon, all seven billion humans on the Earth will live the "ideal lifestyle" as suburban couch potatoes with three hour long daily commutes, jobs in air conditioned offices, abundant leisure time to watch sitcoms on television, and perfectly politically correct views on all ideological matters. This promise of "infinite social progress" is, however, simply a euphemism for fossil fuels and only makes any sense if the subject has first registered the somatic presence of fossil fuels as the dominant resource for survival.

Second, in the gnostic layer, we find the same logic embodied through systems which use an abstract set of values to communicate the same expectation. The pseudo-science of Modern High Finance promises that one can generate infinite economic growth on a finite planet through "lending money which doesn't exist" to people who can't pay it back and then stealing their material possessions as punishment. As David Icke said in his 2017 book *Everything You Need to Know But Have Never Been Told*:

[M]oney is another illusion, another hoax [in which] private banks owned by Archontic Reptilian hybrid families can 'lend' money that doesn't exist called 'credit' and charge interest on it. They can lend some nine or ten times more than they actually have (much more in truth with other manipulations) and charge interest on the lot – charge interest on illusory 'credit' that has not, does not and will never exist. Put a dollar in a bank and it can lend that dollar multiple times and charge interest on every loan . . . People and families are being thrown on the street for not being able to pay back 'money' that has not, does not and will ever exist, and so could not have been 'lent' in the first place. Archon bloodline banks are 'lending' you an illusion that only has value because people believe that it does. In return bankers get the collateral of your house, land, vehicle or business.[48]

The systematic expression of this nonsense differs from the mythological expression insofar as a system uses a set of formalized constructs, such as numbers, mathematical functions, arithmetical operators, or logical connectives rather than simply disclose a compelling event within a narrative. This too, however, only makes sense to a subject who is already situated within an ecological context in which fossil fuels are the crucial resource for survival.

Third, in the counter sense objective layer, the same logic is embodied in the form of an object. One notable example is a student

---

[48] Icke, David. *Everything You Need to Know But Have Never Been Told By David Icke* . David Icke Books Limited. Kindle Edition.

loan, for which a borrower will consistently make extravagant monthly payments yet will somehow find that he or she only ends up deeper in debt the more money he or she throws down a bottomless pit which was engineered to never be filled. Once again, it is only fossil fuels that have temporarily blinded the human race to the despicable criminality of this farce. The day of reckoning when the masses rebel against their student debt slavery will not be delayed for very much longer.

Fourth, the memological layer embodies the same logic through the shape of a geometrical metaphor. Below the surface of the mythological fantasy of a universal middle class, the gnostic system of economics, and the counter sense object of a student loan lies the same abstract shape of an ascending arrow which never plateaus and never retracts. This deep meme is a shape which structures the subject's worldview below the surface, yet it is also simply a euphemism for the ecological context of living under the influence of fossil fuels.

Finally, one might penetrate to the deepest layer of the Soma in itself. If one does so, one will no longer deal with half-clear euphemisms distorted by the transcendental rules of manifestation unique to mythic events, gnostic values, objective forms, or memological shapes. One will instead grasp the Soma as the present body which grounds the entire hierarchy. The following table synopsizes this information.

[1]

Layer	Example	Minimal Unit of Meaning
Mythic	Universal Middle Class	Event
Systematic	Modern Finance	Value
Objective	Student Loan	Form
Memological	Ascending Arrow	Shape
Somatic	Fossil Fuels	Presence

This hierarchy of meanings is not unique to fossil fuels. Each Soma has its own idiosyncratic character which twists all other meanings within its ecological horizon to embody a consistent set of somatic themes.

For the hunter gatherer, for example, the Soma is herds of megafauna such as the woolly mammoths once tracked during the Ice Age. In turn, the hunter gatherer will approach the world through the primordial shape of a level plane which lacks any hierarchical distinction between humans and Nature. Natural forces are anthropomorphized into conscious intelligent agencies which humans can influence through ritual. In addition to personifying nature, humans will naturalize their own cultures and treat them as extensions of the natural habitats they live under. The somatic themes of this context therefore include levelled relations and mutual influence.

In the agrarian context, the Soma is fields of grain. In turn, the agrarian peasant will approach the world as a circular structure with repeating cycles and an intrinsic completeness which lacks any need to grow or multiply. In the medieval era, for example, Thomas Aquinas argued that because God is already completely perfect, there is no need for him to become more perfect, for that would imply that he had some defect which he needed to overcome.[49] The somatic themes of this context include cyclical predictability, stability, completion, and the maintenance of tradition.

In the salvage context, the Soma is industrial era ruins which can no longer be used as intended due to a shortage of fossil fuels; the salvager will then see the world in terms of material which must be creatively retrofitted to serve purposes which would have been previously unimaginable. In addition, the subject will explicitly posit his or her era as one of decline rather than progress. The somatic themes of this context include memory, decline, and repurposing.

In the nomadic context, the Soma is herds of animals like camels or yaks; unlike the stationary herds of the Agrarian Worldview, the nomadic herds are inherently mobile and move

---

[49] St. Thomas Aquinas, *Summa Theologica I*, in *Introduction to St. Thomas Aquinas* (New York: The Modern Library, 1948), p. 127.

across vast tracts of land in search of food. The nomadic subject therefore views the world through the shape of a flock, or a set of elements for which inclusion in the set takes precedence regardless of which geographical location one happens to inhabit at the moment. The somatic themes of this context include inclusion within a set and movement.

Finally, in the Arrakeen or extreme desert context, the Soma is water and the Arrakeen subject will process the world in terms of evaporation, the tendency for scarce and precious materials to vanish if neglected or misused. One also finds frantic resistance against waste; for example, in *Dune* Frank Hebert describes subjects using stillsuits to reclaim their own bodies' escaping moisture as drinking water.[50] The somatic themes of this context include evaporation, scarcity, and preservation.

Each of these somatic contexts provides the minimal standard for how higher order memological, objective, systematic, and mythological meanings make sense. Even the most abstract gnostic system or the most far-fetched mythology can only be given meaningfully if each emerges within an ecological context. Economic systems in the Ancient World, for example, were intrinsically oriented towards maintaining economic stability (what we would call "stagnation" today)[51] rather than pursuing growth, yet this was because agrarian grain had already provided the bias to maintain completion and to faithfully uphold traditional cycles. In our era, any economical "science" not founded on pursuing limitless exponential growth and needless "innovations" would represent the greatest contradiction in terms, but this is only because fossil fuels have already provided the basis that guaranteed surpluses and constant change are rational things to expect and to actively pursue.

---

[50] Frank Herbert, *Dune* (New York: Ace Books, 1990), p. 436.

[51] John Michael Greer has repeatedly mentioned that Ancient Egyptians did the unthinkable by actively pursuing economic stagnation, though arguably his earliest written reference to this fact occurred in a December 31, 2008 *Archdruid Report* post titled "History's Meaning, History's Choices."
John Michael Greer, "History's Meaning, History's Choices", in *Archdruid Report*, Vol. 2 (Chicago: Founders House, 2017), p. 277.

Thus, even an abstract science supposedly founded on hard numerical figures, such as Economics, can only emerge meaningfully if it carries the Soma up along with it, no matter how far from the Earth it seems to float. Just as Icarus found that he had to carry his all-too-earthly wax wings up with him no matter how high he flew above the ground but then found out far too late that these were fragile somatic bodies which the Sun easily melted, we too shall find out the hard way that the very Soma behind our current mythological fantasies of limitless technological domination of Nature are just so many fossil fuel sources which are burning out of existence even more conclusively than a pair of wax wings too close to the Sun.

A somatic context can only provide a foundation for higher order meaning's structures to emerge if it has first allowed the subject to be authentically situated within a real ecological context. Both Kant's transcendental ego and Fichte's "I in itself" are fictions, since both seek out a purified subject who can exist above and beyond a horizon of ecological limitation. Admittedly, Oswald Spengler accomplished enormous leaps in demonstrating the impossibility of a pure standpoint of neutral objectivity, yet we shall argue for an even more radical shift than Spengler's appeal to cultural and historical relativism.[52] Ecology, properly understood, influences subjective interpretation even more primordially than culture and history because the deep meme is more fundamental than any cultural worldview. It simply condenses the somatic context's themes into the logic of a shape by providing a direct geometrical metaphor for the crucial resource which limits a subject's survival within an ecological situation.

Just as Aristotle realized in Book IV of *The Physics* that it is impossible for a void to exist within Nature,[53] we shall see that a hypothetical "ecological void" which is not dominated by a particular Soma is just as self-contradictory. The only reliable measure to evaluate whether a "radical environmentalist" is really

---

[52] Spengler, Oswald. *Decline of the West: Volumes 1 and 2* . Random Shack. Kindle Edition.

[53] Aristotle, *The Physics*, in *The Basic Works of Aristotle* (New York: The Modern Library, 2001), p. 280.

serious about critiquing fossil fuels is therefore to see whether that person has any plans to actually transition to a different somatic context after the global capitalist system they claim to despise really does collapse. Such a person can only be proven sincere if he or she demonstrates a willingness to become an agrarian peasant, a nomadic yak herder, a post-industrial salvage ruin-man (as in John Michael Greer's *Star's Reach*), an Arrakeen water warrior, or some other determinate somatic identity. One cannot simply "escape capitalism" without fleeing to some other Soma. Anyone who laughs at such a proposition as "wildly unrealistic" should bear in mind that the most committed critics of Modern Industrialism proved their allegiance by literally abandoning the somatic context of fossil fuels, yet this move could only be accomplished through finding another ecological context to exist within. Ted Kaczynski's decision to live as a hunter gatherer in the woods in Montana is just as admirable in this regard as Pentti Linkola's work as a traditional fisherman in Finland who used an old-fashioned boat, a horse-drawn cart, and a traditional cabin with no running water.

Needless to say, virtually every climate change protester holding a sign on a street corner and yelling for someone else to solve global warming for them is only interested in finding some way to keep inhabiting the somatic context of fossil fuels, but with all of the nasty side effects removed. It is no exaggeration to say that the "major change" they really crave is for some clever scientist to find a way for them to run all of the technological appliances in their suburban homes or uptown condos on some mystery clean energy source which generates no pollution and is infinitely renewable. They certainly aren't interested in inhabiting a world where smartphones, personal cars, hot showers, and air conditioning are luxuries which even emperors cannot afford, though this is exactly what one would find if one actually transitioned to a world beyond fossil fuels to some other Soma. Nomadic camel herders tend not to generate the kind of material surpluses which can drive a modern consumerist economy. The following table synopsizes each somatic context and its corresponding themes.

[2]

Ecological Context	Soma	Somatic Themes
Hunter Gatherer	Wooly Mammoths	Levelled Relations, Mutual Influence
Agrarian	Fields of Grain	Predictable Cycles, Completion, Tradition
Fossil Fuel	Petroleum, Coal, Natural Gas	Growth, Progress, Surplus
Salvage	Industrial-Era Ruins	Decline, Memory, Repurposing
Nomadic	Yaks, Camels	Inclusion in Set, Movement
Arrakeen	Water	Evaporation, Scarcity

In addition, the following table summarizes this discussion of the six deep memes. Each deep meme condenses the somatic themes of a worldview into a purified shape which captures the logic of that worldview in an isomorphic geometrical form. In the Hunter Gatherer Worldview, the deep meme is the shape of a level plane. In the Agrarian Worldview, it is a circle. In the Fossil Fuel Worldview, it's an ascending ray of progress. In the Salvage Worldview, a bell curve of decline. In the Nomadic Worldview, a mobile set with elements. In the Arrakeen or Extreme Desert Worldview, it is an evaporating cloud of mist to denote scarcity.

[3]

Worldview	Deep Meme	Soma	Transcendental Shape
Hunter Gatherer	Level Plane	Woolly Mammoth, Deer, Wild Roots	▬▬▬▬▬

Agrarian	Circle	Grain, Cattle, Sheep	
Fossil Fuel	Infinite Ray	Petroleum, Natural Gas, Coal	
Salvage	Bell Curve	Industrial-Era Salvage Materials	
Nomadic	Set	Camels, Yaks	{a, b, c, d . . .}
Arrakeen	Vapor	Water	

Somatic Hermeneutics

Somatic Hermeneutics is the hermeneutical interpretation of one's ecological context as such. Penetrating all the way to this foundation is the sole meaningful pathway for ecological awareness and the only solution to break free from the impasses which have paralyzed mainstream environmentalists thus far. The author's decision to speak of hermeneutics will likely surprise some readers who might think of ecology as strictly a matter of scientific objectivity; in fact, such readers might argue that relying upon hard empirical facts alone will provide a credible pathway to enact a serious political response to impending environmental crises. The only problem with such a stance, of course, is that it has *never* proven sufficient in bringing about even the smallest change in personal behavior. Ted Kaczynski, John Michael Greer, and Pentti

Linkola have provided abundant evidence to demonstrate why no amount of exposure to scientific data regarding environmental crises will ever be sufficient to bring about even the most modest change in one's lifestyle and consumerist habits, as will be discussed in much greater detail in the third chapter. In other words, the hypothetical pathway for one to transition from learning theoretical information to making a serious practical change effectively does not exist. This is an inconvenient truth which renders null and void any hope that scientific objectivity alone will be sufficient to confront the impending ecological crises. One must instead turn to hermeneutics.

Even if one accepts this unpopular fact, one might still object that getting lost in the intellectual labyrinth of poetical interpretation would be even worse, since this would only threaten to squander the opportunity for practical action by burying it under countless layers of obscurantist mystifications in the dizzying circular movement from part to whole which characterizes the hermeneutical circle of understanding. This criticism, however, only makes sense if one assumes that the hermeneutical circle is a strictly linguistic structure which would trap one on the inside of a poem, effectively immobilizing one from engaging with the real world outside the text. Although such a view of hermeneutics is taken for granted today, this radical emphasis on language and language alone is actually quite new and is contradicted by centuries of history on the topic. We shall briefly consider this trajectory before proceeding.

One might define the hermeneutical circle through the idea that when one is trying to understand something, one cannot inductively build up one's understanding of the "whole" simply through concatenating one piece of it at a time until the last fragment is exhausted. Rather, the paradox of the hermeneutical circle is that one can only even begin to understand the first part if one already has some understanding of the whole. In turn, one's understanding of the whole changes as one continues to amass information from the parts; this is why one speaks of a circular rather than linear movement of interpretation.[54]

Contrary to currently-fashionable theories on the topic, the hermeneutical circle has not always been defined as a movement between one linguistic fragment of a text and the written text as a whole. In fact, there has been significant disagreement over the centuries regarding what exactly "the whole" refers to. Originally, in classical rhetoric, "the whole" was the ideal of perfect speech, which was understood to have the same relation to its parts as the human body has with its arms, legs, head, and other organs.[55]

During the Reformation, Martin Luther adopted this model from classical rhetoric but significantly modified it to fit his own theological needs. Luther adopted a revolutionary stance towards scriptural interpretation primarily in order to castigate the hermeneutical abuses of the Church magisterium in Rome. This was necessitated by the simple fact that the "official interpreters of scripture" were not even any good at it. In fact, Luther noted that they often avoided the hard work of interpreting difficult scriptures from the Old Testament by simply designating them as allegorical symbols for passages from the New Testament which were intrinsically easier to understand from the standpoint of Medieval Christianity. Worse still, they would sometimes even excuse themselves from interpreting New Testament passages by claiming that they were mere allegorical symbols for the current Church hierarchy.[56]

Luther appropriated the hermeneutical circle in order to salvage the possibility of scriptural interpretation which the Papacy had long since squandered, as much out of institutional corruption as sheer intellectual laziness. Luther argued, however, that all of these abuses were unnecessary to a reader with a proper understanding of the whole. There was no need to posit random ad hoc allegorical connections among unrelated fragments because any textual passage from the Old or New Testament, however inherently obscure, could eventually be elucidated through the guarantee that it was an integral part within the sacred unity of scripture. For him,

---

[54] Hans-Georg Gadamer, *Truth and Method* (New York: Continuum, 1989), p. 190.
[55] Ibid., p. 175.
[56] Ibid.

this whole bore an inherent promise of comprehensibility because it was divinely inspired by God to communicate a single, internally-consistent message for human salvation. Likewise, for Luther, "the whole" referred to the canonical unity of all of the books of the Bible. Yet even more specifically, the whole referred to the divine message which Luther believed God had inscribed within it.[57] This message was somehow present both in every fragment of the text, however small, and within the canon in its entirety, yet it would be absurd to think that it was merely a linguistic set of information. One had only truly understood the whole if one had grasped that it was a spiritual truth which opened the pathway for the soul to achieve eternal life.

With the rise of secularist and rationalistic viewpoints within the West, Luther's idea of the whole came to be devalued as overly-dogmatic and unacceptably archaic. Over time, the Bible itself was no longer seen as a single book with one divine author and one coherent spiritual message but was instead seen as a number of distinct texts with many different human authors, each of whom was influenced by all too human concerns. This shift from divine inspiration by an omniscient deity to a plurality of disconnected human authors who lived in many different geographical regions in many different eras naturally led to a rise in historicism, since a god exists outside historical finitude but a human subject does not.

This requirement was not, however, applied to all texts equally. Spinoza argued, for example, that historical context is necessary to understand passages of scripture which are inherently ambiguous but he did not see any need to extend this requirement to scientific or mathematical treatises.[58] In his view, these latter texts were sufficiently clear on their own, so there was no need to supplement them with unnecessary historical information. Spinoza memorably noted that one does not need to know anything about Euclid's biography to faithfully follow along with his geometrical reasoning. Hermeneutics was therefore largely a response to a problem of incomplete understanding, a problem which only affected a certain subset of texts such as scripture and poetry. In this

---

[57] Ibid., p. 176.
[58] Ibid., p. 181.

phase, therefore, the "whole" in the hermeneutical circle became the historical context, specifically, the biographical context of the author's life.[59]

Spinoza was not alone in his belief that the meaning of the whole could be a biographical context. In more recent times, however, the emphasis shifted from trying to reconstruct the life of a classical author from the vastly distant past to instead considering how one's own life could be a hermeneutical whole to which particular major events relate. The German term for such an experience within a life, *Erlebnis,* is a common word today but it has something of a mysterious origin. In Gadamer's own research for *Truth and Method*, the earliest reference he could find for it actually occurred in a letter written by none other than Hegel himself. In the letter, Hegel appears to have coined the term in order to talk about a moving experience he had while traveling abroad.[60] He apparently chose to modify the older term *Erleben,* which meant "to be alive when something happened," in order to emphasize that the major experience occurred within the broader whole of his lifetime.[61]

Afterwards, the term *Erlebnis* fit well with hermeneutical theories of life which posited an "adventure" as a particular experience which was so intense that it allowed the whole of one's life to be felt at one time.[62] To this day, we continue to oppose "mere living" to "living well" to convey this idea that in the absence of adventures, one never really gets to experience life. Thus, life (*Leben*) came to play a greater role in aesthetic theory after Hegel, as great art was judged for its ability to manifest the infinity of *Leben* in the finite medium of art.[63] On an epistemological level, mere concepts also came to be opposed to this primordial force of Life, as Neo-Kantians favored defining aesthetic feeling as that which heightens the feeling of Life (*Lebensgefuhl*). This goal allowed them to shift away from transcendental neutrality, the cold

---

[59] Ibid., p. 177.
[60] Ibid., p. 60.
[61] Ibid., p. 61.
[62] Ibid., p. 69.
[63] Ibid., p. 64.

rationalism of the Enlightenment, and the ugliness of Industrialism.[64] Unlike Spinoza's attempt to restore ancient biographies, the context of life as *Leben* could only really be given hermeneutically if it was the living presence of one's own life.

Although there were subsequent developments in this historical trajectory, these examples are sufficient to demonstrate that none of these definitions of "the whole" are equivalent to the Linguistic Turn notion of "the whole text," outside of which supposedly lies nothing at all. Classic rhetoric's perfect speech, Luther's divinely-inspired good news, Spinoza's biographical context, and Hegel's *Leben* all flatly contradict the Linguistic Turn ideology that the hermeneutical circle is a movement from a fragment of the text to the whole of the text within the medium of linguistic understanding alone.

This prejudice that language is the only acceptable definition of the whole can in many ways be attributed directly to Gadamer himself. In fact, his emphasis on language was taken way too far, as he literally elevated linguistic understanding to the very ontological standard of Being. Zizek aptly synopsized Gadamer's thesis as "to be is to be understood," [65] a fanatical over-emphasis on language which the present text shall reveal to have no justification. Gadamer's "Linguistic Turn Ontology" misses the point that all linguistic understanding is founded upon a type of understanding which is fundamentally non-linguistic in nature, a standard of understanding which is ultimately ecological. Purely linguistified interpretation only occurs as a perversion of genuine understanding and a deviation away from the five originary modes of hermeneutics, none of which is purely linguistic in nature. We shall briefly consider all five before proceeding.

Mythological understanding, for example, is successful only to the extent that it provides a pathway for spiritual absolutes to appear within consciousness through events, symbols, and rituals, all situated within a broader narrative.[66] Although it is fashionable

---

[64] Ibid., p. 63.

[65] Zizek characterizes Gadamer's stance with this phrase in his 2012 book *Less Than Nothing*.

Slavoj Zizek, *Less Than Nothing* (London: Verso, 2012).

to mock the very idea of spiritual absolutes (certainly one of the reasons why Julius Evola's monumental work remains ignored within the academic industry), one should bear in mind that love magic all too often yields fruitful results, despite seeming flatly impossible to the materialist skeptic. The explanation for its success can only be grasped on hermeneutical rather than scientific grounds. For example, some love magic rituals use the color green to summon Venus and the energies of ἔρος.[67] Such attempts to capture the essence of love often "really work," provided one utilizes the power of magical symbols. These allow a spiritual absolute to be disclosed to a human subject in a form which can be grasped hermeneutically.[68] One would completely miss the point, however, if one claimed that in such an operation the whole is a linguistic text and nothing more. The whole is, in fact, not even limited to being only spiritual. Because mythology can only appear within some determinate somatic context, in this layer the whole is a composite essence containing both pneumatic[69] (spiritual) and somatic elements. The whole is both a pneumatic and a somatic whole because a finite human subject cannot just directly "see" the spiritual absolutes without any symbolic intermediation bound to some real ecological context. The subject cannot overstep this horizon of ecological limitation without ceasing to exist.

Similarly, systematic understanding is successful only to the extent that it provides a pathway for gnostic absolutes such as numbers, logical relations, and grammatical universals to manifest themselves within consciousness through rational constructs and coherent systematic contexts. A finite human subject cannot just directly "see" the number 3 without an underlying system for it to appear within. Somehow, although no two systems are fully consistent with one another, any one of them still provides an

---

[66] Julius Evola, *Revolt Against the Modern World* (Rochester: Inner Traditions International, 1995), p. 82.

[67] Eros or erotic love. The Greeks had four terms for love which are difficult to distinguish in Modern English, which has only the one term.

[68] John Michael Greer mentioned this magic symbol in his August 2019 discussion on Occultism on the Hermitix podcast.

[69] From the Ancient Greek word πνεῦμα

equally legitimate window into the same gnostic absolute. Even something as fundamental as the definition of number can vary drastically without affecting this hermeneutical requirement. Descartes, for example, held that numbers are innate ideas of the Cogito, while Russell held that numbers are higher order logical classes of classes. Somehow, both can provide a window into the same gnostic essence equally legitimately, even though both are considered "outdated" by the standards of contemporary mathematics. Like mythology, a system can only appear within an ecological context. In this layer, the whole is also a composite essence, made up of both gnostic and somatic elements.

Objective understanding is successful only to the extent that it provides a pathway for the human body itself to be understood hermeneutically through ergonic labor processes involving sense object tools ("ergonic" is the author's own term derived from ἔργον, the Greek word for "work."). Contrary to expectation, understanding the tool itself is just a means to an end to understand one's own body. Examples include blacksmithing, traditional farming, and woodworking. In our era, this hermeneutical experience has almost entirely disappeared, as work itself has been transformed from a physical process of the human body oriented towards satisfying serious survival needs into an empty surrogate activity in which passivity literally becomes one's ethical duty.[70] Bestselling financial author Jim Rickards has noted that in many cases "working on Wall Street" literally means playing golf with the other company employees while the company AI runs on autopilot behind the scenes.[71] Needless to say, in an era where even one's "work" is a surrogate activity, one's pastimes are equally meaningless and immobilizing. Collecting every Mariah Carey album or cheering for a football team displayed on a television set only disconnect oneself from one's own body by turning passivity into one's ethical duty. Surprisingly, it was precisely because the traditional tools have disappeared through Modern Technology's

---

[70] Ted Kaczynski, *Industrial Society and Its Future* (Scottsdale: Fitch & Madison, 2019), para. 39.
[71] Jim Rickards, *The Death of Money: The Coming Collapse of the International Monetary System* (New York: Penguin, 2014).

invasion into every area that the human body has lost nearly every ergonic outlet to discover itself in meaningful processes of work with real sense objects. In this layer too the hermeneutical whole is a composite whole, containing both ergonic and somatic elements. The whole is the human body disclosed through labor with tools within a specific ecological context.

Memological understanding is successful only to the extent that it allows one to grasp the different deep meme shapes which consciousness can hold in different somatic contexts, such as the agrarian circle, the hunter gatherer level plane, fossil fuel ray of progress, the salvage bell curve, Arrakeen vapor, and the nomadic mobile set. Memological shapes of consciousness are all mentatic essences, or essences of non-robotic consciousness in itself. This terminology is borrowed from Frank Herbert's *Dune*, since in that novel the mentat is a conscious thinker who develops his or her mind and power of awareness in order to salvage genuine subjectivity against the artificial intelligence standard of nefarious thinking machines.[72] In our terminology, though, we might go even further and say that only a mentat is capable of holding a memological shape of consciousness. This is because only a mentat authentically exists within an ecological context. Robots have no deep memes, because they are incapable of sustaining a somatic context of meaning. Only the mentat is capable of grasping limitation as such.

In 2018, the NPC Meme began circulating online in response to the need for a universally-recognizable symbol to express the difference between a conscious human and a mindless robot. Whereas a playable character is controlled by a real human agent who exists outside the virtual limits of the game and can act creatively in accord with free will, a non-playable character is a sheer figment of algorithmic execution, a set of digital instructions masquerading as a free entity. Interest in the meme was primarily driven by a desire to identify robots even among those *within* the human population, by exposing that these supposed "free thinkers"

---

[72] Herbert, Frank, *Dune* (New York: Ace Books, 1990), p. 208.

were nothing more than fully-passivized puppets of the System's programming.

Over time, the NPC Meme became sufficiently controversial to motivate a social media purge. It was supremely ironic, however, that the meme was banned because it was deemed "de-humanizing" by the same institutional forces which routinely dismiss anyone who opposes the Democrat Party establishment as "Russian bots" in disguise. In 2019, this accusation was extended even to movements *within* the party itself, as Hillary Clinton publicly "outed" Tulsi Gabbard's presidential campaign as a front operation for foreign interests propped up by Russian bots rather than real human agents,[73] an ironic claim to emerge from someone whose rallies drew the tiniest crowds yet somehow was promoted by the media as a leader with a massive popular following.

On a philosophical level, proponents of the NPC Meme defended its content by alleging that an NPC was someone who had willingly surrendered his or her human freedom in exchange for the perceived benefits which conformists could expect to receive from the System; it was claimed, in other words, that these figures had willingly given up their humanity in order to become robots simply out of a hope that they would receive thirty pieces of silver in exchange for selling their mentatic souls. Although the meme was primarily directed against perceived "political sellouts," the ultimate NPC's are, without any question, the technophiles who mindlessly promote Modern Technology and actively work to dismantle the last remaining somatic contexts on the Earth. These figures rank even lower than mindless promoters of Fossil Fuel Industrialism, because whereas Fossil Fuels form a legitimate Soma that can ground and sustain an ecological context of meaning and a shape of consciousness (albeit a thoroughly dysfunctional one), Modern Technology is not just one more Soma among all the others. It is the anti-Soma that destroys the very possibility of an ecological context. Modern Technology in Kaczynski's sense of the term can never become the Soma or generate a new deep meme of meaning, for it is merely the end of ecology and the destruction of the

---

[73] Jeanine Santucci, "Tulsi Gabbard's lawyers sent a letter to Hillary Clinton demanding she retract Russia comments", *USA Today*, 12-11-2019

mentatic subject. The ultimate NPC is one who has lost the ability even to embody a deep meme. Our project shall be to salvage this composite essence of the mentatic-somatic whole against this onslaught while what little hope there is still remains.

Finally, somatic understanding is successful only to the extent that it provides a pathway for one's ecological context as such to manifest itself; in this layer "the whole" of the hermeneutical circle is the Soma itself, such as the woolly mammoth, agrarian grain, fossil fuels, or Arrakeen Water. Crucially, the ecological whole can only appear properly if it appears as limitation. In Herbert's *Dune*, for example, Water can only appear as Soma only if it appears as the limitation of existence in an extreme desert planet. If one has merely grasped water as one sense object of many, one has failed to penetrate to the deepest layer of somatic hermeneutics and remains at the higher order layer of the sense object. Ecology is therefore literally the hermeneutical interpretation of limitation, the horizon in which the whole is limitation itself.

The problem of composite essences poses a challenge to the traditional theories of Material Ontology. In the archaic view on the subject, Aristotle believed that the material cause of any object could be unearthed through identifying what type of physical stuff it was composed of. Ultimately this could be reduced to one of the four basic elements: earth, water, fire, or air. In Modern Phenomenology, however, Edmund Husserl took this insight a step further by arguing that even these four elements were all instantiations from the same general class of physical objectivities, but this was only one type within a set including several other distinct regions which lacked any common origin or overarching genus.[74] Physical things, psychic acts, feelings, and even consciousness itself were all genuine types of objects to which the conscious subject had access, yet each was ultimately defined by a set of purified features which lacked common ground with any of the other types'. A physical object, for example, could only ever be given one partial perspective at a time, but this was not a

---

[74] Edmund Husserl, *Ideas: General Introduction to Pure Phenomenology* (Eastford: Martino Fine Books, 2017), p. 134.

requirement which psychic acts or feelings had to respect. Husserl argued therefore that the goal of Material Ontology was to isolate each type from the others through gaining a purified insight into the essence of each.

One might argue that pneumatic, gnostic, ergonic, mentatic, and somatic essences are all unique types. Each one is indigenous to its own distinct "region" of Material Ontology. Spirits, numbers, and even the mentatic awareness itself are not simply materialistic forces which are misrecognized for something else out of ignorance or delusion. There is, however, one crucial privilege which only the Soma holds, as it is the only one which can be isolated in consciousness and grasped purely without influence from the others. Only the Soma can claim an entire layer of understanding for itself. The other regions, insofar as they are accessible to the subject at all, can only be interpreted in impure forms; they can only ever appear if they are mixed with some somatic influence. This is the chief limitation of a subject bound to exist within an ecological context. We shall return to this subject in greater detail.

[4]

Hermeneutical Layer	Essence of Whole	Example
Mythological	Pneumatic-Somatic	Love
Systematic	Gnostic-Somatic	3
Objective	Ergonic-Somatic	Blacksmith Work
Memological	Mentatic-Somatic	Vapor Deep Meme
Somatic	Somatic	Water

Gadamer's Hermeneutics: Language and Ecology

The author's emphasis on ecological hermeneutics may surprise readers who would be otherwise inclined to think of ecology as one of the natural sciences rather than an aesthetic problem of interpretation; however, it is largely due to Gadamer's influence that we should automatically assume that hermeneutics is primarily a matter of linguistic interpretation of literary texts in the first place. In fact, Gadamer took this insight way too far, since he literarily redefined Being in terms of hermeneutical understanding. In his sprawling 2012 book *Less Than Nothing*, Zizek aptly synopsized Gadamer's ontology under the slogan "to be is to be understood":

> [A]s Gadamer put it in his paraphrase of Heidegger's thesis on "language as house of being," "to be is to be understood"; that is, the horizon of understanding sustained by language is the ultimate transcendental horizon of our approach to being . . . [because] the impenetrable background of historical prejudices [always] predetermine the field of what we can see and understand. Every world is sustained by language, and every spoken language sustains a world.[75]

Gadamer was able to uphold this bizarre equation of Being and language by claiming that, contrary to expectation, understanding does not secondarily translate the pre-linguistic objectivity of the world into symbolic words; rather, linguistic understanding is the originary medium in which a thing can achieve Being in the first place, because understanding is to be defined as the "coming-into-language of the thing itself."[76] Presumably, for Gadamer, a thing can only lay full claim to Being if it has been disclosed hermeneutically within a horizon of inter-subjective interpretation, but of course this can only occur within the public medium of language rather than the private medium of Cartesian subjectivity.

Although Gadamer's ontological thesis that "Being is understanding" might sound indefensible when taken as a small sound-bite out of the vast context of his massive text *Truth and Method*, even figures who disagree with him must acknowledge that he had compelling reasons to reach such a strange conclusion. Above all, Gadamer could not accept the one-sidedness of traditional hermeneutical models which portray understanding as a

---

[75] Slavoj Zizek, *Less Than Nothing* (London: Verso, 2012).
[76] Hans-Georg Gadamer, *Truth and Method* (New York: Continuum, 1989), p. 378.

secondary act of reproduction which unfolds inside one isolated human mind.[77] Under this view, the reader would merely reconstruct the original process of creation which the artist performed in composing the text. For example, the novel *Don Quixote* only "really happened" once within Cervantes' mind when he wrote it; each time one of us reads it, we are merely re-staging his unique original act of thinking within our own private mental spaces. A reader, therefore, could only ever hold the position of a spectator, forever consigned to lie outside the "real event" to which the author alone had access.

Gadamer devoted considerable energy near the very beginning of the book to exposing how this belief is simply a logical conclusion of Kant's aesthetic theory in *The Critique of Judgment*. In that work, Kant found that aesthetic experiences differ from ordinary experiences in the following way: whereas one is ordinarily able to subsume an experience under a universal concept which would tell one what something is, in an aesthetic experience of a great work of art, there is no universal concept available.[78] For example, if one sees a monkey while walking on a road in India, subsuming this intuition under the universal concept of a monkey will allow one to understand what it is.[79] However, when one experiences one of Mozart's brilliant musical compositions, one does not have any universal concept readily available to tell one what it is. In fact, it is altogether impossible for one to even speak about "understanding" great works of art, for the entire point is that these experiences only enable the subject's faculties to fall into an exciting, harmonious "free play" because there is no concept readily available to halt the process from carrying itself away.[80]

Of course, Kant did not argue that there are *no* cases where something can both be beautiful and be understood. There are certainly beautiful things which occur as a product of Nature rather than as a product of aesthetic genius and artificial creation, and are therefore subsumable under a universal concept. Everyone has seen

---

[77] Ibid., p. 166.
[78] Immanuel Kant, *Critique of Judgment* (Indianapolis: Hackett, 1987), p. 19.
[79] Ibid., p. 82.
[80] Ibid., p. 62.

natural beauty in a tree in the forest, a cow in a field, or a lovely woman, yet none of these examples of "dependent beauty" are quite the same thing as what one finds a true experience of "free beauty" which lacks a universal concept, such as a Rembrandt painting, a Bach fugue, or a Faulkner novel.[81] Kant had a solid theoretical reason for this opposition, in that for him having a concept available to define the content of an experience of "dependent beauty" would merely limit the pleasure one could feel.[82] One could only overcome this limitation through an experience of free beauty in a genuinely aesthetic mode of appreciation, since this alone would allow the faculties to fall into the harmony of free play which provides the transcendental condition for pleasure to be maximized.

As a result of this distinction between determinative judgments in which one understands through a concept and reflective judgments in which one does not, Kant was forced to portray the artist behind great works through the cult of genius.[83] Just as the spectator's experience of the work cannot be explained conceptually, the genius artist's process of creation cannot be explained rationally. It is not possible to explain how Mozart, Cervantes, and Van Gogh created their masterpieces; this is not merely a limitation which we as spectators endure, for even these geniuses themselves could not provide a coherent theoretical explanation for how their own work was produced.[84] All that we can do is acknowledge that it was only a matter of historical happenstance that these geniuses were born in the first place.

Unfortunately, this overemphasis on a genius whose inspiration is inexplicable even to himself or herself led to a tendency to redefine all genuine understanding as scientific explanation. In fact, Gadamer explicitly blamed Kant's radical "over-subjectivization" of aesthetic experience[85] as the true origin behind the widespread devaluation of all theoretical truths which lie outside the realms of the Natural Sciences to the lowly status of

---

[81] Ibid., p. 76.

[82] Hans-Georg Gadamer, *Truth and Method* (New York: Continuum, 1989), p. 45.

[83] Ibid., p. 54.

[84] Immanuel Kant, *Critique of Judgment* (Indianapolis: Hackett, 1987), p. 175.

[85] Hans-Georg Gadamer, *Truth and Method* (New York: Continuum, 1989), p. 97.

pseudo-truths which cannot claim to hold the dignity of genuine understanding, since that would only be reserved for objective judgments obtained through strict adherence to the scientific method.

Gadamer wrote *Truth and Method* as a desperate attempt to save the hermeneutical tradition of non-scientific understanding from both the naïve attempts to redefine all the Human Sciences in the image of the Natural Sciences[86] and the hasty dismissal of all non-scientific work as idle chatter with no legitimate claim to truth.[87] Against both of these straw-man caricatures, Gadamer argued that we can only save hermeneutics, and indeed the ontological horizon of meaningfulness itself, if we move away from models which favour an isolated subject and instead focus upon language as such.[88]

Gadamer found the hermeneutical model of a subject privately reconstructing the artist's original act of creation to be unsatisfactory because it is simply a poor description for what takes place in language, even in ordinary conversations.[89] It would be absurd to describe linguistic communication as something which merely unfolds on the inside of each person's mind, even if one were to assume that the "same process" could unfold identically at the same time for each subject. Such a hypothesis is inherently questionable, since any appeal to a substitutable procedure which always yields the same pre-determined results is actually just a reference to Modern Technology in disguise. Artificial intelligence is not "perfected interpretation." It is the destruction of hermeneutics and the death of the subject.

It is impossible to speak of anything like an "identical process" in the case of understanding because the entire point of hermeneutics is that no two subjects will ever interpret the same contents in exactly the same way. One of the theoretical justifications for close reading is that even the poet himself or herself would have no privileged position with regard to his or her own works. Walt Whitman himself, for example, could not claim to

---

86 Ibid., p. 65.

87 Ibid., p. 43.

88 Ibid., p. 384.

89 Ibid., p. 388.

have the sole valid interpretation of his own poems, despite the fact that he wrote them. It is easily overlooked, though, that this holds true for both written texts and for live communicative processes such as discussions, speeches, and theatrical performances. Anyone who has attended a heated political rally with a controversial speaker will know that there is bound to be significant disagreement over how to describe what happened at "the same event" afterwards, even by people who were all there in person. Yet despite the fact that each subject's interpretation will be slightly different, it would be absurd to say that only one of them could be correct and all the others are wrong.

In order to address this paradox, Gadamer found it necessary to abandon the most fundamental presuppositions of Western Metaphysics altogether. Rather than be enslaved to the dichotomy of subject and object, he favoured the phenomenological concept of the horizon.[90] Although Husserl and Heidegger had both adopted this concept for their own philosophical purposes earlier, Gadamer himself defined a horizon as "the range of vision including everything which can be seen from a particular vantage point."[91] Horizons are difficult to conceptualize for thinkers influenced by the biases of Western Metaphysics, since they defy all of our expectations about how ordinary objects should behave. For example, unlike mundane things, horizons can be expanded. In addition, new horizons can be opened up. Horizons are, in fact, fundamentally incomplete, since the very concept of a "closed horizon" is something of a contradiction in terms.[92] Horizons are therefore completely unlike the fixed, reified contents presupposed within the standard of truth defined by the scientific method.

Gadamer found that horizons are necessary to describe what happens in communication because a participant in a hermeneutical situation is never located somewhere on the outside of the situation, viewing it in its entirety from a detached standpoint of objectivity. The act of being caught up in a hermeneutical situation is something which is by definition unfinished. For this reason, Gadamer warns

---

[90] Ibid., p. 370.
[91] Ibid., p. 302.
[92] Ibid., p. 304.

that historical self-knowledge is something which can never be complete.[93] Any fantasy of complete historical knowledge is simply an appeal to the outdated metaphysics of objectivity in disguise.

Gadamer was careful to note, however, that in understanding there are not two different horizons, one for each speaker. Rather, the only way to honestly describe what happens in communication, and understanding more broadly, is that there is "a fusion of horizons."[94] In order to explain this obscure idea, Gadamer claimed that Kierkegaard was one of the few thinkers who had seriously grappled with a similar concern.[95] Kierkegaard similarly rejected views which equated truth with objectivity, since the most important truth of all could never be submitted to such requirements. One could never understand Christ's existence from a detached and objective perspective, especially one which was definitively situated many centuries later. In Kierkegaard's view, the professional scholars whose job is literally to do just that are all too often the ones who understand the true point of Christ's existence the very least.

In his classic *Philosophical Fragments*, Kierkegaard contrasted these "followers at second hand" with the "contemporary follower."[96] Rather than adhere to the common expectation that truth must be objective, the contemporary follower realized that truth can only happen if the subject is deeply, personally involved. Unlike the dry geometrical truths which Socrates was content to merely "recollect," Jesus' existence provided a path for the contemporary follower to confront the most important truth of all, the truth of his or her own eternal happiness, as well as the possibility of it being lost.[97]

In his *Concluding Unscientific Postscript*, Kierkegaard contrasted objective communication and subjective communication to explain why the highest truth could never be grasped as an

---

[93] Ibid., p. 302.
[94] Ibid., p. 306.
[95] Ibid., p. 127.
[96] Soren Kierkegaard, *Philosophical Fragments* (Princeton: Princeton University Press, 1987), p. 89.
[97] Ibid., p. 63.

objective datum.[98] On one hand, objective communication concerns itself only with transmitting results; even if the procedure to acquire these results involved a difficult pathway, this process loses its relevance once execution is completed and the final result has been obtained. On the contrary, in subjective communication, the way is precisely what matters, for subjective communication is in itself "a way" rather than a result. For this reason, Kierkegaard insisted that subjective communication must take the form of indirect communication, such as art, humour, or pseudonymous writings (as his own body of work demonstrates all too clearly.)

The loss of subjective communication in favour of objective communication was surely a problem in Kierkegaard's 19th Century Denmark, but in the present year of 2019 Modern Technology has allowed objective communication to take on a life of its own, as vast, impersonal technological networks are now able to transmit electronic data over global distances without any need for a human subject, let alone one whose involvement with the process is motivated by an existentialist crisis regarding the risk of losing one's eternal happiness. Just as Kierkegaard warned that the obsession with results risked devaluing even the most complicated procedures to the status of irrelevance once completed, in our era these algorithmic processes literally unfold outside any human subject's consciousness, as vast armies of artificially intelligent machines execute tasks which are not transparent even to the companies who claim to own the "intellectual property rights" over them. Few smartphone zombies realize that they are willingly contributing to their own subjective extinction by enthusiastically supporting this monstrosity.

Following this distinction between objective and subjective truth, the only way to really understand Christ's existence is to somehow become contemporaneous with him. Kierkegaard did not mean by this that they would have to literally exist at the same time, which would not be possible at any rate; rather, contemporaneity could only be achieved through "bringing two moments together." While Kierkegaard was primarily interested in how this would work

---

[98] Soren Kierkegaard, *Concluding Unscientific Postscript to Philosophical Fragments*, Vol. 1 (Princeton: Princeton University Press, 1992), p. 79.

for the Religious Stage, as a phase intrinsically higher up than the Aesthetic Stage, Gadamer claimed that something like this is also appropriate to describe the Being of the work of Art.[99] For Gadamer, hermeneutics, whether it be concerned with art,[100] law,[101] religion,[102] or history,[103] is the fusion of horizons.

Gadamer went on to argue that, for this reason, a genuine conversation is by definition one which is not steered or controlled to follow any one subject's will. In fact, a "conducted conversation" is inherently contradictory.[104] A conversation is genuine only if what is expressed is not only mine or yours, but something "common."[105] Likewise, Gadamer insisted that the "between" is not an interval between two subjective processors, as though the "real action" were only to occur on the inside of each mind. On the contrary, the between, definitively situated on the outside, is the default space in which any real understanding would have to occur. This is why Gadamer repeatedly contrasted the flawed model of "aesthetic consciousness," which merely occurs inside one mind, with his own idea that art is where an "event of Being" happens on the outside.[106] Near the very end of the text, he explicitly designated this to be an "event of language."[107]

Gadamer admitted himself that his unconventional views on "the outside" were directly influenced by Heidegger's similar shift with regard to how we think of time in his magnum opus *Sein und Zeit*. Interestingly, Heidegger was also motivated to do so by his desire to solve the hermeneutical mystery of how understanding occurs. Because Heidegger found that understanding could only be grasped through the ontological orientation of an "existential" in

---

[99] Hans-Georg Gadamer, *Truth and Method* (New York: Continuum, 1989), p. 127.
[100] Ibid., p. 151.
[101] Ibid., p. 330.
[102] Ibid., p. 309.
[103] Ibid., p. 198.
[104] Ibid., p. 383.
[105] Ibid., p. 388.
[106] Ibid., p. 144.
[107] Ibid., p. 471.

Dasein's mode of being in terms of time, Heidegger concluded that time could no longer be considered merely negatively, as a gulf to be crossed over.[108] Rather, time would have to be the supportive ground of the course of events, in which even the present itself is rooted. After *Being and Time*, temporal distance could no longer be thought of as an empty abyss between two points. Time is rather a positive, productive condition which enables understanding to happen in the first place.[109]

Although Gadamer focused more on language than time, he similarly claimed that the "common between" of hermeneutical understanding is the space in which Being itself must be understood. Anything which falls short of the achievement of intersubjective commonness in the public "between" cannot be considered to hold the status of Being. Or to put it more briefly, anything which is not linguistically understood has no Being. As Gadamer said himself near the very end of the text, as something of a synopsis of the entire sprawling meditation: *"Being that can be understood is [just] language."*[110]

Although this claim is admittedly quite interesting on a theoretical level, Gadamer's reduction of hermeneutics to a type of "Linguistic Turn Ontology" was inherently misguided, since purely linguistic understanding is only ever a secondary perversion. It can only occur as an abstraction away from the more originary modes of understanding considered earlier, none of which is oriented towards language alone. Mythology succeeds as Pneumatic Hermeneutics only if it can disclose transcendent spiritual absolutes. System succeeds as Gnostic Hermeneutics only if it can disclose transcendent gnostic essences such as numbers, logical relations, or grammatical absolutes. Dealing with sense objects succeeds as Ergonic Hermeneutics only if the human body itself can be disclosed through a process of real labour. Memology succeeds as Mentatic Hermeneutics only if the shapes of consciousness are manifested in living awareness which can never be reduced to the robotic imitation of a machine. Finally, Ecology can succeed as

---

[108] Ibid., p. 297.
[109] Ibid.
[110] Ibid., p. 474.

Somatic Hermeneutics only if the Soma itself can be revealed as the very limit of one's worldview. Gadamer's ideal of linguistification defeats the purpose of hermeneutical understanding, for the whole point of each layer of meaning is to provide a space for a non-linguistic, transcendent essence to manifest itself and be understood within a somatic context of intelligibility.

Mythology drained of spirit is every bit as distorted as Mathematics devoid of number, a process of work without the body, a memological analysis with no mentatic consciousness, or an ecology which lacks somatic limitation. In this light, we can see all too clearly how bizarre it was for Gadamer to have claimed that linguistification is what grants Being to a horizon of meaning. Far from bestowing the gift of Being, linguistification is the deterioration of Being into an empty shadow of it. A purely linguistic hermeneutics is therefore actually something of a contradiction in terms, since it would merely block out the non-linguistic essences from manifesting themselves. Most important of all of these is the act of ecological hermeneutics in which somatic limitation could reveal itself, for even the higher order layers of understanding all must be founded upon a context of ecological understanding to be given themselves.

Gadamer was not completely unaware of this incompatibility between ecology and linguistification. However, his fanatical adherence to the Linguistic Turn led him to actively downplay ecological concerns as applicable to lower animals but fundamentally inappropriate to the properly hermeneutical world of a speaker who has access to language. In fact, Gadamer devoted one of the final sections of *Truth and Method* to explicitly contrasting the animal's ecological habitat with the speaker's linguistic world.[111] Whereas an animal is a biological organism which is simply embedded in a habitat and responds to external stimuli in accord with instinct, a speaking subject lives in a linguistic world which cannot be described with either of these motifs. Most importantly, whereas an animal is incapable of rising above instinct and stimuli, Man is by definition free to rise above his world, for language is

---

[111] Ibid., p. 444.

precisely that.[112] Ecological context is therefore literally a euphemism for a type of inhuman slavery to external conditions and internal biology. Freedom fundamentally implies the "linguistic constitution of the world" which the animal lacks, since only a linguistic world could allow even the possibility of human freedom. The very idea of an objectified world in which language was not possible would rule out freedom from having any meaningful realization. Gadamer held that this revelation definitively negated any archaic "dogmatism of 'meaning-in-itself,'" as this is a construct which would not even be possible outside the Metaphysics of an objectified, non-linguistic world.[113]

Gadamer therefore downplayed efforts towards "human ecology" as a fundamental misunderstanding of the difference between a free speaker's linguistic world and an animal's merely objective habitat.[114] Far from being a worthy hermeneutical concern, Gadamer considered ecology to be the purified antithesis of hermeneutics, the ultimate counter-example to the achievement of common understanding worthy of the title of "Being."

Slavoj Zizek and the Divine Violence of Language

Despite considerable disagreements with Gadamer on the fine details of the Philosophy of Language, Zizek has similarly contrasted ecology and language in a number of fascinating passages. We shall examine the most important of these to demonstrate how arguably the only thing Zizek and Gadamer could agree on is that ecology and hermeneutical interpretation are not the same thing. In his classics from the 1990s, such as *Tarrying with the Negative* and *The Ticklish Subject,* Zizek argued that the tendency among professional academics to blame Descartes for every social problem in the world all too often misses the real point of his work, which is far more subversive than almost anyone in the mainstream realizes.[115] This can only be revealed, however, if we first dispel the

---

[112] Ibid., p. 445.
[113] Ibid., p. 473.
[114] Ibid., p. 453.
[115] Slavoj Zizek, *The Ticklish Subject* (London: Verso, 1999), p. 1.

urban myth called "How Descartes Invented the Fiction of Cartesian Dualism Simply out of a Malicious Desire to Dominate the Other." Like any good urban myth, one will get a slightly different answer regarding who exactly this Other was, depending on who happens to be speaking. In the feminist version of the myth, Descartes invented the Cogito out of a sexist desire to dominate women. In the Marxist version of the myth, he did it to dominate industrial workers (never mind that Descartes wrote before the rise of Capitalism). In the Postcolonial version, he did it to dominate "lesser peoples" on faraway continents. In the Queer Theory version of the myth, he did it to dominate those who do not performatively embody heteronormative expectations regarding sexuality. In the environmentalist/ecological version of the myth, he did it to dominate the Earth itself.

This is not hyperbole, as a thinker no less great than John Zerzan has described Cartesian dualism exactly this way. In his early essay from *Elements of Refusal* titled "Number: Its Origin and Evolution," Zerzan claimed that Cartesian dualism misrecognizes the historically-contingent alienation inherent in civilization for a Metaphysical distinction between mind and matter, then uses this hierarchy to justify Man's dominion over Nature:

> The thesis that the world is organized in such a way that there is a total break between people and the natural world, contrived as a total and triumphant world-view, is the basis for Descartes' renown as the founder of modern philosophy.[116]

Zerzan did not, however, think that Descartes had invented anything new with this insight, for he was merely developing the same historical trajectory of domination which had begun with the rise of agriculture near the end of the prehistoric era. Zerzan goes on to explain that Descartes's belief in a "total break" between people and the natural world made him incapable of even recognizing the vitality of the living creatures of Nature. Even animals were reduced to the status of machines, simply because they lacked the

---

[116] John Zerzan, "Numbers: Its Origin and Evolution," in *Elements of Refusal* (Kindle Edition).

Metaphysical principle of *res cogitans* (thinking substance) with which the rational human subject alone was endowed:

> To Descartes the material universe was a machine and nothing more, just as animals "indeed are nothing else but engines, or matter set into a continual and orderly motion." [As a result,] Descartes had asserted that animals could not feel pain because they are soulless, and that man is not exactly a machine because he had a soul.[117]

Zerzan argues, therefore, that Cartesian dualism is the absolute antithesis of ecological awareness, since even Nature itself fails to appear as Nature in this framework. He suggests that the remedy against this distortion must be to restore Man's position as one more natural entity among all the others within the ecosystem. This could be achieved through surprisingly simple means. He claims, in fact, that an anthropological change in how we obtain our food would be enough. Through abandoning agriculture and returning to hunting and gathering, the attitude of domination would lose its material foundation, since domination is simply the memological shape of agriculture in disguise.[118] In its place, we would all view the world once again through the automatic shape of egalitarianism which supposedly was the norm for humans until the rise of civilization occurred.[119]

Although Zizek agrees that Descartes's viewpoint represents something of a break from naïve ecological awareness, Zizek has demonstrated that Descartes's interest in the Cogito is a good deal more complicated than a simple "will to dominate the Other." Nor is it sufficient to simply celebrate this as Man's "triumph" over Nature. In fact, compared with the alienation from ecological harmony which the Cartesian Cogito suffers from, the animal world can easily seem quite romantic.

---

[117] Ibid.

[118] John Zerzan, "The Iron Grip: the Axial Age," in *Twilight of the Machines* (Port Townsend: Feral House, 2008), p. 31.

[119] John Zerzan, "The Beginning of Time, End of Time" in *Elements of Refusal* (Kindle Edition).

According to Zizek, what Descartes really discovered with the Cogito was just that the human subject does not actually "fit" into its surrounding environment, or even into its own physical body. This is not a problem for animals. They fit into their physical bodies effortlessly, since natural instinct alone is sufficient to determine how they should react to a stimulus which confronts them. Humans, however, cannot fall back so easily on instinct, since even instinct itself must be repressed to serve the artificial requirements of culture which are all too often obscured by innuendo and unwritten rules anyway. In addition, animals simply fit into their ecological habitats because there is no need for them to sit around for years wondering what their role within the ecosystem might be. A wolf will not need to question whether it will be a hunter, just as an antelope will not need to question whether it will be a grazer. We, on the other hand, must spend decades contemplating how we will fit into the System; even after investing considerable time and money in order to fulfil the educational requirements to fight for the niche we had decided upon, all too often we find that there is no place for us amidst stiff competition, rapidly-changing conditions, and outright dishonest projections for future employment broadcasted by the media and student loan usury industry for their own benefit. Against this backdrop, it is all too easy to long for the animal world as a space without alienation, a kind of ecological utopia in which everyone knows his or her role automatically and anyone, however strange, is already guaranteed a place within the whole.

In several texts (*Living in the End Times*,[120] *Absolute Recoil*[121] etc.), Zizek has mentioned that documentaries which portray animals in the wild offer a tempting form of escapism for just this reason. Interestingly, there is no alienation in these contexts precisely because there is no need for language, no need to find the right words to express a desire or convince the Other of its legitimacy. Nowhere is this "lack of linguistic alienation" more appealing than in the realm of sex. In fact, the great mystery of the animal world is that whereas humans never quite know when "the

[120] Slavoj Zizek, *Living in the End Times* (London: Verso, 2011), p. 83.
[121] Slavoj Zizek, *Absolute Recoil* (London: Verso, 2014), p. 203.

right moment" to make a move might be, for animals the perfect moment always seems to magically arrive right on time. There is no need to struggle through numerous obscure layers of culturally-conditioned bullshit which lack the guarantee of success anyway; for animals, they just spontaneously "do it."

Zizek has gone as far as to claim that the tendency for modern laws on sexual harassment to progressively become stricter (in the early 2000's, it was decided that even looking at a person "the wrong way" could be cited as a "legitimate case of criminal sexual harassment") misses the point that because there is no "right time" to make a move, any leap of faith in that regard is in a certain sense "harassment."[122] Harassment, perhaps, is simply a word for the attempt that failed.

Zizek accepts that Cartesian dualism is the loss of ecological harmony, but he suggests that this is largely to be attributed to Man's unique requirement to mediate his or her relations with the outside world through the symbolic medium of language. The solution to this impasse, however, could never be as simple as just "un-learning" language and other symbolic forms of alienation (number,[123] time,[124] art[125] etc.), as John Zerzan has promised would happen if we just return to hunting and gathering.[126] Such a hope is bound to fail because Cartesian alienation is not simply a result of empirical contingencies, such as whether we currently rely upon agriculture. Zizek claims that Kant discovered that Cartesian alienation has a transcendental origin which cannot be overstepped through any amount of anthropological tinkering, for it alone provides the very conditions for subjects to experience the world in the first place. Interestingly, Zizek explicitly contrasts this view

---

[122] Slavoj Zizek, *Living in the End Times* (London: Verso, 2011), p. 5.

[123] John Zerzan, "Number: Its Origin and Evolution," in *Elements of Refusal* (Kindle Edition).

[124] John Zerzan, "The Beginning of Time, End of Time" in *Elements of Refusal* (Kindle Edition).

[125] John Zerzan, "The Case against Art," in *Elements of Refusal* (Kindle Edition).

[126] John Zerzan, "Language: Origin and Meaning," in *Elements of Refusal* (Kindle Edition).

with "ecological ideology" and its fantasy that the subject can someday be restored to a position within the great chain of being:

> [While] Descartes was the first to introduce a crack in the ontologically consistent universe, [o]nly Kant fully articulates the inherent paradoxes of self-consciousness. What Kant's 'transcendental turn' renders manifest is the impossibility of locating the subject in the 'great chain of being,' into the Whole of the universe—all those notions of the universe as a harmonious Whole in which every element has its own place (today, they abound in ecological ideology). In contrast to it, subject is in the most radical sense 'out of joint"; it constitutively lacks its own place.

It is important to note that Zizek does not frame this argument through New Age clichés about humans evolving to "higher forms of consciousness" than lower animals embody. On the contrary, linguistic mediation opens up possibilities of perversion which would be unimaginable within the ecological world of animal instinct. For example, in his 2012 *Less Than Nothing*, Zizek argued that "[w]hat distinguishes humans from animals is their ability to pretend as opposed to simply getting caught up in an illusion."[127] One might argue that pretending is a symptom of linguistic alienation, something of an impossibility for an animal truly absorbed within the ecological chain of which it is just one small part. This distinction is far from trivial:

> [For example, w]hen we watch a horror movie, we are pleasurably terrified — pleasurably, precisely because while giving ourselves up to the spectacle we know very well that that it just what it is. But imagine our shock and withdrawal if, all of a sudden, we became aware that what we were watching was in fact a snuff movie depicting real acts of horror. This is also why scarecrows can be frightening: not because we are duped into believing they are alive, but

---

[127] Slavoj Zizek, *Less Than Nothing* (London: Verso, 2012), p. 44.

because we have to confront the fact that they work, while knowing very well that they are just artefacts.[128]

We can understand all too well Zizek's example of what would happen if we switched from pretending to watch a gruesome murder in a horror film to suddenly realizing that it was a real snuff film with no pretending involved. What is truly shocking in such a shift, though, is just that it reveals to us that we would only be sickened by our own behaviour if the linguistic dimension of pretending were banished and the raw animal dimension of violence were all that remained; otherwise, we would simply go on "enjoying it" all the same. This proves Zizek's point that language opens up a horizon of meaning which is wholly Other to what even the most demented animal could be capable of sustaining.

Cartesian dualism therefore does not mean that humans are just "higher animals" with "more evolved features," as the stereotypical view would hold. Cartesian subjectivity is not an improvement over the ecological absorption animals experience; rather, Zizek has repeatedly favoured describing subjectivity as the very crack or rupture within the universe. According to him, the mind and body are not two coherent objects which have somehow inexplicably become mismatched with one another; rather, the Cartesian Cogito simply *is* this mismatch itself.[129] This is why Zizek has repeatedly claimed that the true significance of Descartes's discovery was not a new "thinking substance," but rather that subjectivity is substancelessness itself.[130] The following section from his *Absolute Recoil* is worth quoting in full:

> If a substance is an X which expresses itself in its attributes or representations, even if this representation is failed and partial, then a subject is something much more radical: an X which emerges retroactively through the failure of its

[128] Ibid.

[129] Slavoj Zizek, *Absolute Recoil* (London: Verso, 2014), p. 242.

[130] Slavoj Zizek, *Tarrying with the Negative: Kant, Hegel, and the Critique of Ideology* (Durham: Duke University Press, 1993).

representation, with no substantial content preceding this loss or failure.[131]

Zizek was not content to merely lament this loss of ecological inclusion, as Zerzan seems to do. Rather, he was interested in salvaging the revolutionary potential inherent to language. Bizarrely, one of his favourite examples of this subversive capability was in Jesus Christ's message. In his 2010 *Living in the End Times*, Zizek argued that no one has ever really provided a satisfactory explanation for why Jesus openly promotes violence in scriptural passages such as Luke 12:49 ("I have come to cast fire upon the earth; and how I wish it were already kindled") and Luke 14:26 ("If anyone comes to me and does not hate his own father and mother and wife and children . . . and even his own life, he cannot be my disciple.") Christian apologists who have an ideological reason to insist that Jesus is the "Prince of Peace" often argue that the kind of violence Jesus endorses in these passages is not the mundane "earthly violence" which a power-hungry political leader would favour; rather, Jesus was only interested in the "divine violence" which lies in the spiritual realm. Contrary to expectation, Zizek actually does agree with this stance but exposes how such a reading risks missing the point that the divine violence which is more fundamental than any worldly struggle is none other than language itself:

> [O]ur "earthly" divisions and struggles are ultimately always grounded in a "divided heaven," in a much more radical and exclusive division of the very (symbolic) universe in which we dwell. The bearer and instrument of this division of heaven is language . . . as the medium that sustains our entire worldview, the way we experience reality: language, not primitive egotistic interest, is the first and greatest divider, and it is because of language that we and our neighbours can live in different worlds even when we live on the same street.[132]

---

[131] Slavoj Zizek, *Absolute Recoil* (London: Verso 2014), p. 242.
[132] Slavoj Zizek, *Living in the End Times* (London: Verso, 2010), p. 103.

Jesus' call for violence continues to be scandalous because it does not merely focus on the ontic struggles of a divided Earth, but posits the ontological struggle of a "divided heaven" as the very key for each individual to directly access the dimension of linguistic universality himself or herself:

> Christianity introduces into the global balanced order of *eunomia* a principle totally foreign to it, a principle that, measured by the standards of the pagan cosmology, cannot but appear as a monstrous distortion: the principle according to which each individual has an immediate access to the universality (of the Holy Spirit, or, today, of human rights and freedoms) – I can participate in this universal dimension directly, irrespective of my special place within the global social order.[133]

Zizek claims therefore that Jesus' demand for his followers to disregard their traditional family relations is just a particular example of his more general aversion against the very principle of ecology. One is not bound to his or her ecological niche within the organic social whole, because the whole itself is always already broken. The divine violence of language does not intrude into a coherent, harmonious ecological whole by contaminating it with division in a merely secondary way; rather, the divine violence exposes that any dream for a perfect human ecology is a fiction which is fundamentally ruled out by the very symbolic structures which allow this world to be disclosed to us in the first place, as there is no reality without symbolic mediation.

Although it is true that Christianity forms a community of believers, Zizek warns that even this community cannot be understood as a coherent ecological whole which merely replicates the family which each member had to disregard his or her role within in order to join. In his 2000 *The Fragile Absolute*, a book dedicated to saving Christianity's radical message from the

---

[133] Ibid., p. 105.

fundamentalist reading, Zizek argued that the Christian community is by definition a community of outcasts; for that reason, it is the antithesis to any organic social ecosystem:

> It is precisely in order to emphasize this suspension of the social hierarchy that Christ . . . addresses in particular those who belong to the very bottom of the social hierarchy, the outcasts of the social order (beggars, prostitutes . . .) as the privileged and exemplary members of his new community. This new community is then explicitly constructed as a collection of outcasts, the antipode to any established organic group.[134]

In his 2006 "magnum opus" *The Parallax View*, Zizek similarly cautioned readers that although "universality" plays a fundamental role in Christianity, this Christian universality must not be misinterpreted to mean something like an "all-encompassing global medium where there is a place for all and everyone – it is, rather, a struggling universality, the site of a constant battle."[135] In other words, in Christianity, universality can no longer mean an ecological matrix in which everyone finds a slot to "fit in." Universality under Christianity is rather the name for the divine violence of language itself, a violence which can never be reincorporated into some naïvely-posited ecological totality.

Although this claim might sound unjustifiably abstract at first, it was perfectly consistent with the broader ontological thesis which motivated Zizek to write *The Parallax View* in the first place. The problem of parallax is essentially the problem of how an object will appear differently depending on which location it is viewed from. Historically, parallax has played a particularly important role in the context of viewing stars from different points in the earth's orbit. In the foreword to his *Revolt Against the Modern World*, for example, Julius Evola expressed his own admiration for "the method of parallaxes" as that 'which is used to determine the exact position of a star by reference to how it appears from different

---

[134] Slavoj Zizek, *The Fragile Absolute* (London: Verso, 2000), p. 123.
[135] Slavoj Zizek, *The Parallax View* (Cambridge: MIT University Press, 2009), p. 35.

places."[136] Evola's own methodology was somewhat similar, as the work largely considered the mystery of how the same spiritual absolutes could appear in symbols indigenous to cultures ranging from the Incan and Aztec to the Egyptian and Chinese Civilizations, evidence which Evola affirmed even as the "academic marketplace of ideas" came to demonize such truths as Orwellian thought-crimes against the religious dogma of postmodernist relativism.

Zizek's interest in parallax fit with his general tendency to prefer counter-intuitive thinking, in that he emphasized that the real point about parallax is precisely *not* to fall for the trap of getting lost in celebrating the multiplicity of perspectives as such. Clichés regarding the Yin Yang balance of multiple coherent frames of meaning miss the point that the conflict is not between the two at all; parallax merely reveals that the One has always already failed to be itself. Christian's universality is, as he says himself, a "struggling universality, the site of a constant battle" for just this reason. An empty space of universality can never precede the particular by providing a space for it to occupy as part of some broader ecological totality, because universality itself can only arise from a particular's non-coincidence with itself.[137] Hegel's idea that dialectical movement occurs precisely because the Notion can never succeed in living up to its own criteria is therefore, according to Zizek, an insight into the mysterious fact that Being is, in itself, incompleteness.[138] Reality can never actually succeed in being itself, for Being is itself incomplete.

It is for just this reason that Zizek has made the bizarre statement that "Nature doesn't exist." Any deep ecology calls to save Nature as though she were the coherent and complete One which existed before diabolical Man intervened in her harmonious functioning miss the point that the One is a fiction which even Nature itself cannot live up to. In defence, Zizek has claimed that natural disasters such as earthquakes, hurricanes, and volcanic eruptions are not disruptions *of* Nature, for Nature itself *is* this set of

---

[136] Julius Evola, *Revolt Against the Modern World* (Rochester: Inner Traditions, 1995), p. xxxv.

[137] Slavoj Zizek, *The Parallax View* (Cambridge: MIT University Press, 2009), p. 41.

[138] Slavoj Zizek, *For They Know Not What They Do* (London: Verso, 2008).

disruptions. Nature cannot be saved from disaster for Nature is itself the disaster.[139]

These passages demonstrate that on a political level, Zizek associates ecology with social hierarchy and associates language with the revolutionary potential to disrupt fixed niches and unjust power divisions. We might even argue that Zizek rejects the "false universality" of the harmonious ecological totality and favours the "true universality" of language, since his meditations on Early Christianity proved that the latter notion is closer to the very ontological structure of Being itself. The author of the present text shall find this particular claim to be the most troubling, as it implies that linguistification and the suspension of ecological awareness provide the pathway to overcome dysfunctional political arrangements. One might consider Zizek's view to be the exact antithesis of Zerzan's viewpoint, in that for Zerzan it is language which is a mere symptom of unjust political hierarchies, while the revolution against these corrupt power structures can only occur through restoring the lost ecological balance by returning Man to his status as one more natural hunting and gathering animal among all the others. Despite significant disagreements with Zerzan, the author of the present text agrees that linguistification is not the medium for revolutionary politics; it is the very technology used to destroy the possibility of rebellion against the System.

The Five Layers of Hermeneutical Understanding

While Zizek's and Gadamer's insights remain fascinating on their own terms, neither seem to have grasped that this strict opposition between hermeneutics and ecology can only be sustained if one assumes that the only valid type of hermeneutics is linguistic in nature. While Gadamer has acknowledged that there is some hermeneutical value to interpreting wordless art, such as sculpture,[140]

---

[139] See the video "Slavoj Zizek- Nature Does Not Exist."
https://www.youtube.com/watch?v=DIGeDAZ6-q4&list=PL2JZmtbono_fx3iiLw-BT5SszBpA3BN3T&index=7&t=0s
[140] Hans-Georg Gadamer, Truth and Method (New York: Continuum, 1989), p. 149.

painting,[141] and architecture,[142] he has still insisted that each of these fall short of the ideal of language; or more precisely, their hermeneutical value is intrinsically oriented towards the horizon of language, even if it cannot be actualized as such in a non-verbal medium. He argued that one might consider the following hypothetical example as evidence for the intrinsic link between language and understanding. If some civilization from the remote past had left behind nothing except vast stone monuments, these would certainly be fascinating objects to examine; nonetheless, this past civilization could never truly become a part of our world if it had not left behind any written texts.[143] In the absence of these, the historical dimension as such would forever remain inaccessible to us, since the possibility of a linguistic fusion of horizons would be blocked out.

More specifically, Gadamer claimed that the very ability to disclose a Whole through the hermeneutical circle can only be realized through texts. Vast, impersonal, silent stone monuments cannot disclose any Whole. Likewise, he claimed that writing is "central to the hermeneutical phenomenon,"[144] since writing is something like "hermeneutics purified."

Because Zizek and Gadamer both lacked the hierarchy of five layers of meaning (mythological, systematic, objective, memological, somatic), their analysis of the relation between language and ecology will remain incomplete at best, despite both men's Herculean accomplishments as scholars. As we shall demonstrate, the purified horizon of hermeneutics is not the written text which speaks a truth inaccessible to the silent stone monuments, as Gadamer claimed; rather, hermeneutics purified is ecology, the very thing which Gadamer considered to be the antithesis of hermeneutical understanding. While it is true that Gadamer did not seek to merely reduce ecology to language, since he was more interested in transcending the limitations of ecological objectivism altogether, for reasons which Gadamer did not himself

---

141 Ibid., p. 140.
142 Ibid., p. 157.
143 Ibid., p. 390.
144 Ibid., p. 392.

consider, we must question whether any attempt to replace genuine ecological awareness with a post-ecological horizon of pure linguistification might only lead to massive suffering and perhaps even human extinction in the not so distant future. Linguistification bears no essential differences from Modern Technology, for Modern Technology is in a certain sense merely the technical perfection of linguistification. Far from abandoning ecology to the lower, unfree slaves of instinct and stimuli, we must reclaim ecology as the supreme hermeneutical concern.

Gadamer's reduction of all understanding to a single, common linguistic layer and Zizek's emphasis on the linguistic alienation inherent in submitting to the Symbolic Order both miss the point that there is no one hermeneutical layer of understanding as such. Rather, there are five different layers in which understanding can occur, none of which is purely linguistic. We shall consider each of these before proceeding with an argument for redefining ecology in terms of the final of these, somatic hermeneutics.

Pneumatic Hermeneutics: Mythology

We shall begin our analysis of the five layers with Mythology. In the layer of pneumatic hermeneutics, one does not only understand linguistically because the true standard of success is whether one understands spiritual essences, which are themselves accessible only if they are disclosed in a mythic event. In Hindu Mythology, for example, it is one thing to say that Lord Shiva is absolute emptiness because the Sanskrit meaning of "shi-va" is "no thing." It is another thing to actually disclose the mythological event of Shiva passing months in silent meditation after he had appeared as the Adiyogi in the Himalaya Mountains; as the unenlightened onlookers waited for the miracle to occur, they were too spiritually impoverished to realize that this radical stillness *was* the miracle. In the mythic event, this purely spiritual principle of absolute emptiness somehow manifests itself within a broader narrative which allows the subject a hermeneutical pathway of entry to touch it, however incompletely.

Although it is currently fashionable to ridicule the very idea that independent spiritual essences could be viewed in consciousness, John Michael Greer has provided abundant evidence to demonstrate that this attitude of materialist reductivism requires a fair amount of cognitive dissonance to be maintained. Many readers who primarily know Greer through his writings on Peak Oil and the collapse of Industrial Civilization might be surprised to learn that his most popular work was actually a short 2001 book called *Monsters*. This delightfully-readable text, in fact, very well might have provided some of the source material for Stephanie Meyers' bestselling *Twilight* franchise, since the tradition of werewolf folklore among Native American tribes in the Pacific Northwest was rarely discussed before *Twilight* — with the notable exception of Greer's book.

In *Monsters*, he explored the inconvenient fact that long after scientists had conclusively disproven the physical existence of monsters such as vampires, ghosts, zombies etc., somehow people have still ended up frequently reporting experiences in which they see these supposedly impossible creatures.[145] One certainly *could* take the easy way out and claim that these experiences are always nothing more than hallucinations with an explanation completely reducible to psychological brain processes (a cheap tactic which Greer exposed as an equally problematic approach to the *UFO Phenomenon* in his 2009 book of the same name).[146] But even if one does so, one would still fail to explain why certain recurring identical traits appear in people's paranormal experiences of these beings, even across different cultures, geographical areas, historical eras, and religious backgrounds. These fixed morphological features can only indicate the presence of some spiritual absolute which cannot be explained away on linguistic or physical grounds alone.

For example, the reader himself or herself may be all too familiar with the so-called Old Hag experience. In it, one finds oneself lying in bed, perhaps in half-dreaming state. Next, one hears footsteps rustling near the bed and feels the undeniable presence of

---

[145] John Michael Greer, *Monsters: An Investigator's Guide to Magical Beings* (Woodbury: Llewellyn, 2001).

[146] John Michael Greer, *The UFO Phenomenon* (Woodbury: Llewellyn, 2009).

another malicious being in the room. Frantic attempts to move or speak fail, as the dreamer is frozen in a state of paralysis. The wicked being approaches, though it might not be seen coherently. Although the human subject will often awaken after a certain amount of desperate struggle, there have been a disturbingly high number of cases in which this experience has literally led to death. Greer noted among Hmong refugees who were displaced from Laos after CIA intervention in that nation, medical examiners were puzzled to find that many of them had died in their sleep; these same figures had complained about having Old Hag experiences before their deaths, so one could only assume that the final night of life held the unwanted visit that finally went too far.[147]

What the medical examiners' materialist prejudices failed to allow them to accept with its full relevance was that these experiences tended to arise when Hmong refugees were no longer able to perform traditional rituals to honour their ancestor spirits; one purpose of these rituals was to seek their help to ward off evil spirits. As refugees were forced to relocate to urban apartments after being displaced from their native country, these rituals became nearly impossible to maintain and the defences against hostile spirits started to wear thin. It was only after the Hmong relocated to rural areas in which the physical infrastructure could be restored to perform the traditional rituals that these experiences tended to decline and peace was restored.

The author of the present text would like to suggest that the chief reason why materialist researchers failed to solve the mystery for why Hmong deaths and Old Hag encounters tended to coincide was that they embodied a flawed hermeneutical approach to the experiences. More specifically, their methodology automatically ruled out interpreting these experiences as anything except manifestations of psychological processes of the brain or some other type of physical processes carried out by the human body. It was precisely because their hermeneutical prejudices were distorted to rule out the possibility that any transcendent spiritual essence might exist, let alone that it could ever appear within consciousness,

---

[147] John Michael Greer, *Monsters: An Investigator's Guide to Magical Beings* (Woodbury: Llewellyn, 2001).

that they had to rely on far-fetched explanations which proved ineffective to solve the crisis anyway. Whether one would like to admit or not, it is a fact that Hmong deaths to Old Hag visits only declined after the properly spiritual solution of restoring the old traditional rituals was implemented. One can only remain intellectually honest if one admits that there are certain experiences in which transcendent, independent spiritual essences manifest themselves. The fact that they do not have a physical existence is hardly a refutation, for that was precisely the point of designating them as spiritual essences in the first place. The standard of hermeneutical success for these experiences is therefore whether one allows the spirit to be interpreted or understood as a spirit rather than let it be trivialized or explained away as some unrelated bit of linguistic or physical illusion.

Although Greer was primarily interested in paranormal experiences of monsters as such in this 2001 book, his later *Archdruid Report* posts on the decline of Industrial Civilization revealed that spiritual components are an integral feature of our so-called normal experiences of the world as well. For example, Greer reported in a February, 2007 post titled "The Failure of Reason" that professional engineers were frequently sending him fully-rationalized plans which would allow society to smoothly transition from a petroleum-based economy to a post-petroleum economy.[148] These models tended to embody the highest standard of mathematical rigour and on theoretical grounds alone many of them seemed plausible. However, of the countless plans that had been drafted to transition to a post-petroleum economy, not even *one* has ever been implemented. Greer is one of the few thinkers with the courage to admit that this was not due to a lack of logical rigour. Like the Hmong deaths, the mystery could only be solved through identifying the properly spiritual component. In this case, any engineering plan that prioritizes numerical considerations alone without doing anything to address spiritual problems is doomed to failure, no matter how linearly sophisticated it might be: "What has

---

[148] John Michael Greer, "The Failure of Reason", in *Archdruid Report*, Vol. 1 (Chicago: Founders House, 2017), [. 156.

been lacking consistently is [just] the collective will to put any of these ideas into practice."[149]

Like the Old Hag herself, human willpower is a legitimate spiritual essence which must be hermeneutically interpreted as such if it is to be dealt with in a productive manner. Yet even if one acknowledges that these spiritual essences exist, it may initially remain unclear which path one should take to investigate them. Interestingly, Greer implied in this essay that simply thinking about human willpower in isolation is impossible. One can only find it if one looks within the medium of mythology:

> The crux of the problem, as suggested in an earlier post in this blog, is that human thought is mythic by its very nature. We think with myths as inevitably as we see with eyes and eat with mouths.[150]

The only medium in which willpower might be properly examined is the "underground realm of mythic narratives and magic symbols."[151] It is not enough to short-circuit the seemingly-irrelevant layers of narrative and symbol in order to zero in on the spiritual essence in itself. Somehow, one can only succeed in changing one's relation to the spirit if one changes the mythological infrastructure in which it can appear first. He explicitly warns:

> [Any] attempts to change the course of industrial civilization without changing the narratives and symbols that guide it on its way are doomed to failure, and those narratives and symbols cannot be changed effectively with the toolkit [currently available in the collective psyche.]

Although Greer does not explicitly acknowledge it himself, there are strictly hermeneutical reasons why this is the case. One can only change one's dysfunctional relation to the human will if one first changes the symbolic narrative in which it can appear; yet

---

149 Ibid., p. 157.
150 Ibid., pp. 159-60.
151 Ibid., pp. 157-8.

this is because the mythic event alone provides the hermeneutical horizon in which this spiritual essence can manifest itself in the first place.

One might consider the following for an all too understandable example of this admittedly obscure principle. Greer repeatedly notes the irony that suburban American homes are not at all desired out of any objective recognition of their practical value, which is effectively nothing at all. To this day, no one has ever succeeded in explaining why a flimsy cardboard shack which can hardly withstand even the slightest impact from an unexpected weather event or bulldozer[152] could somehow be valued at over half a million dollars just because it happens to be located one to two hours away from some major American city. Clearly, our irrational fixation with suburban McMansions cannot be understood at all unless we examine their ability to hermeneutically disclose the spiritual desire for security through the magical symbol of a safe house surrounded by a moat of green lawn grass a comfortable distance away from some hypothetical scary place "out there."

Likewise, any plan for a sustainable or green future which refuses to let suburbs disappear cannot be taken seriously. This effectively rules out virtually *all* pseudo-ecological efforts currently underway in established bureaucracies, since these are only carried out with the goal of somehow being able to keep the suburban home at any cost, even ecological death. This refusal to change symbols can only be understood as a refusal to abandon one's pathological attachment to a transcendent spiritual essence, a refusal which tends to be the most deeply-entrenched precisely in figures who claim to have long since abandoned any belief in the same spiritual absolutes which they cannot see beyond.

---

[152] Dmitry Orlov once noted: "[Most] of the suburban housing stock is actually of very low intrinsic value, constructed out of a few sticks, a bit of tarpaper and some plastic and cardboard sheets. These American-style Potemkin villages will be simple to knock down . . . the merest touch from a bulldozer will be sufficient to cause these little market bubbles to fold up into a pile of of kindle and dust with barely a groan." *Reinventing Collapse: The Soviet Experience and American Prospects* (Gabriola Island: New Society Publishers, 2011)

Ironically, one misses the entire point of narrative and symbol if one treats them as purely linguistic games. Indeed, literary studies departments within academia have worked against their own interests in this regard, since they have willingly gone to the greatest extremes to enforce Linguistic Turn-inspired reductivism through postmodernist, deconstructivist, and post-structuralist brands of sophistry. The official gatekeepers of mythology seem to have missed the point that to strip mythology down to nothing more than an empty language game is to distort its very hermeneutical essence. The ongoing decline of Liberal Arts departments in the West and their deterioration to an object of scornful ridicule to anyone outside their own closed circle of entrenched academic careerists is simply an inevitable conclusion of their own deliberate decision to abandon the whole point of their subject matter. The only reason mythology matters in the first place is precisely that it provides the hermeneutical horizon in which spiritual absolutes can manifest themselves and be understood. To disfigure this hermeneutical space into one which actively resists spiritual infiltration by embracing materialism and relativism as secular dogmas will not liberate us from the influence of spirits altogether; it will only enslave us even more to the dominant spirit of our times which drives our mindless sleepwalking into the abyss of industrial collapse.

Nor is this simply a matter of individual spirituality. Julius Evola's monumental work remains ignored within official academic circles because he identified that there is a properly political dimension to Pneumatic Hermeneutics as well. Although Evola's views are undeniably controversial, we have an ethical duty to break the Orwellian censorship which has thus far consigned one of the more interesting thinkers of the past century to the secular equivalent of the Vatican's index of forbidden texts. No discussion of Pneumatic Hermeneutics can be complete without including his *Revolt Against the Modern World*.

Evola's "revolt" consisted in overturning the most basic of all the presuppositions of modernity by systematically dismantling the illusion of "progress."[153] Evola found progress to be an unsatisfactory term to define the ongoing trajectory of our era because the modern world is actually nothing short of a catastrophic degeneration in comparison with the world of Tradition.[154] Rather than affirm democracy,[155] Evola shocked readers by openly endorsing the archaic social structures of Ancient Civilizations, complete with the caste system,[156] divine monarchy,[157] political priesthood,[158] women's roles in the harem,[159] and holy war.[160] In addition, rather than celebrate the scientific materialism of modernity,[161] he performed the unthinkable feat of arguing that the magical rites[162] and spiritual forces[163] of Tradition were not baseless superstitions but were, in fact, powerful realities with an invisible but no less real origin in the higher realm of Being.

He noted near the very beginning of the text that the fundamental doctrine of two natures would be necessary to understand anything else which followed. According to the doctrine, the higher realm of supernatural Being is the true origin and support which grounds the ephemeral realm of naturalistic becoming.[164] In Evola's own words, "the physical plane merely contains effects; nothing takes place in this world that did not originate first . . . in the invisible dimension."[165] It was precisely this belief in the two natures that made up the true thought crime which has consigned Evola to the margins of the world of "professional intellectuals."

---

[153] Julius Evola, *Revolt Against the Modern World* (Rochester: Inner Traditions, 1995), p. xxx.
[154] Ibid., p. 177.
[155] Ibid., p. 24.
[156] Ibid., p. 89.
[157] Ibid., p. 8.
[158] Ibid., p. 14.
[159] Ibid., p. 165.
[160] Ibid., p. 116.
[161] Ibid., p. 163.
[162] Ibid., p. 29.
[163] Ibid., p. 33.
[164] Ibid., p. 3.
[165] Ibid., p. 34.

In modernity, of course, we have denied the existence of this realm of Being through reducing the shallow layer of material becoming to the sole region of existence. The reader may object that appealing to invisible supernatural forces beyond the realm of physical materiality is epistemologically unjustifiable, since these by definition lack any empirical pathway to be investigated. It is only in the hermeneutically-impoverished modern age, however, that it would seem obvious to think that empirical observation is the only "right" standard of interpretation. In fact, Jordan Peterson noted in *Maps of Meaning* that the attitude of scientific objectivity is an historical anomaly which required centuries of purification before it achieved the strict form familiar today.[166] Far from being one's default stance towards the world, the scientific method long remained something of a mystery, since even the most intelligent minds of the Scientific Revolution were unclear on the details for how exactly it should be done. This was because it required something like a wilful deterioration of the hermeneutical horizons of meaning, a degradation which eventually become universalized through major institutions which mandated it through an Orwellian Ministry of Truth. In the world of Tradition, however, the highest knowledge was not the scientific elucidation of matter, but the hermeneutical disclosure of spiritual absolutes. These were embodied in magic symbols, priestly rites, and supernatural myths.

In the author's own terminology, the scientific method is simply another form of linguistification, since it has only progressed at the cost of fundamentally disfiguring our ability to grasp the pneumatic meanings which were a basic feature of the world of Tradition. Like all forms of linguistification, contemporary scientific reductivism only demonstrates how badly damaged the hermeneutical horizon of our era has become and how far the process of decline from Tradition has proceeded. The greatest irony, though, is that rather than rid the Earth of the pneumatic absolutes, the System has simply enslaved us to the dark forces all the more. John Michael Greer has repeatedly called modern advertising "black magic," the abuse of pneumatic forces to convince masses of

---

[166] Jordan Peterson, *Maps of Meaning* (New York: Routledge, 1999), p. 3.

people to waste money they don't have on stupid, ugly, shoddily-made products they don't even want and which won't make them happy anyway. Linguistification has not banished the spirits altogether so much as it has provided a safe haven for malicious forces to reign unchecked; ironically, the surest guarantee that evil will never be challenged is to deny its existence altogether, as the official dogma of materialistic scepticism has ensured.

Evola negated the intellectual relativism which naturally follows from a reduction of all reality to the ephemeral realm of physical matter, as he instead affirmed spiritual absolutes as genuine essences which must be recognized in their ontological integrity rather than be dismissed as empty remnants of pre-scientific ignorance. In order to support his claim that the origins of this cryptic knowledge indeed date back to an era often considered to be so primitive as to barely qualify as human, Evola rejected the official anthropological account about the prehistoric times.[167] Far from being an era of halfway-human "cavemen," the distant past was a Golden Age "naturally and totally in conformity with . . . the traditional spirit."[168] While he admits that caves obviously played a role in the people's life in that era, they appeared to be used for cult and ritual purposes rather than as animal-like dwelling places.[169] Far from being halfway-human, the beings who lived in this time were actually more than human.[170] Contrary to the gospel of Darwinian evolution, the past was a superhuman "era of the gods" rather than a descent into purely animalistic primitivity. The modern world is nothing more than a grotesque deviation and decline from this point of origin, but that is only because the Golden Age embodied a superior horizon for the hermeneutical disclosure of spirit.

In addition to examining the broader process of deterioration from the Golden Age in the vastly-distant past, like Spengler, Evola was interested in the question of why individual great civilizations decline. Ultimately, he found that no naturalistic explanation will

---

[167] Julius Evola, *Revolt Against the Modern World* (Rochester: Inner Traditions, 1995), p. 182
[168] Ibid., p. 184.
[169] Ibid., p. 182.
[170] Ibid., p. 178.

ever be sufficient.[171] Unthinkable though it might be, Evola claimed that the true causes of civilizational decline shall always be found in spiritual errors, such as the neglect of sacred rites, the violation of traditional laws, and the disregard for caste hierarchy ("caste mixing").[172] These undo order and trigger the return of chaos, though Evola meant this in a far more than metaphorical sense.

Evola did not, for example, conceptualize order and chaos as merely psychological factors, as the early Jordan Peterson apparently did in his 1999 *Maps of Meaning*. Peterson correctly identified this interplay between order and chaos as a constant theme within the body of Ancient Mythology. For example, the pagan god slays the dragon of chaos and establishes order for the human subjects living under his dominion. However, for Peterson these terms are largely just euphemisms for naturalistic phenomena.[173] The kind of order Peterson was interested in was really just the order of psychological comfort within a territory which had been rendered sufficiently familiar that it no longer triggered one's fight or flight instincts.[174] In addition, Peterson seemed to view chaos as simply the possibility of finding oneself thrown to a frightening context where naturalistic dangers might threaten one's life because they escape the zone of intelligibility which had been previously mapped out.[175] Likewise, for the early Peterson chaos and order are not spiritual realities grounded in a higher realm of Being, since they are ultimately explicable within the naturalistic layer of material becoming. Order and chaos are simply euphemisms for a physical organism's struggle to function without anxiety amidst countless dangers in the wild. Nor is this even unique to humans, as the instinctual responses to confronting unexpected anomalies within one's environment overlap significantly among humans and

---

[171] Ibid., p. 55.

[172] Varg Vikernes cites caste mixing as the cause of the decline of Egypt as well in the fifth section of *Vargsmål*.
Julius Evola, *Revolt Against the Modern World* (Rochester: Inner Traditions, 1995), p. 56.

[173] Jordan Peterson, *Maps of Meaning* (New York: Routledge, 1999), p. 214.

[174] Ibid., p. 56.

[175] Ibid., p. 55.

non-human animals.[176] It is for this reason that the main task accomplished in *Maps of Meaning* was to crack the psychological code to explain how order is achieved and chaos overcome through an explanation that was fully compatible with the neuroscientific understanding of how the brain functions as a biological lump of flesh.[177] Transcending the illusion of pneumatic absolutes is therefore, under this view, a sign of scientific progress's conquest of yet another intellectual territory. The early Peterson was just another proponent of linguistification.

Evola differed remarkably from Peterson by insisting that the interplay between chaos and order is far more than just psychological. The result of losing sacred order will be nothing short of real supernatural catastrophe, as the ongoing decline of global civilization demonstrates all too well. We can consider the violation of traditional laws as one notable example. Contrary to the modern view, the very notion that laws have a merely humanistic origin was entirely foreign to the world of Tradition. Laws were legitimate only insofar as they had a divine origin grounded in some spiritual and transcendent character.[178] In this context, breaking the law was literally a matter of sacrilege and impiety rather than just an offense against the "social contract" established among humans on an ad hoc basis of consent. Far more than merely risking earthly punishment under the state, such a violation posed a supernatural danger for the fate of the culprit, as well as the people to whom he or she was closely related.[179] In our era, of course, we have completely lost sight of this older view and have instead privileged utilitarianism as the sole meaningful standard to guide political decisions. Any appeal to the usefulness or uselessness of a law is a modern preoccupation which Evola calls the "ultimate materialistic criterion of modern society."[180]

---

[176] Ibid., p. 19.
[177] Ibid., p. 49.
[178] Julius Evola, *Revolt Against the Modern World* (Rochester: Inner Traditions, 1995), p. 21.
[179] Ibid.
[180] Ibid., p. 22.

Although Evola does not use the terms himself, he noticed something of a distinction between a horizon of meaning in which Pneumatic Hermeneutics functions properly, and the distorted fragments of linguistification in which spirit becomes hermeneutically inaccessible. In the non-linguistified contexts of the world of Tradition, for example, the symbol of the "sacred stone" with a "foundation from above" (often, a stone that literally originated from the sky) recurs in various cultural contexts whenever the question of the legitimacy of rule comes up.[181] The spiritual foundation of legitimate rule symbolized by a stone from the sky is of course the exact antithesis to the modern notion of democratic rule, that indeterminate and formless abstraction which lacks any guarantee beyond the vague notion of social agreement. Though it is only a faint echo from the pre-modern past, we are still somewhat familiar with this image through the story of King Arthur in ancient Britannia, but Evola noted that Theseus in Greece and Sohrab in Persia also drew a sword from a stone as a symbol to determine that they were worthy of ruling (just one example of the overlap among many civilizations' symbols' reference to the same pneumatic absolutes).[182] The symbol of the sword in the stone has virtually entirely lost its meaning in our era, however, as the story of King Arthur is seen as nothing more than "good entertainment." We have only preserved the symbol as a linguistified shell which has been disconnected from the pneuma that once animated it in the world of Tradition.

In our modern hermeneutically-impoverished world, we have willingly reduced meaning to the shallow and distorted layer of linguistification alone, even within the political realm. Under democracy, the state's only recognized principle of legitimacy and authority lies in the indeterminate masses. Evola calls this a regression to what was "typical of naturalistic social forms lacking an authentic spiritual foundation, which can alone be held through participating in a higher order."[183] In his critique of Christianity as a fundamentally anti-traditional movement, he similarly claimed that

---

[181] Ibid., p. 23
[182] Ibid.
[183] Ibid., p. 24.

Christianity's so-called "egalitarianism" was really just a prohibition against seeking to achieve a determinate form through some heroic action: "This belief in human equality . . . exercised an antithetical function to the heroic ideal of personality and to the value bestowed on anything that a being, by becoming differentiated, by giving itself a form, is able to claim for itself within a hierarchical social order."[184] We even miss the point, however, if we think of the ideal hierarchy as being based on economic values alone, for it can only be sustained through its embodiment of spiritual forms.

Contrary to the media caricature of him, Evola noted that even the notion of "race" as some biological or naturalistic entity definable only in terms of blood purity misses the point as well, since a great civilization only arises when a supernatural and nonhuman force of higher order Being acts upon the factors located in the lower realm of naturalistic becoming.[185] He noted, for example, that pre-Roman Italy was actually a mixture of a number of different ethnic groups;[186] the Roman Civilization as such only arose through a spiritual rather than naturalistic principle of unity among them.[187] This is the mystery which the secular and materialistic historians have never been able to crack. Losing contact with this higher power is the catastrophe which sets the process of decline in motion.[188] As this process accelerates, the results include the all too familiar phenomena of individualism and anonymous massified social body.

He even devoted the final chapter of the first part of the text to explaining why the "Decline of the Superior Races" could never be solved through strictly genetic methods, contrary to the media stereotypes on Evola. In this chapter, he addressed the crisis of overpopulation which has coincided with this "racial decline" among the formerly-elite bloodlines by designating it just one more example of how chaos has overtaken form in the reduction of

---

[184] Ibid., p. 283.
[185] Ibid.
[186] Ibid., p. 265.
[187] Ibid., p. 264.
[188] Ibid., p. 58.

humans to purely quantitative category.[189] The solution, however, cannot just be to engineer this population growth in a controlled fashion oriented towards yielding "the best results." If we reduce human reproduction, even among surviving aristocratic types, to another application of the same methods used to strategically breed "good horses," we will only get, at best, beautiful animals destined for work.[190] True greatness will forever remain inaccessible if its spiritual foundation remains blocked out through the hermeneutical disfigurement of materialistic linguistification. Kaczynski's warning in the 174th paragraph of the Manifesto about the "domesticated animals" which humans will be reduced to once the technological destruction of freedom is completed is worth quoting as well:

> If the elite is ruthless they may simply decide to exterminate the mass of humanity. If they are humane they may use propaganda or other psychological or biological techniques to reduce the birth rate until the mass of humanity becomes extinct, leaving the world to the elite. Or, if the elite consists of soft-hearted liberals, they may decide to play the role of good shepherds to the rest of the human race. They will see to it that everyone's physical needs are satisfied, that all children are raised under psychologically hygienic conditions, that everyone has a wholesome hobby to keep him busy, and that anyone who may become dissatisfied undergoes "treatment" to cure his "problem." Of course, life will be so purposeless that people will have to be biologically or psychologically engineered either to remove their need for the power process or to make them "sublimate" their drive for power into some harmless hobby. These engineered human beings may be happy in such a society, but they most certainly will not be free. They will have been reduced to the status of domestic animals.[191]

---

[189] Ibid., p. 167.
[190] Ibid., p. 170.
[191] Ted Kaczynski, Industrial Society and Its Future (Scottsdale: Fitch & Madison, 2019), para. 174.

Interestingly, in addition with these demographic factors of overpopulation, anonymous collectivism, and individualism, Evola listed the technological phenomenon of mechanization as a symptom of abandoning the order of Being for the chaos of becoming.[192] In the second part of the book, he discussed Japan's decline from Tradition after its defeat in World War II. It is no coincidence that the flight of the traditional spirit coincided with a rise in the frenzied proliferation of technological mechanizations: "Because of the Dark Age and its laws, wherein technological and industrial potential as well as organized material power play a decisive role in the clash of world powers, the fate of this tradition has been sealed with the outcome of the last war."[193]

This tendency for technological exploitation to coincide with the loss of spiritual realities was also confirmed in his chapter on "Space, Time, Earth," in which he warned that the new property laws which had come in to replace the sacred laws of aristocratic land ownership have not brought about the social egalitarianism they promised so much as they have effectively reduced the land to something "only valued from an economic point of view and . . . exploited as much as possible with machines and with other modern technical devices."[194]

The demographic correlate of this technological monstrosity is, as Ellul and Kaczynski also noted, collectivism.[195] Evola warns that Marxism is not at all a heroic act of revolution against the beast of Modern Technology, for it is precisely the social form which naturally results from allowing this runaway train to continue on its path of destruction:

> That being the case, it is natural to encounter other typical traits of a degeneration such as the property increasingly shifts from the individual to the collectivity. Parallel with

---

[192] Julius Evola, *Revolt Against the Modern World* (Rochester: Inner Traditions, 1995), p. 59.
[193] Ibid., p. 236.
[194] Ibid., p. 156.
[195] See Chad A. Haag's *The Philosophy of Ted Kaczynski* for a more detailed discussion of both men's thoughts on collectivism and technology.

the collapse of the aristocratic title to the lands and the economy having become the main factor, what emerges first is nationalism, which is followed by socialism and finally by Marxist communism. In other words, there is a return to the rule of the collective over the individual.[196]

It will likely strike the reader as inherently self-contradictory to associate technology with the loss of order and the victory of chaos, for Modern Technology would seem to represent the very highest standard of ordering ever devised. After all, Jacques Ellul defined Technique precisely in terms of its hard-wired tendency to replace spontaneous natural actions with strict, calculated, technical forms.[197] However, one could only claim that Modern Technology restores order against chaos through upholding a very subtle equivocation in these terms. In the world of Tradition, the very concept of "form" had a much more specific meaning than would be accessible in the modern worldview, in which we tend to think of form as any ordering of matter whatsoever. The reason for this ambiguity is that the old distinction between form and matter loses something of its original meaning when interpreted outside the context of the fundamental doctrine of the two natures, in which the physical was distinguished from the metaphysical, and Being was distinguished from becoming.[198] As Evola said himself near the beginning of *The Revolt Against the Modern World*, in the world of Tradition, mere "matter and becoming express the reality that acts in a being as an obscure necessity or as an irrepressible indetermination, or as the inability to acquire a perfect form and to possess itself in a law."[199] In other words, materialism was simply the failure to obtain the higher ordering of form which could only be achieved through rising up from the lower realm of becoming to the higher ground of Being to reach a form which was not the result

---

[196] Ibid., p. 156.

[197] Jacques Ellul, *The Technological Society* (New York: Vintage Books, 1964), p. 20.

[198] Julius Evola, *Revolt Against the Modern World* (Rochester: Inner Traditions, 1995), p.3

[199] Ibid., p. 5.

of materialistic contingency but was instead a manifestation of some pneumatic absolute: "The incessant becoming and the perennial instability and contingency of the inferior region appeared to the man of Tradition as the cosmic and symbolic materialization of that predicament."

Modern Technology is the ultimate example of such a failure for matter to rise up to embody a genuine form, as the pseudo-forms embodied in Modern Technology are not reflections of spiritual absolutes with a transcendent origin; technological pseudo-forms are all invented on a whim by feeble humanistic interests, solely in order to plunder the Earth in pursuit of economic wealth. Far from even realizing that this is a shortcoming, however, Modern Technology actively inhibits this upward movement through promoting materialism as a religious dogma. We are forbidden from seeking any principle of ordering beyond what was artificially engineered on an ad hoc basis under the command of corporate and government agencies motivated solely by financial greed and political power hunger. Far from embodying order, Modern Technology is simply "institutionalized chaos," a monstrosity that has legally mandated formlessness and indeterminacy by threat of Orwellian excommunication to anyone foolhardy enough to speak out against it.

Modern Technology is therefore just another brand of linguistification, even if it occurs within media which appear to lack any linguistic component. One should be reminded that linguistification is anything which causes the hermeneutical horizon to deviate from its proper orientation of transcendence towards, in this case, real spiritual absolutes. Democracy and the Modern Technology which it serves are simply political linguistifications, symptoms of the failure for the horizon of Pneumatic Hermeneutics to disclose itself, as the spirits of Being take flight and abandon the lower level to fragmentation and emptiness.

Gnostic Hermeneutics: Systems

Linguistic reductivism is every bit as inappropriate to the hermeneutical horizon in which gnostic systems (such as systems with mathematical, logical, or scientific content) are understood by the subject. In Systematic Hermeneutics, the true standard of success is whether one can understand gnostic essences which have a transcendent and independent origin. Notable examples of gnostic absolutes include numbers, logical constructs, and grammatical universals. We shall begin by analysing numbers' requirement to be manifested only within the context of a system, which itself requires a somatic context to be actualized.

Even in the absence of the ecological memology which we shall favour, Oswald Spengler noticed numerical systems' dependence upon cultural worldviews to manifest themselves and even devoted a great deal of energy towards efforts to solve the great gnostic mystery why numbers can only be given in a system, yet a system can only be given in a particular cultural context, which itself can only be given within history. Spengler devoted the second chapter of *Decline of the West* to exploring why a plurality of mathematical systems have actualized themselves over the course of history, yet each one was beholden to a specific cultural and historical context which allowed it to appear in the first place but could not be transferred to another cultural context without serious distortion.[200]

In the fifth chapter of that work, Spengler expanded on this argument by observing that even so-called "pure numbers" cannot be properly understood outside a recognition of how symbols in general function within a cultural worldview.[201] The key to a understanding the broader set of cultural symbols, of which mathematical symbols were just a subset, lay in identifying what Spengler called "the prime symbol" of a culture. Spengler believed that the prime symbol was a basic presupposition unique to a particular culture's worldview, which in turn provided an underlying condition for its other symbols to make sense. For example, he noted that for the Ancient Greeks, the prime symbol was the "[compressed] material and individual body." For the Western Europeans, the prime symbol continues to be "pure infinite

---

[200] Spengler, Oswald. *Decline of the West: Volumes 1 and 2* . Random Shack. Kindle Edition.
[201] Ibid.

space." For the Arabians, the prime symbol remains the enclosed "cavern." Spengler claimed that one could reliably identify the prime symbol's influence over cultural artefacts as diverse as architecture, music, and sculpture. For example, the Western European fixation on "pure infinite space" provides the cultural rationale behind Gothic Cathedrals' tendency to have raised ceilings, even if these do not serve any utilitarian purpose as such. Similarly, the Arabian prime symbol of the cavern provides the rationale behind the construction of mosques even to the present day. The Classical Greek prime symbol of a compressed body provided the rationale for their tendency to believe that absolute perfection should be embodied in the medium of temple statues, for in these statues the gods' and goddesses' bodies could defy logic by being both eternal and yet more youthful than any mere mortal who stands in their presence.

Interestingly, Spengler did not believe that the prime symbol was simply a word, for he held the prime symbol to be something more originary than any linguistic construct. Although a culture had countless linguistic symbols, these were all merely derivative relative to the prime symbol which provided their condition of intelligibility in the first place: "the prime symbol . . . is not presentable by words, for language and words are themselves *derived symbols*."

Spengler believed that Mathematics, like language, would be impossible to actualize within a specific culture outside the influence of a particular prime symbol. Despite our tendency to claim that Mathematics is the purified form of scientific objectivity, Spengler realized that the prime symbol would subtly influence even one's best intentions toward mathematical rigour by coercing the results to reflect a certain cultural worldview which was anything but objective. There is not even any such thing as an unbiased, non-cultural answer to the question over the fundamental definition of numbers.

Spengler's own example contrasting Greek and Indian views on something as basic as the ontological status of the number 3 is worth examining in detail. Because their prime symbol was a compressed body, for the Greeks the number 3 could not be anything except a positive integer. For the Indian mathematician, however, the number 3 was in itself neither positive nor negative, for it was not yet a "something" at all. This Indian concept would be impossible to imagine from the Greek standpoint, but that is only because the Greeks' worldview was grounded in a compressed body. The Indian worldview lacked this restriction precisely because it had a different prime symbol.

The Indian concept of Nirvana has similarly posed enormous challenges for Western understanding because it also escapes the constraints of the Greek positive body and other Western prime symbols. Just as for the Indian mathematician the number 3 in itself is neither positive nor negative for it is not yet a something at all, Nirvana is neither life nor death, neither sleeping nor waking. Spengler's discussion of this opposition is worth quoting in full:

> For us, 3 is always *something*, be it positive or negative; for the Greeks it was unconditionally a positive magnitude, +3; but for the Indian it indicates a possibility without existence, to which the word 'something' is not yet applicable, outside both existence and non-existence which are *properties* to be introduced into it. +3, -3, 1/3, are thus emanating actualities of subordinate rank which reside in the substance (3) in some way that is entirely hidden from us. It takes a Brahmanic soul to perceive these numbers as self-evident, as ideal emblems of a self-complete world form; to us they are as unintelligible as is the Brahman Nirvana, for which, as lying beyond life *and* death, sleep *and* waking, passion, compassion, *and* dispassion and yet somehow actual, words entirely fail us[202]

It is no coincidence that the concept of zero arose within the context of the Indian worldview, in which the prime symbol allowed what would have been flatly impossible in the Ancient Greek mindset. We must be careful, however, to avoid the Western

---

[202] Ibid.

cliché that the Indian concept of zero is simply a metaphor for numerical abstraction away from positive givens, something with only a negative value relative to the "real numbers." Zero could only be truly understood within the unique cultural context of the Indians, in which the prime symbol could allow it to be a "true number" rather than a mere privation of value:

> Only this spirituality could originate the grand conception of *nothingness as a true number, zero*, and even then this zero is the Indian zero, for which existent and non-existent are equally external designations.[203]

Nor was this problem of cultural influence limited to Indian Mathematics. Spengler noted that the theoretical systems of Ancient Greece underwent a previously unimaginable revision when appropriated by Medieval Arab thinkers who were freed from the cultural constraint of having to posit a compressed body as the basic starting point of analysis. This freedom from the Greeks' prime symbol allowed them to posit what would have been outright contradiction to Aristotle: a space-less body:

> Arabian thinkers of the ripest period (and they included minds of the very first order like Alfarabi and Alkabi) in controverting the ontology of Aristotle, proved that the body as such did not necessarily assume space for existence.[204]

Spengler's consistency as a thinker lay in his insistence that *no culture* could escape its own historical finitude, not even his own Western European worldview. He warned his readers: "So also will the Western world be incomprehensible to the men of Cultures yet unborn."

As brilliant as his insights on the topic were, we shall take this question even further than Spengler was willing to by arguing that systems are not only beholden to historical contexts, but to something even more primordial than that: even cultural contexts

---

[203] Ibid.
[204] Ibid.

are subordinate to ecological contexts. For example, Plato, Descartes, Frege, and Russell all somehow managed to deal with an overlapping set of numbers without being able to agree on something as basic as what the definition of number is in the first place. Their answers to this question, however, betray a bias rooted in their own ecological relation to the Soma. For Plato, numbers were Ideas from the World of Forms. For Descartes, numbers were innate ideas which the cogito always already had in a mental storage unit. For Frege, numbers were the logical extension of concepts.[205] For Russell, numbers were higher order classes of classes.[206] Each thinker presupposed a radically different overall system in which any number would have to appear, and yet somehow, no matter which system we adopt, we are still able to hermeneutically access the same numbers from each standpoint. It does not matter whether we consider a 3 to be an innate idea, extension of concept, Platonic form, or class of classes. No matter which systematic context the number 3 happens to temporarily inhabit, it is still able to manifest itself hermeneutically in each of these. Just as Greer's analysis of monsters leads one to acknowledge that certain spiritual absolutes exist and that they can manifest themselves hermeneutically within mythological contexts, a study of the History of Mathematics will reveal that certain gnostic absolutes such as numbers, logical relations, and grammatical universals also exist transcendentally; each, however, can only be given through a specific system, yet a system can only be given in some determinate somatic context.

Even one's sincerest efforts towards mathematical objectivity still betray biases which are even more primordial than Spengler's "prime symbol." Despite nearly two millennia of historical distance and two distinct cultures (Ancient Greek and Western European), Plato and Descartes share a common memological expectation, rooted in a common ecological somatic context under agrarian farming.

---

[205] Gottlob Frege, *The Foundations of Arithmetic* (Evanston: Northwestern University Press, 1980), p. 85.
[206] Bertrand Russell, *Introduction to Mathematical Philosophy* (:Merchant Books, 2014), p. 185.

For example, despite otherwise notable differences, both Plato and Descartes assumed that numbers should effectively already exist, whether in the Platonic World of Ideas or in the Cartesian Cogito's inventory of innate ideas. Both held the expectation that the system of numbers should already be complete and that counting through them is merely another iteration of a recurring cycle which other great minds have already traversed. In both cases, this belief is simply the memological worldview of agrarian farming in disguise.

On the contrary, as fossil fuel-based thinkers living in the era of Modern Industrialism, Frege and Russell both sought to de-substantialize numbers. Both Frege and Russell questioned the very expectation that a number could be a pre-given element from a system, especially a system which was intrinsically complete. In fact, both distinguished themselves through their aversion to think of numbers as traditional "things" at all.

Although such a claim may initially seem unjustifiable, there were bulletproof logical reasons to argue against the idea that numbers could be objects in the traditional sense of the term. While Frege revolutionized the study of Logic and Mathematics by revealing that because mathematical statements are really logical statements in disguise, numbers effectively cannot exist without the concepts of which they are the extension. Unfortunately, in its early phases, the theory resulted in certain paradoxes, most importantly the paradox that the set of all sets which are not themselves is a member of itself if it is not, and is not a member of itself if it is.

Russell revealed, however, that such paradoxes are more apparent than real, since they violated the rules inherent to a logical hierarchy; a better understanding of this infrastructure would reveal the paradoxes to be meaningless pseudo-problems. Before Russell, for example, few thinkers realized the difference between first order concepts and second order concepts. Plato more or less assumed that all concepts were effectively located "on the same level" of eternal universality in the World of Ideas, but Russell argued that this stemmed from a misunderstanding between concepts which are about individuals (first order) and concepts which are about concepts (second order).

As classes of classes, Russell's numbers were literally on a different level than that of real things; thus, confusing one for the other was explicitly ruled out by the very logical infrastructure of his system. Russell said in his introduction to the second edition of *The Principles of Mathematics* that his theory of Logicism progressed precisely insofar as it came to remove any illusion that numbers are Platonic entities with a real existence:

> [N]ot even the most ardent Platonist would suppose that the perfect 'or' is laid up in heaven, and that any 'or' here on Earth is merely an imperfect copy of the celestial archetype. But in the case of numbers this is far less obvious. The doctrines of Pythagoras, which [literally] began with arithmetical mysticism, influenced all subsequent philosophy and mathematics more profoundly than is generally realized. Numbers were immutable and eternal, like the heavenly bodies. Numbers were intelligible: the science of the numbers was the key to the universe . . . Consequently, to say that numbers are symbols which mean nothing appears as a horrible form of atheism. At the time I wrote the 'Principles', I shared . . . a belief in the Platonic reality of numbers, which in my imagination, peopled the timeless realm of Being. It was a comforting faith, which I later abandoned with regret.[207]

Russell noted in retrospect that by the mature stage of his thought, "the numbers 1 and 2 ha[d] entirely disappeared" as such. Russell believed that his success as a mathematician could be measured by the extent to which he had succeeded in reducing these numbers from their previous status as real things to their new status as "merely symbolic or linguistic conveniences, not genuine objects."[208] Yet this belief that numbers must be un-reified simply demonstrated his own memological aversion against the agrarian circle, the deep meme which provides the foundation for systems

---

[207] Bertrand Russell, *The Principles of Mathematics* (London: Routledge, 2012), pp. xxxvi-ii.
[208] Ibid., p. xxxvii.

which are always already complete, incapable of growth, and fully enclosed upon themselves.

Similarly, Russell's own preferences were rooted in memological biases which were even more fundamental than any cultural worldview. Because his own somatic context was rooted in fossil fuels, his ecological biases explain even more conclusively than Spengler's cultural "prime symbol" why Russell would insist on devising a gnostic system which would forbid even numbers from originating out of a complete reserve of eternally-existing objects.

There is, however, an undeniable danger inherent in this realization that mathematical systems, however seemingly "objective," are always beholden to memological biases. It is no coincidence that John Zerzan, one of the thinkers most heavily-invested into the project of exploring ecological contexts' influence over thought processes, would reach the conclusion that mathematics is, in fact, just language in disguise, rather than a distinct field of thought with a unique set of transcendent and independent truths. Mathematics, he claims in the essay "Number: Its Origin and Evolution" from his *Elements of Refusal*, is simply the end result of allowing language to continually deteriorate under the alienation inherent in favouring civilization over natural modes of life. Language has progressively become emptier, yet this was precisely insofar as it has become more mathematically formalized over time:

> An impoverished present renders it easy to see, as language becomes more impoverished, that math is simply the most reduced and drained language. The ultimate step in formalizing a language is to transform it into mathematics.[209]

Numbers, for Zerzan, are just the most impoverished words; numerical symbols cannot provide a window for transcendent gnostic absolutes to manifest themselves, because there are no gnostic essences behind the mesmerizing illusion of *a priori*

---

[209] John Zerzan, "Number: Its Origin and Evolution," in *Elements of Refusal*, Kindle Edition.

validity. As strange as such a claim might sound initially, this is simply the logical conclusion of Zerzan's view that *all* symbolic systems are equally empty, since any system, however seemingly "true" or necessary, is simply a side effect of existing within an anthropological context that favours agriculture over hunting and gathering. His *Elements of Refusal* similarly devoted individual essays to exposing the emptiness of art,[210] natural language,[211] and even the system of time.[212] Such a dismissal will likely shock students of philosophy, since these are often thought of as the same features which define Man and elevate him above the lower animals who lack the need, not to mention the ability, for such things as aesthetic appreciation or creative generation of art; linguistic rationality or λόγος; as well as Man's historical situatedness within temporality, whether understood as the synthesizing activity of the transcendental ego or the very horizon of Being itself. One could hardly imagine what would be left if one subtracted these seemingly-necessary features from Man.

However controversial such a claim might seem, Zerzan had admittedly-convincing reasons to defend these unusual positions. In the context of mathematical systems, for example, he warned that numerical figures are favoured over natural language because they satisfy the need for generality, formalization, and abstraction even better than the already-artificial medium of natural language can. He warns, however, that these are precisely the features that negate any need for a human subject. Even at the beginning, seeking finer and finer grades of formalized abstraction is prized for its elimination of subjective judgment, as the human user is completely accidental with regard to the objective "truths" which would hold the same status regardless of who thought about them. This process can only end with the outright destruction of human subjectivity:

---

[210] John Zerzan, "The Case against Art," in *Elements of Refusal* (Kindle Edition).
[211] John Zerzan, "Language: Origin and Meaning," in *Elements of Refusal* (Kindle Edition).
[212] John Zerzan, "The Beginning of Time, End of Time" in *Elements of Refusal* (Kindle Edition).

This abstracting process and its formal, general results provide a content that seems to be completely detached from the thinking individual; the user of a mathematical system and his/her values do not enter into the system. The Hegelian idea of the autonomy of alienated activity finds a perfect application with mathematics; it has its own laws of growth, its own dialectic, and stands over the individual as a separate power.[213]

Zerzan questions the idea that mathematics even can be considered to be "human thought," let alone the most perfect form of it. Rather, Zerzan argues that this can only be called "the virtual abandonment of [human] thinking."[214]

Claims to "scientific objectivity" are therefore laughably unfounded, for numerical abstraction lacks any connection with an external world. Behind the façade of providing the best kind of descriptions, it remains incapable of actually capturing the flow of Nature, for the "colourful movement of life" remains fundamentally inaccessible to it:

> [I]t does not convey truth about the external world. Its essential attitude toward the whole colourful movement of life is summed up by, "Put this and that equal to that and this!" Abstraction and equivalence of identity are inseparable; the suppression of the world's richness which is paramount in identity.[215]

Zerzan argues, in fact, that the very things one uses language to talk about have shifted over time. In prehistoric eras, most words referred to things which were immediately experienced with the senses; the only numbers were typically one, two, and a generic symbol for "many." There was no need for a more sophisticated system of numbers because direct engagement and face to face

---

[213] John Zerzan, "Number: Its Origin and Evolution," in *Elements of Refusal*, Kindle Edition.
[214] Ibid.
[215] Ibid.

contact proved sufficient even to accomplish tasks which would seem to require numerical procedures today. For example, Zerzan notes that even in the present era, if a large family sits down to dinner, they will not need to explicitly count the members to notice if someone is missing. Over time, however, language came to refer to more and more abstract referents, not coincidentally, just as the mathematical systems exploded in complexity far beyond the "primitive" origins one could observe in the prehistoric era.

Symbolic systems are problematic on more than just an epistemological level, as Zerzan claims to have identified a political dimension which is always at work behind the scenes. Numbering, he argues, is not merely a side effect of domestication and agriculture, but was likely one of the tools used to bring about the agricultural catastrophe in the first place. Arguably the first use for number systems was to "control domesticated flock animals." Numerical abstraction allowed "wild creatures" to suddenly become "products" of artificial manipulation, though the metaphorical gun was quickly turned back on its human masters as well. Zerzan claims that naming and numbering cannot be understood outside this "new attitude towards the world," which in addition to dominating the Other, even inflicts alienation, fragmentation, and distancing on the namer himself or herself:

> If naming is a distancing, a mastery, so too is number, which is impoverished naming . . . In distancing and separation lies the heart of mathematics: the discursive reduction of patterns, states and relationships which we initially perceived as wholes.[216]

As compelling as Zerzan's arguments might be, there are serious objections which must be made against them. Above all, Zerzan argues that all hermeneutical horizons of meaning which involve symbols are actually just frames of linguistification in disguise. For Zerzan, linguistification is not an accidental result of some tragic distortion of these hermeneutical frames; it is the true

---

[216] Ibid.

essence of any symbolic system, insofar as each is merely a euphemism for the alienation and distancing inherent in abandoning natural modes of life for a civilization founded on domination. Zerzan's dismissal of gnostic essences is not only problematic on numerical grounds, for even language itself provides a legitimate space in which to grasp certain gnostic universals, the ontological integrity of which must be respected. We shall consider these grammatical universals briefly before proceeding.

Although there have been numerous attempts to prove that language is just mathematics or logic in disguise, none of these has ever solved the mystery of grammatical universals.[217] It is impossible to reduce grammatical universals to logic or mathematics because although they are principles which no known natural language contradicts, a translation from natural language to logical or mathematical representation cannot be guaranteed not to violate the same principles.[218] For this reason, at least some linguists have speculated that these principles are indigenous to a "language faculty" which is a distinct "mental organ" from the "logic faculty" or the "mathematical faculty."[219] According to this theory, one never has to learn these linguistic principles because they are already innate features of the human brain, a raw biological product of millions of years of evolution.

One example is the Locality Principle. An instance of this principle can be found in the way that "a reflexive pronoun can only refer to an antecedent within a limited area of the sentence known as the local domain."[220] In the sentence "Paul thinks that George cut himself with the knife," it is clear that the reflexive pronoun "himself" refers to George, not Paul. Although both are men and could theoretically agree with the masculine pronoun, it would not even seem possible to think otherwise. Even if we don't know that we know it, we can all see that that the shorter reference is grammatical and the longer one is not. This cannot be reduced to

---

[217] V. J. Cook and Mark Newson, *Chomsky's Universal Grammar* (New Delhi: Wiley, 2007), p. 37.
[218] Ibid., p. 23.
[219] Ibid., p. 49.
[220] Ibid., p. 39.

one grammatical rule, for we find the same principle exemplified in the unrelated example of movement. When one transforms the statement "Jimmy has read that book" into a question, it is clear that the corresponding question is "Has Jimmy read that book?" rather than "Read Jimmy has that book?" Because moving the word "read" would cover a greater distance than moving the word "has," it is ungrammatical. The following table demonstrates that the same rule would hold whether the language be English, French, German, or Italian.

[1]

Language	Grammatical Movement	Ungrammatical Movement
English	Has Lars read the book?	Read Lars has the book?
French	Lars a-t-il lu le livre?	Lars lu-t-il a le livre?
German	Hat Lars das Buch gelesen?	Gelesen Lars das Buch hat?
Italian	Lars ha letto il libro?	Lars letto ha il libro?

From the standpoint of physical materialism, it is understandable that linguists would opt for the theory that these principles are hard-wired into the brain and are therefore perhaps nothing more than biological contingencies. Under this view, it is just an accident of evolutionary history that we ended up with these principles rather than some other ones. This crass materialism is, however, something of a distortion of the hermeneutical horizon of gnostic essences. The locality principle is a genuine gnostic essence which can manifest itself across many unrelated linguistic problems and even across countless natural languages for the same reason that the gnostic essence of a 3 can appear in many different mathematical systems with no common origin. Even if one does accept that there is some physical component in the brain that "stores" the locality principle, even this neuroscientific feature would be just one more systematic instantiation of the gnostic essence rather than its ultimate origin. Locality in the brain, locality of reference, locality of movement, and locality in other languages are all instantiations of the same gnostic absolute in just the same way that Descartes realized that a point on a graph and a tuple of numbers (i.e., (2,4)) are two different systematic windows into the same gnostic essence.

To fully appreciate why linguistification is not the "true definition" of mathematics but rather the destruction of it, we must consider the following example of how numbers can be treated as pneumatic objects within the horizon of mythology rather than as gnostic essences within the horizon of a system. Such a view would doubly offend modern sensibilities, as linguistification is the idea that mythological symbols have no connection to transcendent spiritual essences. This is because under this view there could be nothing beyond language. Rather than be anchored to a single pneumatic absolute, mythology would seem to be set free to explode into an unbridled dissemination of signifiers which lack any centre, as the Postmodernist cliché would hold. One problem with this view that mythology can be divorced from spirit is that the linguistified content alone is not sufficient to determine a symbol's meaning. This is particularly true for religious symbols which seem, on a purely morphological level, to be identical but which open pathways to access rather different spiritual truths.

Because it has become unfashionable within academic circles to discuss the very possibility of such a distinction, this topic is only seriously contemplated by figures who lie far enough outside the mainstream to be able to disregard the Orwellian Ministry of Truth's current definitions of "thought crime." Norwegian Black Metal musician and pagan ecophilosopher Varg Vikernes, for example, wrote in his notorious 1994 prison manifesto *Vargsmål* that the pagan belief in reincarnation and the Christian belief in the resurrection might appear to be the same thing (that is, the belief that one will live again after dying) but are actually quite different. Moreover, the mythological symbol for each is unique, despite superficial appearances of similarity.[221] In the 48th section of the text, Vikernes claims that "many times" he had heard it claimed that the image of Odin hanged in Yggdrasil and the image of Jesus crucified are essentially the same image, insofar as the pagan image is supposedly a mere "copying" of the Christian original. Vikernes demonstrates, however, that if one goes beyond the brute surface level content to examine the properly spiritual truth disclosed in each hermeneutical horizon, one will find two very different messages. Although in each case the symbol merely portrays a figure hanging without any further explicit qualification, the mythological context is quite different in each case. Jesus, for example, was crucified by the Roman soldiers, but Odin hanged himself by his own agency. Odin was also hanged alone, while Jesus was accompanied by two common thieves. These details demonstrate that a mythic event is significant only insofar as it is situated along some narratological pathway. These images are not just linguistified blobs of "data" but are events within a story. Most importantly, however, the results of the hanging are quite different in each case. Odin ends up in a stage between life and death, whereas Jesus definitively died and then was resurrected back to life again three days later. To say that these are the same image is to miss the point of each.

Interestingly, Vikernes goes on to explain that the numerological significance is quite different in each case as well. Whereas Jesus only hung for one day on the cross before being taken down for burial, Odin spent nine days and nine nights in this state. Vikernes argues that these numbers are far from arbitrary, for while one is the number representing a beginning, nine is the number representing an end. According to Vikernes's own interpretation, Jesus' one day hanging represents the beginning of a new and unfortunate disruption in world history, as the trajectory which would eventually lead to the de-paganization of Norway was launched on that day. On the other hand, he claims that Odin's nine days of hanging represent something like a productive destruction of a problematic worldview, a destruction which allows a new cycle of historical time to begin unfolding. Paradoxically, the true number

---

[221] Varg Vikernes, *Vargsmål* (unpublished, unofficial 1997 English translation from Norwegian manuscript).

to affirm life is not the number of the beginning (one), but the number of the end and of destruction (nine.) He argues, for example, that it is no coincidence that pregnancy also finds its "ending" after nine months but this is the symbol of a productive ending, since the conclusion of pregnancy is actually just the dawn of a new life. The number of life and the number of destruction are the same number.

Vikernes's analysis of the numbers one and nine therefore complicates the standard expectation that numbers are always gnostic essences and that they can only be disclosed within systems rather than within mythology. This view, so casually taken for granted in our era, is actually something of a recent innovation; it is a product of the tendency to banish all pneumatic essences from the realm of hermeneutical interpretation, under the guise of promoting rationalism and scientific materialism as the only options available. In reality, such a view is merely the result of disregarding the distinction among the five layers of hermeneutical disclosure by restricting oneself to the single pseudo-hermeneutical layer of linguistification. Numbers certainly can be viewed as gnostic essences within the hermeneutical layer of a mathematical system, but this is only one of several possibilities. The spiritual study of numerology is not merely a primitive, failed attempt to do modern mathematics; it is, rather, the window through which an entirely different type of essence, the pneumatic rather than gnostic, must disclose itself.

Ergonic Hermeneutics: Work and the Body

In objective hermeneutics, the standard of success is whether a sense object can allow one to understand an ergonic process of work ("ergonic" is the author's own term derived from ἔργον, the Greek word for "work."). For example, a bucket of well water is a sense object which manifests a certain process of work, in that one must use physical labour to lower it into the well, gather water, retrieve it from out of the well, and then carry it to its final destination. If one has not understood the full process of work, one has not understood the object. Nor is this understanding merely intellectual. One has only truly understood the ergonic process, and therefore the sense object itself, if one has understood the particular movements which one's own body must perform if the process is to be carried out correctly. In some cases, failure to execute even one of these movements properly could potentially ruin the entire operation. For example, spilling the well water on the ground while carrying it away will only demonstrate that one has not understood the true meaning of the bucket. This is even truer for complicated ergonic processes which require the highest standard of bodily precision to be performed correctly, such as blacksmithing, wood carving, or sculpting.

On the other hand, a kitchen faucet in an American suburban home is a counter sense object in which no ergonic process of work can manifest itself. One simply turns a knob and what appears to be an infinite supply of water will emerge. The irony, of course, is that this water from the tap requires an even greater energy cost to be transported from some distant water processing facility to the clueless suburbanite's kitchen sink but because the process has been taken over by machines, the ergonic process as such vanishes entirely and the hermeneutical horizon ceases to be. Automation is a type of hermeneutical death that removes the very possibility for ergonic processes to manifest themselves or be understood. As a result, the ergonic hermeneutical subject has all but vanished out of existence in our era, replaced by countless smartphone zombies who have willingly immobilized themselves into a state of passivity before smartphone screens and brought about their own hermeneutical deaths.

While mythological hermeneutics allows the transcendent essences of spiritual absolutes to be disclosed in a context for understanding and systematic systems do the same for gnostic absolutes, one might argue that objective hermeneutics also allows another type of real, non-linguistic essence to manifest itself. This is none other than the human body itself.

It will likely seem controversial to claim that the body could be a hermeneutical whole to be discovered through ergonic processes of work, yet the fact such a claim is "shocking" is only a testament to how thoroughly the System has deprived us of

147

opportunities to do just that. It is no exaggeration to say that the System has virtually made it illegal to work. Any task which could be automated away has been, even in cases where the collateral damage for doing so was mass unemployment and, in some cases, even human deaths. Recently, it was reported in the news that a pedestrian was killed by a self-driving car for the simple reason that the A.I. was never taught to search for pedestrians outside cross-walking zones. In addition to demonstrating that inexcusable design flaws in the machines have literally cost innocent people their lives, we must not miss the deeper point in this story: the System has made no allowances for the possibility that human agents might not behave in accord with the strict regulations which are dictated to them by oppressive bureaucracies. People have literally died simply because they did not act robotically enough. If one's movements fail to conform to arbitrary zoning requirements which the System has demanded, one cannot count on receiving sufficient protection to avoid a premature death. We are quite near to reaching the point where any humans who are allowed to continue existing must be, for all intents and purposes, robots.

As early as David Icke's 1994 classic *Robots' Rebellion*, he similarly warned that the vast majority of humans on the Earth today are actually robots in disguise. Icke justified this shocking claim through exposing the extent to which virtually every thought in people's minds has been implanted from an exterior origin generated by the System and disseminated through its media, educational institutions, advertising agencies, and political puppets. Near the end of the text, Icke forcefully insists that there is a strict dichotomy between slavery and freedom: one is either a robot or a rebel.[222] There is no third option or grey area. In his slightly later *I am me, I am free: The Robots' Guide to Freedom*, he argued that the rebel seizes the freedom to think for himself or herself and affirm the infinite consciousness which is its true identity, while the robot conforms to the System's demands and accepts its weak, fragile, and subservient "phantom identity" as one more cog in the machine as its only option.[223]

---

[222] David Icke, *Robots' Rebellion: The Story of the Spiritual Renaissance* (Bath, Gateway: 1994), p. 339.

Although the author agrees with Icke's decision to designate those who lack freedom as "robots," it is still troubling that Icke emphasized intellectual slavery as the *gom jabbar* to test whether one is a real human or merely a thinking machine.[224] While no one could deny that intellectual freedom has become an Orwellian thought-crime in our era which even the supposedly "radical thinkers" in the academic industry vehemently censor, it is arguable that the System has actually succeeded in eliminating even more opportunities for ergonic freedom. This elimination is admittedly quite subtle, since the System has preserved the illusion of ergonic freedom through a set of front operations that have nearly conclusively destroyed it.

For example, even the small handful of heretics who express a desire to grow their own food at home have effectively lost the ability to do so. Anyone who has purchased the so-called "tools" available at the mainstream hardware stores will find that they are more like overpriced recreational toys or ornamental trophies to be hung on a garage wall than instruments for serious labour. It is quite literally the case that these "tools" are designed to force one to fail at gardening, since they will break down almost immediately after being purchased in order to ensure "job security" for the shady overseas factory owners and for the corporate boardroom members at the hardware store headquarters. Even when they are still brand new, however, they will hardly accomplish anything beyond allowing one the opportunity to "play around" in the backyard for fun, and maybe snap a few selfies in the process to "social media celebrate" a garden which will never yield any results and will likely be abandoned after a few weeks anyway once the half-serious suburbanite gets bored with it. Yet even when one does have sincere intentions to do the real thing, one doesn't even have the option to do this as anything *except* a Kacyznskian surrogate activity.

---

[223] David Icke, *I am me, I am free: The Robots' Guide to Freedom* (Ryde: David Icke Books, 1996), p. 1.

[224] When Paul asked the Reverend Mother why she submitted him to extreme physical pain with the gom jabbar, she responded, "To determine if you're human."
Frank Herbert, *Dune* (New York: Ace Books, 1990), p. 9.

There is a properly ecological explanation for this unfortunate turn of events. A farming tool which actively prevents one from farming cannot be described as anything except counter sense embodied in the physical form of an object. Even the items which appear to be traditional agrarian sense objects are all too often just fossil fuel counter sense objects in disguise if they originate within the ecological context in which fossil fuels are the Soma. We can only truly gain access to agrarian farming tools if we switch ecological contexts and restore agrarian grain to its privileged status as the Soma.

Virtually no one among the millennial generation in the West may be able to appreciate this distinction, since even the author himself almost never saw a real tool before leaving the United States. The only notable exception was a traditional donkey cart which an elderly neighbour's blind grandfather once relied upon for transportation, but even this was only a true sense object tool because it was built in the 19th Century and was owned by a peasant from rural Canada who still inhabited a world disclosed by the Soma of agrarian grain. We are not far from the point where such things will be confiscated by the System as illegal contraband, since any real ergonic labour with sense objects will be deemed an Orwellian "body crime."

After years of wasting hundreds of dollars on ornamental pseudo-tools from hardware stores in the United States, the author found upon living in India that the best tools here are the ones which have been handed down over generations within the same families. Since the author's wife's ancestors were, even as recently as one generation ago, tapioca farmers in rural Central Kerala, we continue to use the same tools they did to accomplish serious farming tasks whenever they happen to arise. The reason why a decades-old tool constructed by a local blacksmith so easily outcompetes the overpriced, flimsy, fraudulent trash manufactured just this year by factory machines in China is quite simple: tapioca farming in rural Kerala was not a surrogate activity. Under a true agrarian somatic context, farming is a life or death activity upon which a people's survival hinges. It is only under the Soma of fossil fuels that gardening could be trivialized as a "fun pastime" which is valued more for its ability to generate social media likes than for its ability to put food on one's own table.

Without any doubt, in our era the same level of seriousness once given to donkey carts and hand tools is still reserved for the machinery directly relevant to our Soma of fossil fuels. Anyone who has lived in an oil-producing locality knows that this is the one area where we absolutely *do not* play games. In fact, other vital elements of the lifeworld are expected to just "take one for the team" for the sake of the ecologically-destructive oil producing operations. The author recalls living in an oil producing region where buying bottled water shipped in from afar was a mandatory expense even for the poorest citizens, since drinking the water from the tap was completely out of the question. It is no exaggeration to say that even the precious resource of *water* had to suffer a type of destruction in order to allow the oil extraction to go on, despite the fact that this town was located in a desert with extreme water shortage problems. The author recalls receiving a bill for $850 for just one month of city water use; worst of all, this water was mostly just wasted on watering the front lawn, one of the signs of the madness of trying to maintain suburban living arrangements in the middle of a harsh desert which was hardly suitable for *any* human settlement, let alone history's most shamefully wasteful one.

Above all, this demonstrates that ecological contexts determine what objects are allowed to appear to a subject living under the domination of the Soma. Although this was desert, the Deep Meme of Vapour did not structure this world because the Soma had shifted to petroleum. Far from living the Arrakeen existence under the Soma of Water where wasting moisture on green lawns with no utilitarian value would be ruled out as utter insanity, even water was considered unessential in comparison with the Soma of Petroleum and suburban homes with green lawns were normalized as mandatory features of life.

Mentatic Hermeneutics: Memological Consciousness

In mentatic hermeneutics, one seeks to understand a geometrical shape of consciousness as such. Because for us mentatic consciousness can only occur within an ecological context dominated by a Soma, consciousness can only ever occur through the geometrical shape of one of the deep memes. Non-memological consciousness is as impossible as the void which Aristotle forbid in Book IV of *The Physics*.[225] Aristotle's rejection of the void must not be misinterpreted as a primitive attempt to do the same thing as Modern Physics, for his real point had far more to do with ecological hermeneutics than empirical science. Aristotle seemed to realize that if a subject is given at all, this can only occur within a real ecological context. An absolute subject existing without memological bias is a fiction for the simple reason that an ecological context without some founding Soma is strictly impossible. This is why Aristotle warned that if a pure void did exist, it would have to be free even from containing air, as air was one of the four basic elements. In order to be a true void, it would have to be an "empty interval in which there is *no* sensible body" at all.[226] Likewise, the mysterious "void" which holds no somatic body is simply the fantasy of an absolute space with no Soma. This fiction lies behind any hope for a non-ecological subject which would be granted entry to directly gaze at the pneumatic and gnostic absolutes without the intermediation of mythologies, systems or the deep memes upon which they depend. Non-memological consciousness is, however, a contradiction in terms, for the very essence of mentatic consciousness must be one of the deep memes. A pure void in subjectivity is just as impossible as a pure void in the world.

In a certain sense, what Descartes really discovered with Cartesian dualism was just the hermeneutical distinction between the ergonic discovery of the body and the mentatic discovery of the mind, albeit in an incomplete form. One of Descartes's great insights lay in the paradox that although the body is me, I still have to discover it (and by extension, discover myself) through an act of phenomenological investigation which isolates the body as a different kind of substance than the mind is. Descartes opened the

---

[225] Aristotle, *The Physics*, in *The Basic Works of Aristotle* (New York: The Modern Library, 2001), p. 280.
[226] Ibid.

Meditations by guaranteeing that this difference between mind (*res cogitans*) and body (*res extensa*) as two types of substances embodied the highest standard of certainty because it qualified as one of the "clear and distinct" ideas. For Descartes, this epistemological standard of certainty was simultaneously a metaphysical proof of existence: "[We have] this assurance that all objects which we clearly and distinctly think are true (really exist) in that very mode in which we think them."[227]

Descartes believed that the mind was not simply a special type of body (the error of Psychologism) and the body was not just an extension of the mind (the error of New Age solipsism) because the eidetic features of each were unique. Specifically, he noted that while the extended body is a substance with accidents, the mind is a "pure substance" not made up of accidents. Descartes's proof for this lay in the fact that the mind itself does not change, even across countless variations in the content of the Ideas which it entertains in thought.[228] A body, on the other hand, cannot sustain major changes to its physical form without ceasing to be the same body. One might argue, perhaps, that physical bodies are subject to natural decay and corruption but the mentatic substance of the conscious mind is not. Awareness is like a light which is either switched on or off.

Contrary to expectation, this means that death is not properly a problem of the body but rather a problem of the mind. The body shuts down, but only the mentatic mind really *dies*. Frank Herbert examined something like this paradox in *Dune,* since even the most powerful mentats who have an amazing power to see into the future will find that death is the one event which can never actually be disclosed in their predictions. Near the end of the novel, Paul suspects that he might be standing in the presence of his killer but remains uncertain because although "he had seen his own dead body along countless reaches of the time web," he had "never once . . . seen his moment of death" as such.[229] It has perhaps never been acknowledged that there is a thoroughly Cartesian reason for this.

---

[227] Descartes, Rene, *Meditations on First Philosophy*, in *The Rationalists* (New York: Anchor Books, 1974), p. 109.
[228] Ibid., pp. 109-10.
[229] Frank Herbert, *Dune* (New York: Ace Books, 1990), p. 473.

Paul can find his own corpse within the scattered moments of the future but he cannot find the moment of his death because while the corpse is an extended body which can be disclosed even to the one who will die, death as such occurs to the mentatic cogito and not to the body.

The destruction of the pure substance of the cogito is not like a normal event, since it happens to the cogito only insofar as it is does not happen. Heidegger realized something similar in *Being and Time*. Since Being *is* time for Heidegger, Dasein is always ahead of itself, but due to finitude, Dasein is always ahead of itself towards death. Death, however, is not like other events, because when it finally arrives the very clearing in which it could "take place" simply vanishes. Death only guarantees that Dasein will never succeed in catching up with itself and liquidating the final outstanding balance of what remains unaccomplished, for the one event which Dasein will never actually disclose as such is death.[230]

We can go beyond Heidegger, Descartes, and Herbert to explicate how death is, above all, a hermeneutical problem, since even death is indigenous to a very specific layer of meaning. Death can only be properly interpreted within the transcendental register of mentatic problems, the layer of memology, for death is the name for the non-event in which mentatic consciousness perishes. Death remains one of the most widely-misunderstood problems precisely because it is almost never situated within the correct hermeneutical layer of meaning. We live in an era, in fact, in which one of the most popular responses to death is to misconstrue it as a gnostic problem which could be solved through finding a systematic fix to prevent it from occurring. Ray Kurzweil's claim that machines will eventually become smart enough to invent other machines which are smarter enough than their parent computers to solve death with a "super fancy mathematical algorithm" is built upon a fundamental misunderstanding, since it confuses two distinct layers of meaning. Death can never be solved gnostically, for it is inherently mentatic and cannot be transferred to another layer of meaning without ceasing to be what it is.

---

[230] Martin Heidegger, *Being and Time* (Albany: State University of New York Press, 1996), p. 234.

Of course, it has become ever more fashionable within the academic industry to thoughtlessly demonize this Cartesian dualism and to instead posit the fantasy of a perfect union between mind and body. No matter how piously such a religious creed might be parroted in the desperate hopes of beating the odds to secure a tenure track job within the cult of boot-licking conformists, *no one* has ever succeeded in explaining what the hell this actually means. All too often, this zealous "celebration of the non-alienated body" has simply served as an excuse to promote crass sexual experimentation in the guise of a "deeply intellectual refutation of Cartesianism."

It is troubling, for example, that Judith Butler's mediocre theories on Gender Performativity remain one of the favourite sources of material for such movements, since buried behind all of her intentionally-obfuscated layers of deconstructivist blabbering, there is really just one very simple proposition: *people with "weird sexual practices" should be marginalized no more!* Zizek noted (in a talk on ecology, of all things) that it is peculiar to cite Judith Butler as a radical critic of the System, since her stances are actually fully compatible with the spirit of Modern Capitalism.[231] Above all, she is just calling for more people to be included within the System, yet this is indistinguishable from the universalizing tendencies which are already hard-wired into the logic of consumerism. It is peculiar for her to act as though the System of Modern Technology is not *already* oriented towards cracking the marketing codes to break ground in all the remaining niches within the social body, until every square inch of human real estate has been colonized by some corporate patent. Nowhere is this truer than in the category of sex. In a footnote in *Revolt Against the Modern World*, Evola noted that the sexual revolution was not much of a revolution after all, since it was just the ultimate act of modern consumerism: "The reaction of the so-called sexual revolution [to the decline in traditional gender roles] has only led the masses to a regimen of quick, easy, and cheap sex treated as an item of consumption."[232]

---

[231] See "Ecology: A New Opium for the Masses by Slavoj Zizek - Tilton Gallery, November 28 2007", available at
https://www.youtube.com/watch?v=D1FeHcTl614

Ted Kaczynski similarly downplayed the myth that unusual sexual practices represent the highest expression of freedom, since these are not only harmless against the System of Modern Technology, but are in fact *mandated* by it. In an unpublished letter to a researcher dated July 30, 1991, Kaczynski responded to a request to participate in a study over individuality by enquiring into the meaning of this term. He noted that most of the outlets for individualism which are celebrated today are "mere games" with almost no meaning in challenging the System on a serious level. For example, he lists bizarre sexual practices right alongside "wearing kinky clothes," producing avant-garde art, and "developing eccentric philosophical ideas."[233] What all have in common is that no matter how far someone might claim to push the bar in one of these areas, that same person is guaranteed to have zero interest in challenging his or her dependence upon Modern Technology. Even the person with the weirdest sexual fetish will still insist on driving a car, owning a smartphone, posting regularly to multiple social media accounts, and consuming copious amounts of processed junk food.

We can go even further than Kaczynski, Evola, and Zizek did, however, by speaking an inconvenient truth which virtually *no one* is comfortable acknowledging in public. Much of the sexual deviancy within our society does not originate spontaneously from some innate principle of Life within the human subject which the System would seek to repress unjustly, such that the most profound avenue for rebellion would be to "take one for the team" by "orgasming for a higher cause." On the contrary, much of this sexual deviancy is directly generated by the System itself through strictly technological means. Professional sex addiction therapists have noted that many of their clients express frustration that they find it virtually impossible to find a woman in their First World native country who is willing to do the kinds of things which these

[232] Julius Evola, *Revolt Against the Modern World* (Rochester: Inner Tradition, 1995), p. 166.

[233] Ted Kaczynski, "Letter to a Researcher, Dated July 30, 1991" (unpublished letter), Ted Kaczynski Papers, Labadie Collection at the University of Michigan's Special Collections.

men have been conditioned by years of porn consumption to expect. As a result, these men often feel forced to travel to nations like Mexico, Thailand, and Brazil as sex tourists to just cut to the chase and "buy it" outright. It is deeply unfortunate, though, that many of the women involved in these operations are likely to be victims of human trafficking scams, as women are routinely tricked into traveling to a foreign nation under the mistaken impression that there is a legitimate job waiting for them there, only to find upon arrival that their passport is seized and they are sold into slavery. It would be peculiar to describe flying across the globe in order to pay money to solicit Third World sex slaves in order to live out physically-punishing fantasies which virtually no one would agree to otherwise as a "courageous act of rebellion against the System," since the very need to resort to extreme (not to mention, illegal) means to satisfy ever stranger sexual desires is precisely a result of the technological manipulation inherent in contemporary electronic pornography. Even without any reference to "Victorian moralism," one must acknowledge that Modern Technology continues to fundamentally disrupt delicate ecological balances and will only disfigure human nature even further as it is allowed to progress. We shall return to this topic in greater detail in our discussion of Varg Vikernes in the final chapter of the book.

We might argue that even the drive for sex has lost its status as a life-instinct and has dropped down to the status of just another surrogate activity. One should keep in mind that Kaczynski defined a surrogate activity as an iteration through the Power Process which is *not* based on some serious survival need. It is chilling to think that even the natural drive to reproduce has been disfigured into just another outlet for technological slavery. Kaczynski noted himself in the 39th paragraph of the Manifesto that whereas the drive for sex is not ordinarily an outlet for a surrogate activity, excessive domination by Modern Technology has increasingly made it into one:

> On the other hand, the pursuit of sex and love (for example) is not a surrogate activity, because most people, even if their existence were otherwise satisfactory, would feel deprived if

they passed their lives without ever having a relationship with a member of the opposite sex. (But pursuit of an excessive amount of sex, more than one really needs, can be a surrogate activity.)[234]

The Power Process is therefore something like a skeletal form which all the different ergonic essences instantiate in a slightly different way. There is, however, a fundamental distinction between an authentic instance of the Power Process and its degradation to a mere surrogate activity. Surrogate activities come to be defined more and more as linguistification the further they deviate from the ideal of authentic ergonic labour. Against Judith Butler's claims to the "performativity" of the body in weird sexual practices, it is ironic that even these fail to disclose the body to itself as a hermeneutical object, for even sex has been degraded to just another form of technological linguistification.

The Mentatic Essences: The Deep Memes

We shall briefly consider the six deep memes before concluding the discussion. Under the Hunter Gatherer Worldview, the crucial resource of survival is wild food sources such as big game. In this context, humans anthropomorphize natural forces such as animals, plants, seasons, weather, and even the Sun and treat them as human-like agents which can be influenced through ritual. In turn, humans naturalize their own cultures and treat them as extensions of the natural flora and fauna surrounding them. The automatic shape or deep meme is therefore a level plane in which humans have no hierarchical position above Nature.

Under the Agrarian Worldview the crucial resource of survival is large fields of grain. In this context, humans build their lives around repeating cycles of planting and harvesting grain, as well as around the life cycles of the domesticated animals which are born, reach maturity, reproduce, and then die. The automatic shape through which humans experience the world in this ecological

---

[234] Ted Kaczynski, *Industrial Society and Its Future*, in *Technological Slavery* (Scottsdale: Fitch & Madison, 2019), para. 39.

context is the agrarian circle, in which completion and cyclical predictability become the standard of perfection.

Under the Fossil Fuel Worldview, the crucial resource for survival becomes coal, petroleum, and natural gas. These fuel sources contain unprecedented levels of concentrated, storable, and usable energy which in turn normalize rapid growth and constant change into the default shape of Being. Under this view, progress is no longer seen as an historical anomaly with a fragile dependence upon a finite resource, but is instead misrecognized as the default shape which everything within the world should have.

Under the Salvage Worldview, the crucial resource for survival becomes industrial materials which linger from the earlier era of the Fossil Fuel Worldview but must be repurposed to uses which the original designers could never have imagined. Harvesting raw materials from the ruins of the industrial ages will provide a competitive advantage which will re-standardize consciousness to fit the shape of a bell curve, the shape which isomorphically corresponds to the trajectory of Hubbert's Curve of fossil fuel depletion. In this worldview, ongoing decline and lingering memories of the past will take precedence over unfounded hopes for progress and reckless leaps into the future.

In the author's previous books, only these four deep memes were discussed. In more recent times, the author has identified two more deep memes and acknowledges that other deep memes very well might exist both in the past and in the future, since a deep meme is not an a priori rational construct but is rather a higher order representation of an ecological context. The amazing thing about ecology, properly understood, is just how much more variable and open-ended it is than the single-dimensional notion of progress to which it is usually force-fitted.

Under the Nomadic Worldview the crucial resource of survival is flocks or herds of domesticated animals, such as yaks, camels, sheep, and goats; these herds differ from the wild herds tracked by the hunter gatherer and the stationary herds kept by the agrarian farmer because the nomad's herds are inherently mobile. They constantly move across vast tracts of land in search of fresh sources of food. One might argue that in the absence of fossil fuels, a great fraction of the total landmass on the Earth mandates just such a worldview. In his 1999 essay "A Look at Vegetarianism," Finnish ecophilosopher Pentti Linkola noted that politically correct calls for universal vegetarianism are impossible to satisfy on ecological grounds alone because much of the Earth is unfit for intensive vegetable gardening but is suited as grazing lands for herds of herbivore animals instead (a hard ecological fact surely confirmed by the historical record for how these lands were used in pre-fossil fuel eras, and by the fact that the diet in deep Central Asia continues to be quite heavy on sheep and goat meat.) Calls for mandated vegan diets across the global population might even be interpreted as a dog whistle for mass genocide in disguise.[235]

Because many Ancient Civilizations were immediately preceded by nomadic pastoralists, remnants of the Nomadic Worldview can even be identified in later civilizations which were no longer nomadic ones as such. For example, certain motifs from the Nomadic Worldview lingered in the Ancient Egyptian Worldview even after the Soma had shifted to agrarian grain. Michel Foucault himself had observed this in the fifth lecture of his 1978 series *Security, Territory, Population*.[236] Foucault found that the Ancient Egyptian view of the pharaoh's power over the population could not be understood through more recent notions of disciplinary control over a fixed territory (the model of power prevalent in his classic study of penal institutions, *Discipline and Punish*). Rather than exercise power over a definite geographical space which was carved out artificially, a model perfected by the modern prison, the pharaoh provided leadership to a population which could be compared to a flock of sheep. This was because the Egyptian population and the flock of sheep were both considered a "multiplicity on the move" rather than a static territory under disciplinary control.[237]

---

[235] Pentti Linkola, "A Look at Vegetarianism", in *Can Life Prevail?* (Helsinki: Tammi, 2008).

[236] Michel Foucault, *Security, Territory, Population* (New York: Palgrave, 2007), p. 125.

[237] Ibid.

The single most fundamental criterion in this worldview is inclusion within a set; to be included within the flock, no matter where it happens to move geographically, takes precedence over any other concern.[238] The deep meme of the Nomadic Worldview is the mobile set with elements.

Although the Deep Meme of the Set is not strictly equivalent to the mathematical definition of the set, it is notable that much of Badiou's argument in favour of redefining Fundamental Ontology in terms of Set Theory in the early sections of *Being and Event* revolved around the impossibility of subordinating set theoretical membership to any other systematic construct; set theoretical inclusion cannot be defined, for example, "on the basis of properties and their extension," as Frege's Logicist position would hold; nor "on the basis of intuition and its objects," as Cantor's earliest attempts at set theory would hold. On the contrary, the Zermelo-Fraenkel formal system's "lexicon contains only one relation, $\in$, and therefore no unary predicate, no property in the strict sense."[239] To be a member of the set is irreducible to any higher order notion of predicate or collection.

Remnants of the nomadic worldview are identifiable in the canonical gospels of the New Testament as well. The Deep Meme of the Nomadic Set provides an easily-overlooked explanation for Jesus' parable in Luke 15 regarding a shepherd who goes out of his way to find one lost sheep which had accidentally been disconnected from the other 99 in the flock:

> Then Jesus told them this parable: "Suppose one of you has a hundred sheep and loses one of them. Doesn't he leave the ninety-nine in the open country and go after the lost sheep until he finds it? And when he finds it, he joyfully puts it on his shoulders and goes home. Then he calls his friends and neighbours together and says, 'Rejoice with me; I have found my lost sheep.'[240]

---

[238] Alain Badiou, *Being and Event* (London: Bloomsbury, 2005), p. 43.
[239] Ibid., p. 47.
[240] Luke 15:3-6

Even if a member of the flock had accidentally broken away from the rest of the group, this physical isolation was not considered sufficient to override its intrinsic inclusion within the mobile set. Memological inclusion is not reducible to geographical location, since the sheep retained its membership in the group even after finding itself in a different physical area than the rest of the flock had migrated to. The Jesus of Luke's gospel goes as far as to argue that the true point of the story is that heaven itself will embody the same structure, since one sinner who had broken away from the rest of the mystical flock of the body of Christ will similarly be sought out by God himself until that sinner's restores the position he had always already had as a member of the religion:

> I tell you that in the same way there will be more rejoicing in heaven over one sinner who repents than over ninety-nine righteous persons who do not need to repent.[241]

Millennia of readings of this text have arguably missed the fact that, above all, Jesus suggests here that heaven itself shares the same deep meme as the Nomadic Worldview. The memological structure of the flock with members is not merely an empirical contingency of pastoral peoples, but an eternal structure which heaven itself holds for those initiated into it.

Jesus was not alone in promoting the idea that heaven itself is memologically structured by the Nomadic Flock, as though this were some Ancient wisdom which was quickly forgotten as the religion came to be institutionalized. This deep meme provides the missing link to make sense of the paradoxes of Calvinist predestination which continue to baffle and enrage even devout Christians. Above all, Calvin believed that fallen sinners cannot earn their salvation because salvation is quite simply not the kind of thing which could be grasped within the ergonic horizon of human work and sense object tools. One cannot earn one's salvation with good works because there is no such ergonic process which could be carried out by the body within the corrupted space of the material

---

241 Luke 15:7

world. Salvation could only be understood through the memological frame of the nomadic flock, for the elect are merely the flock which God had chosen himself to be saved. In the Second Book of *Institutes of the Christian Religion*, Calvin himself calls predestination a "sublime mystery" which "represses all the wantonness and prurience of the human mind" because its secret lies outside the reaches of historical time altogether: "[it is] what God predetermined before all ages, when he was pleased to provide a cure for the misery of the human race."[242] To have been always already included in the flock of the elect "before all ages" is fundamentally incompatible with any ergonic process, for the latter can only unfold within historical time and according to the agency of some embodied human person.

Even without an explicit understanding of the hermeneutical layers involved in such a distinction, this attitude is similarly observable in some other great Protestant ideas of the Reformation era, such as in Edmund Spenser's massive epic poem *The Faerie Queene*. In Book 1 of the text, a devout ascetic seems to courageously renounce the ways of the world by hiding himself away in a secluded hermitage and rigorously carrying out pious acts of Roman Catholic devotion, no doubt in order to go through the Pope-approved motions of "earning his salvation" through good works.[243] When night falls, however, our "saintly" hermit breaks open his spell books of black magic in order to stir up trouble for the unwitting sleepers, for he is none other than Archimago, the devil himself.[244] In this poem, Spenser literally went as far as to argue that "good works" are so empty and so useless for salvation that even the most devout rituals done by Roman Catholic "saints" can just as easily be performed by Satan himself.

Even before the Reformation began, one could find a mismatch between the worldly pastorate of the Church hierarchy and the mystical pastor of God himself, yet these too must be interpreted through the nomadic deep meme. In his *Security, Territory, Population*, Michel Foucault examined the outlets which

---

[242] John Calvin, *Institutes of the Christian Religion* (Kindle Edition).

[243] Edmund Spenser, *The Faerie Queene* (Book I, Canto I, Stanzas 34-5).

[244] Edmund Spenser, *The Faerie Queene* (Book I, Canto I, Stanzas 36-8).

Medieval Christians had available to challenge or circumvent the institutionalized pastoral authority of the Roman Church. Eschatological beliefs provided one such avenue, for the simple fact that if Jesus Christ were coming back to Earth again soon, there would be no need for the bishops to provide a temporary substitute for his authority; Jesus could simply reign himself as the "true shepherd."[245] In one medieval formulation later condemned as heresy, Joachim of Fiore went even further; he argued that God's final return to the Earth would not be limited to being a second incarnation of Jesus Christ, since that had already been accomplished to launch the second age of history.[246] Instead, the third age of history would begin when God returned as the Holy Spirit itself, a force which would no longer be centred in a single messianic figure but would be "spread over the entire world," embodying "a particle, a fragment, a spark of the Holy Spirit in each of the faithful, so they will no longer need a shepherd." We should be careful not to miss the point in this claim; far from abolishing the concept of a flock, Joachim of Fiore radicalized it by promising that in this final age of history, the earthly flock will simply transform into the heavenly flock itself. No longer would it be an imperfect imitation separated from the "real flock" in heaven and headed by an all-too-human figurehead; rather, in this age, the heavenly flock would be materialized in each member of the faithful on Earth. In the previous era, the divine pastor became an Earthly man; in the final age, the heavenly flock itself would undergo incarnation.

One finds an equally dogmatic attachment to remnants of the Nomadic Worldview in Roman Catholicism as well, even extending to the present day. In this case, nomadic remnants persist after the Soma had definitively shifted not only to grain but even to fossil fuels. Although it is rarely mentioned openly these days, it was not that long ago that Catholics understood that their political loyalty was owed primarily to the Pope, and was owed only secondarily to the king or president of the nation in which that

---

[245] Michel Foucault, *Security, Territory, Population* (New York: Palgrave, 2007), p. 214.
[246] Ibid.

person happened to live. Especially if one had immigrated to Protestant-majority nations such as the United States, Australia, or South Africa, this clear hierarchy would have to be remembered and would influence one's political decisions. Even if such a statement has currently become somewhat politically incorrect at the level of language these days, it continues to persist in the financial arrangement which requires even the poorest Roman Catholics in the global population to pay their yearly taxes to the Vatican, under the euphemisms of "tithing" or (in the worst cases) "sending their money to God." The Pope primarily exercised lordship over a global population spread out in countless nations; his formally-recognized political sovereignty over the geographical location of Vatican City today or the Papal States in earlier times was only secondary to this true global empire which transcended national boundaries altogether. The proper memological shape of Roman Catholicism is the nomadic set with members whose only criterion is inclusion and whose geographical location is merely accidental.

One might use the term pseudo-memology to describe this tendency for an outdated memological remnant to persist even after its underlying Soma had vanished. This is somewhat similar to Oswald Spengler's notion of "pseudomorphosis."[247] Spengler used the term "pseudomorphosis" to describe a morphological feature which had been artificially brought into a cultural worldview from a foreign origin, such as the tendency for early buildings in Washington, D.C. to mimic the Classical Architecture of Ancient Rome; this was to be contrasted with the organic morphological development of a culture over its own proper life cycle in history. Spengler dismissed Modern European fascination with Classical

---

[247] One of Spengler's earliest references to pseudomorphosis occurs in the sixth chapter of the first volume; here, Spengler notes that Western Christianity borrowed the "Magian hierarchy of heaven" with its angels, saints, and persons of the Trinity, but these had "grown paler and paler, more and more disembodied, in the sphere of the Western pseudomorphosis." Even the Devil, once so important to its original Magian context, had "disappeared unnoticed from among the possibilities" of the Faustian Worldview because the Magian "duality of world powers" could not be resolved with the "solitude of the Faustian soul."

Culture as just an engagement with a fossilized relic from a foreign origin:

> [We Faustian Europeans] think that we are [the] pupils and successors [of the Classical,] whereas in reality we are simply its adorers.[248]

In a 2018 *Ecosophia* post titled "Twilight of the Intelligentsia," John Michael Greer argued that the tendency for elites around the world today to wear business suits and meet in skyscrapers is another great example of a cultural artefact from the Western European Worldview which has been artificially implanted into numerous other cultures around the world.[249]

One can even find some remnants of the nomadic pastoralist pseudo-meme as early as the Book of Genesis; according to that text, the victim of the first murder ever to occur was a nomadic pastoralist whose Soma was sheep and goats. He was killed by an agrarian farmer whose Soma was grain and vegetables:

> Abel was a keeper of sheep, but Cain was a tiller of the ground. And in process of time it came to pass, that Cain brought of the fruit of the ground an offering unto the Lord. And Abel, he also brought of the firstlings of his flock and of the fat thereof. And the Lord had respect unto Abel and to his offering: but unto Cain and to his offering he had not respect. And Cain was very wroth, and his countenance fell. And the Lord said unto Cain, Why art thou wroth? and why is thy countenance fallen? If thou doest well, shalt thou not be accepted? and if thou doest not well, sin lieth at the door. And unto thee shall be his desire, and thou shalt rule over him. And Cain talked with Abel his brother: and it came to pass, when they were in the field, that Cain rose up against Abel his brother, and slew him.[250]

---

[248]See the first chapter of the first volume.

[249] John Michael Greer, "Twilight of the Intelligentsia," available at https://www.ecosophia.net/the-twilight-of-the-intelligentsia/

[250] Genesis 4:2-8

The fact that nomadic Abel is portrayed as the hero and agrarian Cain is condemned to be a "fugitive and vagabond in the Earth"[251] after the crime bears remnants of a worldview in which the nomadic pastoralist is to be portrayed as a sympathetic figure whose worldview suffered somatic death through the violent force of an alien people with a strange way of life founded on a new crucial resource. The Legend of Cain and Abel is therefore not only a story of brotherly hate, but is also a snapshot that captures the somatic transition from one worldview to another, as the agrarian farmer killed the nomadic goat herder and brought his ecological context to nothingness.

The tendency to overemphasize the familial element of brother killing brother has made it all too easy to overlook this legend's properly political dimension: above all, this story demonstrates that Cain overwhelmed Abel through generating larger raw surpluses of resources through shifting to agriculture. This process would recur on a much more devastating scale with the rise of fossil fuels, but the time is quickly approaching when it too will meet the fate of somatic death.

The pope's and pharaoh's styles of domination demonstrate that pseudo-memology indicates an ecological mismatch with one's environment. Rather than allow the Soma to genuinely structure one's worldview, one remains beholden to the memological biases of a previous era. Because they lack an authentic somatic context, these must often be brutally enforced with raw violence or threats of supernatural damnation. Rather than allow Limitation to be hermeneutically grasped in the somatic context which allows it to appear to an ecologically finite subject, a worldview is forcibly imposed through political Domination. It would be incorrect to call the heretics burned at the stake for challenging papal supremacy Orwellian "thought-criminals"; above all, by challenging the nomadic pseudo-meme against the backdrop of the Agrarian Circle, these figures were guilty of "meme crimes" rather than "thought crimes" as such. One might argue that Martin Luther's Reformation

---

[251] Genesis 4:12

was primarily a memological revolution and only secondarily a religious one, since his calls to downplay the universal flock headed by the Pope in Rome was truly a call to end an unnecessary and dysfunctional mismatch between Soma of agrarian grain and the pseudo-meme of the nomadic set.

It is uncomfortably easy to imagine that some lunatic dictator in the far future will similarly insist that his or her subjects continue to embody the pseudo-meme of progress long after the last drop of commercially viable petroleum had been burned. This is a crime of the most fundamental kind, since pseudo-memology blocks out the very possibility of ecology; this is because it arbitrarily dictates a memological shape through which a subject must view the world rather than allow one to emerge organically from a somatic context in which the subject is embedded. Pseudo-memology is therefore inherently a matter of Domination and actively blocks out Limitation (Being) from being grasped as such. This distinction between Limitation and Domination shall be treated in much greater depth in the second volume of *Being and Oil*, as the very foundation of understanding ethical, political, and religious problems shall depend upon it.

Finally, although Frank Herbert's *Dune* is a work of Science Fiction, one might argue that the residents of Arrakis display a unique memological worldview founded on the properly ecological problem of living on a desert planet with no natural precipitation. On Arrakis the crucial resource for survival is Water (spelled with a capital "W" in some cases)[252] and the automatic shape through which any object is viewed is therefore founded upon it. Both positive and negative valences manifest themselves through water, as it is more primordial than either a good or a bad feeling as such. For example, near the end of the novel, Paul's mother longs for better days but automatically portrays these "better days" through the filter of abundant rainfall and a land lush with well-watered vegetation:

---

[252] Frank Herbert, *Dune* (New York: Ace Books, 1990), p. 443.

"My mother is sick with longing for a planet she may never see," Paul said. "Where the water falls from the sky and plants grow so thickly you cannot walk between them."[253]

Earlier in the novel, she had made a similar comment regarding the southern lands they had once seen. One might argue that under the Soma of Water, the oasis is the sense object to manifest one's desire for a favourable location:

> Jessica said, "The oases were so beautiful when we left. Do you not long for the day when the whole land may blossom thus?"[254]

It is not only pleasant items which manifest themselves through an image of water, however. Even the ghastliest thing of all, death, is contemplated through the image of a poisoned cup in a fragment of a song near the end of the novel:

> Why do I think of an ambush
> And poison in molten cup?
> Why do I feel my years?[255]

Yet the oasis and the poison cup are in a certain sense deviations away from the standard way that water is experienced on an unbearably hot and dry desert planet. The ordinary frame in which water is experienced is one of evaporation, a testament to water's sheer rarity on the planet. The stillsuit, for example, captures the body's own evaporating moisture and reclaims it as drinking water.

> He found his stillsuit's watertube in its clip at his neck, drew a warm swallow into his mouth, and he thought that here he truly began an Arrakeen existence- living on reclaimed moisture from his own breath and body. It was flat and tasteless water, but it soothed his throat.[256]

---

253 Ibid., p. 469.

254 Ibid., p. 439.

255 Ibid., p. 436.

Likewise, giving up moisture for a higher cause is portrayed as the supreme act of sacrifice, the highest ethical act one can perform. At a funeral for a man he had killed himself, for example, Paul shocks the audience by publicly crying. Giving up moisture for the dead was an act even the dead man's lifelong friends had not done:

> Jessica, hearing the voices, felt the depth of the experience, realized what terrible inhibitions there must be against shedding tears. She focused on the words: *"He gives moisture to the dead."* It was a gift to the shadow world — tears. They would be sacred beyond a doubt.[257]

In fact, this experience leads Jessica to realize that among all the sense objects on the planet, quickly-evaporating tears for the dead overlap with Water's deep meme the most memorably:

> Nothing on this planet had so forcefully hammered into her the ultimate value of water. Not the water-sellers, nor the dried skins of the natives, nor the stillsuits or the rules of the water-discipline. Here there was a substance more precious than all the others — it was life itself and entwined all around with symbolism and ritual. Water.[258]

Somatic Hermeneutics: Ecology

It may seem redundant to speak of a layer dedicated to Somatic Hermeneutics, since each of the four other layers are, in a sense, somatic layers as well. The four preceding discussions all confronted the mystery of ecological finitude in their own way, since even if a transcendent essence can be given in consciousness, it can never be given without an ecological context. A spiritual absolute, for example, can be given through a magical symbol

---

256 Ibid., p. 204.
257 Ibid., p. 314.
258 Ibid.

situated within a mythological event, but the mythological event itself can only be given within a determinate ecological context.

We can see this in the way that the same religion can "update" its mythological structures without changing which spiritual absolutes it relates to, since the spirit appears without purity no matter which Soma dominates it. In all eras of Christianity's existence, it has been understood that the Kingdom of God would be inherited by the poor. However, the precise mythological structures in which the spiritual truth of ascetic poverty could appear had to change massively as the religion shifted from one somatic context to another. In the ancient and medieval worlds, it was understood that the "blessed poor"[259] were the peasants, fishermen, and daily wage labourers who had to physically work with their hands just to struggle for a hand to mouth existence in which there was no question of ever getting ahead (one might be reminded that Jesus himself was one such daily wage labourer); the wicked rich who play so prevalent a role in Jesus' own words within the gospels were, of course, the idle aristocrats who had outsourced ergonic tasks to slaves and enjoyed the unearned luxuries reaped from others' labour. The Jesus of the gospels was quite clear that such a lifestyle was a one-way ticket to Hell, as the parable of Lazarus and the rich man from the Gospel of Luke demonstrates particularly memorably:

> There was a rich man who was dressed in purple and fine linen and who feasted sumptuously every day. And at his gate lay a poor man named Lazarus, covered with sores, who longed to satisfy his hunger with what fell from the rich man's table; even the dogs would come and lick his sores. The poor man died and was carried away by the angels to be with Abraham. The rich man also died and was buried. In Hell, where he was being tormented, he looked up and saw Abraham far away with Lazarus by his side. He called out, 'Father Abraham, have mercy on me, and send Lazarus to dip the tip of his finger in water and cool my tongue; for I

---

[259] Luke 6:20-3

am in agony in these flames.' But Abraham said, 'Child, remember that during your lifetime you received your good things, and Lazarus in like manner evil things; but now he is comforted here, and you are in agony. Besides all this, between you and us a great chasm has been fixed, so that those who might want to pass from here to you cannot do so, and no one can cross from there to us.'[260]

With the rise of fossil fuel industrialism, however, the "blessed poor" suddenly had to appear within a very different set of mythological motifs. On one hand, the ergonic tasks which once defined the daily struggles of the blessed poor literally vanished, as Modern Technology automated away every ergonic job it possibly could and made it illegal to perform traditional tasks without a dizzying array of licenses, permits, and certifications. On the other hand, the ideology of a "universal middle class" cast shame upon physical work and simple lifestyles. Even self-proclaimed "devout Christians" felt compelled to brutally force their children to study subjects they had no interest or competence in, simply out of raw financial interest, such as forcing a child with no mathematical aptitude to pursue an engineering career simply because of the high pay.

The motif of the "blessed poor" remained amidst this frenzy of blatant greed but the mythic structure in which it appeared shifted from the toiling peasant to the "generous donor." Donating a share of one's pay to a list of charities proved a very useful arrangement, since it allowed even multi-millionaire CEO's to still claim, somehow, to be counted among the "poor in spirit" simply because they had written big checks to fund research to cure cancer or to build schools in Africa. In addition, it fit perfectly with the spirit of consumerism, since building up one's own personal list of favourite charities became just another act of shopping around for causes which appealed to one's personal tastes while passing on others which did not. Paradoxically, casting the "generous donor" as the mythic symbol for the "blessed poor" somehow made even ascetic

---

[260] Luke 16:19-31

poverty into a luxury of the well to do, since it suddenly required more and more money just to be wealthy enough to contribute to a dozen different charities each month. Under Fossil Fuel Christianity, one had to be rich just to be poor.

It is peculiar that even among practicing Christians today, virtually no one notices this contradiction. It is not enough, however, to attribute this to religious hypocrisy, for one will never realize such things simply from remaining within the layer of mythology itself; only penetrating all the way to the deepest layer of the Soma will make this clear. This deepest layer is therefore a legitimate hermeneutical horizon of meaning, but it differs from the higher order layers in that it no longer deals with composite essences which combine a somatic essence with a spiritual, gnostic, ergonic, or mentatic one. The layer of Somatic Hermeneutics is distinguished as the only layer which is pure, as the following table shows:

[3]

Hermeneutical Layer	Essence Type	Example
Mythological	Pneumatic-Somatic	Willpower, Absolute Emptiness, Stability, Motivation
Systematic	Gnostic-Somatic	π, 0, Grammatical Locality, 3
Objective	Ergonic-Somatic	Fishing Work, Blacksmithing, Woodworking

Memological	Mentatic-Somatic	Ascending Ray, Circle, Set, Vapor
Ecological	Somatic	Petroleum, Grain, Yaks, Water

This table demonstrates that there are five types of essences accessible to hermeneutical interpretation. These include the pneumatic type of the spiritual absolutes referenced by occultists such as John Michael Greer and Julius Evola; the gnostic absolutes which are partially captured in systems in Mathematics, Logic, and Universal Grammar; the ergonic essences of authentic forms of work which the body might perform by going through the Power Process; the mentatic essences which the deep memes capture in geometrical representations of the Soma; and finally, the Soma itself. Although there are five types, only one of them can be given purely. Only the somatic type can be isolated without mixture from one of the other types. This is not possible for the others, since the spirit can only be given through a symbol but the symbol itself can only be given through a mythological narrative, which in turn can only occur within a memological framework situated within a somatic context. Similarly, a number cannot be given in isolation but can only occur within a system, which in turn can only occur within a somatic context. The same requirement holds for the ergonic and mentatic essences. Somatic hermeneutics is a special case of hermeneutical interpretation which transcends the shortcomings which the other layers suffer from, in that the Soma is the only essence which can be given without being mixed with another type.

We must resist the temptation to misinterpret this idea through the lens of Marxist Materialism. It is not at all the case that the other essences are really just instantiations of the somatic type in disguise, such that pneumatic spirit and gnostic number are nothing more than misrecognitions of material forces. The Soma appears in every layer of meaning accessible to a finite human subject only because the subject is bound by a horizon of ecological limitation which can never be transcended without causing the subject to cease to exist altogether. Overstepping ecological limitation would not grant the subject the immortal gaze of absolute knowledge; overstepping this limitation would simply cause Being to vanish, as Being qua Being simply is limitation. David Icke's primary error remains this mistaken belief that the "phantom self" could reunite itself with the "infinite self" through overstepping the illusion of limitation. Far from being granted absolute freedom, destroying limitation would deprive the subject of its sole foundation of existence.

This is not a requirement for all knowers, only a requirement for ones with ecological limitations. It is possible to imagine that some other type of intelligences might exist which could access some of these types of essences without mixing them with a somatic element.

One could imagine, for example, that the disembodied spirits of the pagan universe would be able to see each other without being bound to an ecological horizon with a somatic component mixed in. Because they are not living beings in a physical sense, they would have no limitation imposed by a Soma.

One might also imagine that the gnostic Ideas themselves would be able to gaze at each other within the hypothetical World of Forms which Plato proposed. Indeed, Plato's entire point was that this world would be free of ecological limitation, for this was a higher realm beyond the world of corporeal limitations of an Earthly existence. This is why Plato proposed that the soul could only return to this realm if it had left its physical body behind after death.[261]

In addition, it is not totally unreasonable to think of viruses as pure ergonic bodies which execute hard-wired physical processes even in the absence of conscious rational thought. After all, viruses are not living things at all but are nonetheless teleologically oriented

---

[261] See Plato's *Phaedo, Meno*, and Books VII and VIII of *The Republic*.

towards Natural Selection competition as self-propagating systems.[262] One might hypothesize that they lack the horizon of ecological limitation, for there is no Soma upon which they depend for survival because they are not alive in the first place.

Finally, one might imagine a pure mentatic awareness which is free to think outside the horizon of somatic limitation. In the Lambda section of *The Metaphysics*, Aristotle hypothesized that God could be defined as a "γνῶσις γνῶσις γνῶσις," a "gnosis gnosis gnosis."[263] We might translate this triple reference to "knowledge" as a "knowing" caught up eternally in a process of "knowing" with "knowing" (itself) as its object. A similar idea was later incorporated into the Abrahamic religions in the Middle Ages, with Thomas Aquinas positing the pure act of intelligence as the Christian God and Abu-Nasr Al Farabi making a similar claim within Islam. This pure mentat would be conscious without having ecological limitation for the simple reason that it would not be a mortal caught up in a struggle for ecological survival. Such a God has no Soma, for there is no crucial resource upon which his life depends.

Admittedly, these ideas can only remain highly speculative, since we are fundamentally prohibited from entering such modes of experience. None of us has access to these frames of meaning because we have consciousness only insofar as the horizon of ecological limitation remains intact. Ecology therefore provides a potential solution for the fundamental mystery of Phenomenology, which is how consciousness can go beyond itself to be aware of transcendent objects which have a real existence "out there." Given these findings, we shall propose a very different definition of Material Ontology than Husserl had identified in his classic work *Ideas: General Introduction to Pure Phenomenology*.

Contrary to widespread misunderstanding, Husserl was not primarily interested in the case of how consciousness could become aware of physical objects, since he identified these as only one type within a broader set of regions within his Material Ontology.[264] Not

---

[262] Ted Kaczynski, *Anti-Tech Revolution: Why and How* (Scottsdale: Fitch & Madison, 2016), p. 71.
[263] See Book XII (Lambda) of Aristotle's *Metaphysics*.

every object of consciousness is a physical entity, for Husserl insisted that the meaning of the term "object" must be extended to include a range of other things which are equally legitimate phenomena accessible to consciousness.[265] One could also investigate psychic acts, formal laws, and even pure consciousness itself. These were all located in separate "regions" which held no common ground with physical objects.

Husserl's justification for maintaining this strict system of categorization lay in the fact that the eidetic features of each class of phenomena were unique to only one region. For example, no matter which physical object one happened to see, it could never appear in its entirety in one single glimpse. One could never see all of the sides of the same cube at once, since the essence of a physical object is that it can only appear in a set of partial perspectives.[266] This eidetic rule does not hold for all classes of objects. As he said himself regarding the experience of feelings, "The experience of a feeling has no perspectives. If I look upon it, I have before me an absolute. It has no aspects which might present themselves now in this way, now in that."[267] Psychic acts were also not subject to this limitation, nor were formal laws or even consciousness in itself. Likewise, Husserl argued that Material Ontology had to be broken up into a set of non-overlapping regions which were more like a set of separate peaks than a single tree with one common origin.[268]

Husserl found the notion of a "Science of Being" to be unacceptably vague because speaking of Ontology as only one thing missed a very important distinction between material and formal concerns.[269] On one hand, Ontology could mean Formal Ontology, or the science of categorical constants which remain valid no matter what regional "type" of object one considered. Husserl's idea of Formal Ontology was quite similar to Kant's notion of a

---

[264] Edmund Husserl, *Ideas: General Introduction to Pure Phenomenology* (Eastford: Martino Fine Books, 2017), p. 134.

[265] Ibid., p. 55.

[266] Ibid., p. 137.

[267] Ibid., p 139.

[268] Ibid., p. 153.

[269] Ibid., p. 67.

Transcendental Logic which provides the rules for thinking of some object. According to Kant, the a priori resources of Transcendental Logic rule out the very option of *not* thinking of some object. Even if it is just the empty transcendental object with no content, one is still thinking of some object if one is thinking through the transcendental categories.

On the other hand, Husserl noted that Ontology could mean the Material Ontology which explicitly identifies the distinctions among the different regions of objects of experience. Husserl's motivation for claiming that the intellectual pathway to unearth all of these truths was Phenomenology (the Science of Experience) lay in his realization that there was no need to go somewhere beyond consciousness to find these results. Provided one had properly suspended the "natural attitude" that defined one's naïve stance towards the world, all of these could be found within the realm of experience itself. Phenomenology's uniqueness as a science therefore lay in its ability to isolate the eidetic features of the purified essences within the common realm of consciousness rather than deduce them secondarily from a set of systematic axioms (as in Euclidian Geometry) or achieve them as symbolic results with no strict equivalent within experience itself (as in much of contemporary mathematics).

We shall differ from Husserl, however, in several important ways. For one, Husserl largely thought of the regions in terms of a set of purified transcendental features which *did not* depend upon ecological context; ecological context was simply one more distortion to be "put out of use" with the transcendental reduction and the suspension of the natural attitude. We have already demonstrated, however, that this transcendence of ecological context is an impossibility. *Nothing* can appear to a finite human subject unless the Soma appears along with it. Even the transcendental features of the five layers of meaning can only appear within an ecological context. Overstepping the ecological dimension would not lead one to understand the difference between systematic value and memological shape any better, for the very horizon to do so would vanish.

In addition, Husserl stressed that each of the regional essences could appear in isolation from the others. He argued, in fact, that the primary source of others' errors lay in mixing up distinct regions, such as mistaking psychic acts for physical objects (the error of Psychologism which motivated his *Logical Investigations*). We have already demonstrated, though, that there is only one regional type which can be isolated in its purity. Only the Soma can appear unmixed with some other type, and this can only occur if one has succeeded in penetrating to the deepest hermeneutical layer of ecology. Somatic Hermeneutics is therefore unique among all the layers of meaning, for it alone provides a pathway to grasp an essence without distortion from some other influence. "Pure Mathematics" is a contradiction in terms, but "pure ecology" is not.

Any claim to ecology or environmentalism which does not penetrate to this deepest layer, the purified somatic layer as such, cannot be taken seriously as a viable path out of our current dysfunctional relation to the Earth. Anyone who claims to reject fossil fuel pollution but does not intend to transition to one of the other five somatic contexts is simply blowing the trumpet of self-righteousness, probably with the hope of receiving spoils of fossil fuel imperialism as a reward. Any social justice college student protester, for example, who screams that the Republican Party needs to solve global warming for them has to realize that the only "solution" to global warming is for that same person to literally become a hunter gatherer, agrarian farmer, salvage ruinman (as in Greer's novel of the far future *Star's Reach*), nomadic herder, or Arrakeen water warrior. Of course, these options are literally unthinkable to virtually all of the climate protesters who busy themselves with street corner activism, but that is only a testament to their complete lack of freedom under Modern Technology. We might say that the true definition of an NPC is that it is one who cannot break free from one somatic context to adopt another. The technophile is the worst NPC of all, for this one has actively surrendered living under *any* somatic context by openly endorsing the anti-Soma and destroyer of ecological consciousness.

We have already observed that the most serious thinkers in the anti-technology and peak oil movements have distinguished themselves through actually adopting lifestyles as hunter gatherers (Kaczynski), pre-industrial fishermen (Linkola), or, at the very least, intensive organic gardeners (Greer). The author of the present text has also found that his life improved radically by clinging to the remnants of the agrarian world which still survive, albeit in discontinuous fragments, in the rural village in India where he lives. These include drinking water from the well on one's own land, using decades-old hand tools to clear weeds and plant crops, carrying water by hand with buckets, storing fish curry in clay pots at room temperature without refrigeration, cooking rice over firewood outdoors, living without AC in a tropical region near the equator, eating eggs from the hens in the backyard, recycling food scraps with a compost pit, and showering with room temperature water by hand with a bucket. Far from "dropping down to Third World poverty," the author has found these remnants of the agrarian past to be a source of freedom which finally breaks the stranglehold of Modern Technology. Ironically, the author recalls being far poorer in the United States, where these alternatives were not even an option and the financial burden to remain a cog within the System was devastatingly high. Somehow, even *slavery* has become extraordinary expensive!

In his 2017 classic *The Retro Future*, John Michael Greer noted that technological choice is the greatest heresy of our era. Getting to choose which technologies one wants to use, even if they are "outdated," is the most certain proof that one is a conscious mentat and not an NPC robot. For this reason, refusing to use the latest product is the highest Orwellian thought crime. The term "heresy" is not at all hyperbole in this context. Greer noted in this book that one woman from Oregon was featured in the news because she lived in a Victorian house and continued to use the 19th Century technologies which were compatible with her particular home.[270] Bizarrely, the response from readers was a flurry of death threats. We are arguably not far from the point at which anyone

---

[270] John Michael Greer, *Retrotopia: Looking to the Past to Reinvent the Future* (Gabriola Island: New Society Publishers, 2017), pp. 71-2.

caught using an outdated tool might be publicly hanged or burned at the stake by the mob of technophile zombies, simply because he or she has demonstrated the freedom to live in a real somatic context amidst a population of robots who have lost the ability even to be ecological beings.

Part II
Ecology and Politics

"Give a man a gun and he can rob a bank. Give a man a bank and he can rob the world. Give a man control of the banking system and he can own the world." —David Icke, *Everything You Need to Know But Have Never Been Told*

"I have found nothing good that was ever brought about by progress" —Pentti Linkola, *Can Life Prevail?*

Chapter Three
The Failure of Scientific Objectivity:
Linkola, Greer, Kaczynski, Zerzan

The author's appeal to hermeneutics may surprise those who tend to think of ecology as strictly a matter of empirical science and who might think of hermeneutics as a concern restricted to the interpretation of literary texts, a bias no doubt worsened by Gadamer's monumental text on hermeneutics *Truth and Method*.[271] However, it would be absurd to claim that ecology has devolved to its current sorry state primarily due to a lack of scientific progress; on the contrary, research related to ecological problems is enthusiastically supported both ideologically in the media and financially in the university budgets. Yet no matter how much scientific information we amass warning us that fossil fuel emissions, mass extinction, topsoil destruction, and water pollution will bring about massive suffering in the near future, virtually *no one* is able to make even the most modest adjustments to his or her consumption habits simply as a result of learning this information on a theoretical level. The greatest ecological thinkers of our era have noticed precisely this shortcoming within the environmentalist movement, even after arriving at this realization from paths as distinct as the critique of Modern Technology (Ted Kaczynski), the eco-crime of human overpopulation (Pentti Linkola), the role of magic in achieving spiritual changes to human motivation (John Michael Greer), and the devaluation of *all* symbolic systems as signs of technological alienation (Zerzan). We shall consider each thinker's stance in detail.

In his super-rare 1971 essay "Progress Versus Wilderness," Ted Kaczynski attempted to provide an answer to the following paradox: no matter how linearly-advanced a supercomputer's problem solving capabilities might become, it remains fundamentally incapable of learning to stop pursuing economic growth, even if this becomes necessary to prevent ecological

---

[271] Hans-Georg Gadamer, *Truth and Method* (New York: Continuum, 1989), p. 4.

catastrophe.[272] Put briefly, the one thing which the System can never learn is that it should stop growing. Decades later in his 2016 fragmentary magnum opus *Anti-Tech Revolution: Why and How*, Kaczynski would reach the troubling conclusion that a self-propagating system will continue to advance until it literally advances into self-destruction, simply because there is no "stop button" hard-wired into the System.[273] Kaczynski's insistence on a revolution against Modern Technology[274] is simply the logical conclusion of this fact, since a system which literally cannot stop itself can only be stopped forcibly by the deliberate decision of some revolutionary group like "Freedom Club."

In the context of his 1971 essay, the grand irony is that this lesson does not lie out of reach to the supercomputer due to technical shortcomings or a lack of raw computing power. In fact, the lesson is not at all complicated; rather, it is only shocking just how astonishingly simple it is. Even human minds with feeble intelligence are in principle capable of grasping that achieving more economic growth will prove useless to a system which must destroy itself in the process, yet the most powerful supercomputer is ruled out from learning it. Likewise, the problem is altogether unrelated to scientific data or explicit theoretical information. The very methodology one uses to approach it must be altogether different from a stance of empiricist objectivity.

Kaczynski goes on to warn that it is not only supercomputers which have proven incapable of grasping the lesson to wilfully forsake economic growth in order to serve higher ecological ends. None other than self-proclaimed environmentalists have proven incapable of taking this lesson seriously, since environmentalists virtually always have roughly the same consumerist habits as the rest of the population; this is deeply

---

[272] Ted Kaczynski, "Progress Versus Wilderness," Ted Kaczynski Papers, Labadie Collection at the University of Michigan's Special Collections Library, Ann Arbor, p. 5.

[273] Ted Kaczynski, *Anti-Tech Revolution: Why and How* (Scottsdale: Fitch & Madison, 2016), p. 55.

[274] Ted Kaczynski, *Industrial Society and Its Future*, in *Technological Slavery* (Scottsdale: Fitch & Madison, 2019), para. 3-4.

troubling because environmentalists represent the segment of the human population who have wilfully exposed themselves to the largest number of scientific data warning them of the consequences of their own behaviour. The quest for the bit of theoretical information which will finally make the big difference by leading a person to change his or her lifestyle once and for all is an infinite loop from which one will never escape; this is an intellectual journey which is futile even to begin pursuing. Clearly, a lack of scientific research is not the problem. Rather, the issue lies in the hermeneutical problems of interpretation and understanding, primarily regarding how one understands the very ecological context in which one is embedded and which provides the foundation for one's higher order layers of meaning to emerge in the first place.

Finnish fisherman and ecophilosopher Pentti Linkola's essay "A Refresher Course in the State of the World" similarly emphasized that ecological inaction cannot be blamed on a lack of scientific "enlightenment" (the term he prefers).[275] As he notes himself, the following are all "generally accepted scientific facts": the seas are polluted with oil; food chains are fundamentally disrupted; deforestation is rampant; entire ecosystems are poisoned; and we are somehow willfully converting productive, renewable green spaces into the most unproductive, not to mention just plain ugly, monstrosity of all by turning them into *parking lots!* There is no debate whether these points might be challenged on the level of scientific factuality. If disputes do occur, they are usually restricted to adjusting specific figures, yet the underlying ecological problem remains the same regardless of any numerical variations.

No one could possibly claim that there is any doubt whether these crises are scientifically validated. The real issue is instead something much more uncomfortable to contemplate, since the true question is only whether learning this data will play any role in affecting individuals' actions. Like Kaczynski, Linkola notes that there is so little difference in personal behavior between the "unenlightened" and the "enlightened" that we can effectively

---

[275] Pentti Linkola, "A Refresher Course in the State of the World", in *Can Life Prevail?* (Helsinki: Tammi, 2008).

186

conclude that exposure to scientific data will never be enough to bring about a change in one's lifestyle. In fact, he claims that the only notable difference between the two groups is that among the enlightened there is "more chattering to be heard" over the issues (or in the present day, there is "more tweeting to be read" among the enlightened). In its worst form, this chattering devolves into an ongoing "rustling of papers" within the First World bureaucracies where so-called "experts" are paid generous salaries in order to go through the motions of drafting up solutions to precisely the same ecological crises which their own agencies bring about. Needless to say, the only solutions the experts will pursue will be ones which do not threaten their own standard of living, let alone harm economic growth for the nation at large.

In fact, Linkola claims in this essay that Finns are relatively well-educated on ecological problems yet they constantly demand that their own purchasing power increase, without realizing that this increase in economic agency is simply a euphemism for more damage to the environment; the two absolutely cannot be separated. National efforts are unanimously harmonized to prevent economic recession, yet if anyone were actually serious about prioritizing ecological truth over political expediency, one would have to adopt the supremely-unpopular policy of pursuing economic depression in order to drastically reduce ecological damage by cutting consumption.

Needless to say, no credible candidate has ever run a political campaign on the promise of bringing about an economic depression. The one thing which every politician in the United States can agree on is that economic growth, rising standards of living, high-paying jobs, and crass materialistic wealth are absolute goods which can justify the most hypocritical violations of the official political ideology or religious creeds which they might otherwise pretend to espouse. Even where debate occurs between conservative and liberal factions, the topic of disagreement is never economic growth in itself, only how to achieve it. In 2009, for example, clergymen within the Roman Catholic Church opposed the Obama stimulus package and other "socialist" reforms only because these were not efficient enough at generating wealth, as though failing to yield a reasonable financial return on the tax payers' investment were literally a sin. One priest on EWTN's World Over news program asserted that socialism should be opposed by the faithful catholic laity because it merely redistributes the wealth that already exists but does little to "grow the pie larger." Voting for the (Neo-Con Republican) candidate who can bring about stronger economic growth had therefore literally become one's ethical duty as a "good catholic," dictated by the Church hierarchy itself.

Anyone with even the slightest familiarity with pre-modern Christian writings will realize that this attitude is completely unprecedented in the history of the religion. Dmitry Orlov, for example, once mentioned that because the Russian Orthodox Church developed its dogmas and traditions before the rise of industrialism, it more or less continues to reflect the archaic Christian understanding that heaven will be inherited by the poor and humble who appear to be "losers" in this temporary, fallen Earth but will get their reward in the next life.[276] While it is customary to think of Protestant Christianity as the primary sect to have reversed this old belief through perversions like Weber's "Protestant Work Ethic," as well as the more recent "prosperity gospel" hoax run by televangelist con-men, this attitude that "greed is good" is every bit as rampant among American Roman Catholics who share this understanding that financial success is God's reward for the "good people" if they work hard, while poverty is an Earthly punishment for those who neglected their studies, dropped out of school, or simply lack motivation to "do better" with their lives.

Even more troubling than theological contradiction is the ecological problem with such an attitude. Anyone who believes that God himself wants a high GDP driven by more speculative bubbles and more printed money (or more precisely, by rampant fossil fuel pollution) must somehow provide an answer for the environmental consequences which these will inevitably bring about. Sadly, many people seem to believe that ecological destruction has become a religious obligation which even God himself supposedly endorses

[276] Orlov, Dmitry, *Reinventing Collapse: The Soviet Experience and American Prospects*, (Gabriola Island: New Society Publishers, 2011).

with a stamp of approval, so long as it serves as a means to an end to make people who are already wealthier than ancient emperors even richer.

Linkola's proposal that we consciously engineer an economic recession is far from the only example of his willingness to acknowledge controversial ecological facts which would otherwise be censored equally vehemently by both conservative and liberal and by both devout catholic and radical atheist alike. In his essays "The Suppressed Nightmare of Conservation" and "Cat Disaster" he had the guts to attack one of the most beloved dysfunctional features of his fellow Finns' personal lives: the house cat.[277] Although cats are beloved pets which are often considered to be members of the human family itself, Linkola noted that on ecological grounds alone their presence in Finland simply cannot be justified. However much they are personally "liked" by their owners, a truly objective ecologist would agree that the cats have got to go.

Once again, such a statement is not at all controversial on scientific grounds, since cats are not even native to Finland in the first place. They are Egyptian predators which had been artificially introduced into a foreign ecosystem with no regard for their inherent incompatibility with it. The result has been devastating for the indigenous wildlife. Although cats might be prized simply for their "cuteness," their natural instincts drive them to do far more than just sit around the house looking "adorable." It should not come as a surprise that natural predators would be driven to hunt local animals, since Linkola notes that this was precisely the reason why cats were brought to Finland in the first place. The result has been devastating, particularly to local bird species. Even after considerable time, money, and effort were devoted to coordinated efforts to stabilize endangered populations, all of this was easily negated by the house cats' rampant unmonitored hunting.

The true extent of our blindness to ecological reality is measured by the fact that although these cats are literally

---

[277] Pentti Linkola, "The Suppressed Nightmare of Conservation", in *Can Life Prevail?* (Helsinki: Tammi, 2008).
Pentti Linkola, "Cat Disaster", in *Can Life Prevail?* (Helsinki: Tammi, 2008).

committing massive unjustified violence which threatens to drive some animals into extinction, they have become the beneficiaries of extravagant legal protections which effectively place them above the law. Although drowning cats has long been a normal, humane practice for dealing with cats who for one reason or another could not be maintained, under Finnish law this practice has literally become illegal. On ecological grounds, what this really means is that we have legally mandated cat populations to explode by threatening to jail anyone who places even the slightest restraint upon them.

The same people who claim that drowning a cat, however justified the individual case might be, is "murder" would likely claim to be "animal lovers" who categorically oppose all violence against animals. This is supremely ironic, since this same prohibition against controlling cat populations is simply a guarantee that countless other animals will suffer violence at the claws of a merciless hunter with no right to be in this ecosystem.

Yet the house cat is far from the only example of a foreign predator which had been artificially introduced into Finland to the detriment of the local ecosystem. In his essay "Violence: The Animal Protector as an Apostle of Doom," he exposes the absolute madness behind proposals that there should be a conservation program for *minks!* From an ecological standpoint, nothing could more absurd, because minks are arguably the Finnish equivalent of the dingoes which had infiltrated Australia. It is not at all controversial to acknowledge that the only ethical stance for dealing with dingoes is forceful, violent extermination because they are vividly terrifying animals, but because minks and cats are intrinsically "cuter" such a statement would seem unthinkable, even to the environmentalists who claim to take ecological issues seriously. Linkola does not mince words on the issue: "This vermin mink raccoon should be vanquished down to the last."[278] According to him, the only ecologically-justified response is that *you have to kill them!*

---

[278] Pentti Linkola, "Violence: The Animal Protector as an Apostle of Doom, in *Can Life Prevail?* (Helsinki: Tammi, 2008).

It is perhaps understandable that leftist environmentalists would lack the motivation to favor violent extermination for animals like minks or cats which do not directly harm them, yet we can find the same idiocy applied even to rodents which threaten to infect human populations in major cities with none other than the bubonic plague and other medieval diseases. Despite a growing typhus epidemic in the city of Los Angeles as a result of exploding rat populations fueled by mountains of stagnant garbage and rising homelessness, some "radical environmentalists" have gone as far as to seek legal action to ban rodenticides, despite the fact that the consequences for publicly "loving the animals" will literally be a series of epidemics which will kill many of the very poorest residents of the city.

The idea that one can preserve Nature and simultaneously eliminate violence is one of the silliest symptoms of an environmentalist movement which has little regard for ecological reality. In one of his letters written from prison, Ted Kaczynski exposed the idiocy of "environmentalist pacifism." This is itself a contradiction in terms, since few things are quite as natural as violence. Some hard-core leftist animal rights activists might be surprised to learn that wolves, tigers, and bears are not "enlightened vegans" who get their food through shopping at the kind of overpriced, upscale organic foods markets frequented by rich yuppies in Boulder, CO and other elitist college towns. The grand irony about this fantasy of "environmentalist pacifism" is that if violence were entirely removed from Nature, the ecosystem as a whole would be destroyed as a result. Ted Kaczynski noted in a letter to M. K.:

> [V]iolence is . . . a necessary part of nature. If predators did not kill members of prey species, then the prey species would multiply to the point where they would destroy their environment by consuming everything edible.[279]

[279] Ted Kaczynski, "Letter to M. K.", in *Technological Slavery* (Port Townsend: Feral House, 2010), p. 377.

We could argue for the following rule of thumb: if anyone believes that Nature can be preserved without any of the violence included, then that person is not really talking about Nature. Such a person could only be referring to a caricature put on display for tourists in the form of National Parks and recreational campgrounds.

This was a subject which Ted Kaczynski also addressed in his 1971 essay "Progress Versus Wilderness." In it, he argued that the term "wildness" should be favored over the more common term "wilderness" to denote something which genuinely exists outside the influence of the System of Modern Technology. Even in the early 1970's, real wildness had already almost entirely vanished even from spaces ordinarily considered wilderness, since these were reduced to the status of "museum-pieces artificially preserved for the entertainment of the affluent."[280] Appeals to preserve Nature without violence are therefore calls for Modern Technology to strangle the last few remaining zones of genuine wildness and transform them into politically correct selfie-sites to be admired simply for their photogenic value. Needless to say, the participants of this farce will have no intention to break their own enslavement to Modern Technology.

In addition to openly promoting violence against minks and cats, anyone who sincerely desires to reclaim the lost ecological balance from its modern disruptions would have to endorse a project even more unpopular than "killing the cats." One would have to call for the end of modern sanitation. Anyone today who argues that this cannot possibly be done seems to forget that even Caesar himself, let alone the peasants he ruled over, did not carry a personal bottle of hand sanitizer everywhere he went in order to instantly "kill the germs" every time he had to touch an object. However, some suburban children today who are forced by their parents to do exactly that have often ended up suffering far more as a result of developing auto-immune disorders, a not so surprising result of using technology to tamper with a complex natural system.

---

[280] Ted Kaczynski, "Progress Versus Wilderness," Ted Kaczynski Papers, Labadie Collection at the University of Michigan's Special Collections Library, Ann Arbor, p. 4.

Ted Kaczynski's comments, from a letter written in prison, on the negative effects of modern sanitation are worth quoting in full:

> It's worth mentioning, by the way, that improved sanitation too seems to have had unanticipated negative consequences. [There is] evidence that modern sanitation has brought about a sharp increase in autoimmune disorders such as allergies, inflammatory bowel disease, and type 1 diabetes. Furthermore, while the poliomyelitis virus has probably been around since time immemorial, paralytic polio was relatively rare prior to the Industrial Revolution. Only after industrialization were there epidemics of paralytic polio that left large numbers of people disabled for life, and it is hypothesized that these epidemics were a result of improved sanitation.[281]

Likewise, it is all the more ironic that many hand sanitizer companies literally use claims of "boosting immunity" as a marketing slogan for their products. In addition to emphasizing sanitation's negative effects on the human body's health, Linkola noted in his essay "Humbug"[282] that sanitation bears an unspeakable economic cost, since the traditional fishermen who had kept Finns fed for centuries violated every health code on the books. This is because it would be impossible for them to satisfy the ridiculous expectations of modern health inspectors, because keeping everything at exactly the right temperature, at exactly the right time, with facilities sanitized with exactly the right brand of artificial chemicals are simply euphemisms for Modern Technology, fossil fuels, and an enormous amount of money. As a result of this unspeakable fact, the traditional fishermen lost their livelihoods and were forced either into unemployment or into wage slavery for impersonal industrial operations. The worst part is that these fishermen were casualties of unnecessary regulations which ironically enough turned out to be both more costly and more

---

[281] Ted Kaczynski, "Letter to David Skrbina, November 23, 2004," in *Technological Slavery* (Scottsdale: Fitch & Madison, 2019), p. 173.

[282] Pentti Linkola, "Humbug", in Can Life Prevail? (Helsinki: Tammi, 2008).

harmful to the consumers anyway. One should also keep in mind that the corporations themselves turned out to be just plain bad at distributing food, since nearly half of all food produced in the United States ultimately ends up in the garbage, just as some 16 million children in the United States struggle with hunger.

Linkola has suggested, in fact, that if one were really serious about preventing ecological catastrophe, one would have to adopt a policy even more unpopular than a consciously-engineered recession, a ban on cats, the violent extermination of minks, and the end of modern sanitation practices: one would have to actively pursue a reduction in global *human* population. One could hardly imagine a more controversial, yet more necessary, move than this. Linkola spends much of the essay "A Refresher Course in the State of the World" arguing that human overpopulation is an eco-crime of the gravest sort which lacks any ecological justification. Its sole justification has been a set of irrational philosophical beliefs which might be grouped under a general heading: the cult of the "unique, irreplaceable individual" who must be saved at any cost.[283] Contrary to expectation, this belief is rampant both within the Religious Right and the Secularist Left and cannot be reduced to any religious or political persuasion as such. Its origin is more primordial than any explicit system of ideology: it is simply our dysfunctional relation to Nature itself, the symptom of an inherently-flawed somatic context which has made ecological madness into the chief requirement of oversocialization.

On one hand, he calls the Pro-Life Movement a "collective mental illness" fighting for the "inalienable rights" of every single fetus; yet he similarly notes that liberal opposition to the death penalty demonstrates an equally mystical fetishization of human life, since even the "most diabolical of criminals" are no longer allowed to be put to death under progressive governments due to political correctness.

In addition, more and more leftists have enjoyed getting to take the moral high ground by condemning police officers for shooting *anyone*, even criminals engaged in violent rampages

---

[283] Pentti Linkola, "A Refresher Course in the State of the World", in *Can Life Prevail?* (Helsinki: Tammi, 2008).

against innocent bystanders. In 2016, an Ohio State University student born in Somalia launched a religiously-motivated attack on his fellow students on campus, presumably against people he did not even know personally. The car ramming and stabbing spree left one person dead and nearly a dozen injured. The police were clearly justified in shooting him dead on the scene, but one well-known far left feminist radio host responded by attacking the police for using deadly force, even against someone who was clearly intent on killing as many anonymous strangers as possible and who likely expected not to survive to the end of the event himself anyway.

This irrationality is not, of course, limited to leftists. In his 2009 classic *Confronting Collapse* Michael Ruppert similarly criticized the "pro-life" fanaticism within the Roman Catholic Church as a supremely ironic title for a stance which is actually just contributing to the destruction of human life through religiously-mandated overpopulation:

> If the Roman Catholic Church were to ever rethink its positions on birth control and growth, then the door would be opened for the whole world to rationally discuss the subject. [People] must be somehow breached with a simple awareness that there are too many of us. We are harming or killing everything and committing suicide in the process. Essentially the Catholic Church's position is that the human race must kill everything—including itself—in order to make more babies.[284]

The Vatican is far from the only guilty party in the collective resistance to even the slightest effort towards confronting human overpopulation. Ruppert also casted blame on tribal peoples who maintain irrational cultural prejudices that having numerous children is a "sign of prestige." He even devoted a whole paragraph to the so-called Octo-Mom, the notorious California woman who surgically modified her face in a bizarre attempt to resemble Angelina Jolie[285] and then drew numerous death threats in early

---

[284] Ruppert, Michael C.. *Confronting Collapse* . Chelsea Green Publishing. Kindle Edition.

2009 after giving birth to octuplets despite being "an artificially inseminated, unemployed, single woman."[286] The source of this anger lay in the perception that she had needlessly resorted to unnatural means to bring eight more "freeloaders" onto the Earth, all on the taxpayer's dime. Ruppert found this mass denunciation ironic, since this woman merely symbolizes the collective madness of overpopulation which otherwise goes unquestioned.[287]

Linkola has been similarly skeptical of the majority's judgment and has even gained notoriety for suggesting that the very belief in Democracy is a roadblock preventing serious action on overpopulation, as well as every other impending ecological crisis. Rather than be held hostage to politically correct demands to respect democratic political procedures, Linkola has suggested that some strong centralized authority should mandate strict policies and implement a "green police" force to drastically reduce both population and economic growth and should remain firm in these admittedly controversial convictions even in the face of widespread public disapproval.

In addition to opposing Democracy on practical political grounds, Linkola finds it questionable even as a basic philosophical stance towards human persons, since Democracy is really just the ideology that we're all the same. Linkola is one of the few thinkers with the courage to openly ask: "How can anyone be so crazy as to think that all human life has the same value?"[288] Even according to the democratic ideology that every life is equal, this would make no sense; from a strictly numerical perspective, human overpopulation is actively *reducing* the value of each individual life, since every new baby born causes the value of all other lives to slightly drop, simply as a matter of supply and demand.

Although this pseudo-religious dogma that "all lives are equal" is a universal belief held by any oversocialized subject of

---

[285] "Angelina Jolie 'creeped out' by octuplets mother after receiving letters from her - and hearing rumours of her plastic surgery", DailyMail, 20, February, 2009.
[286] Ruppert, Michael C.. *Confronting Collapse* . Chelsea Green Publishing. Kindle Edition.
[287] Ibid.
[288] Ibid.

Modern Technology, in recent times there was a notable example of an attempt to expand it into a theoretical manifesto to justify, of all things, a criminal act of leftist political terrorism. In 2019, an Antifa terrorist was shot dead while trying to firebomb an ICE facility in the United States; apparently, he had launched the attack under the delusion that he was "liberating concentration camps." Before his death, he shared a fragmentary "manifesto" with friends to provide an explicit theoretical framework for his motivations, albeit a rather small and unimpressive one. The manifesto begins by arguing that because there is an objective difference between right and wrong, he had a moral obligation to take concrete (violent) action against evil. Interestingly, he simply defines this "evil" as the belief that "one life is worth less than another." In other words, evil is any philosophical disagreement with the belief in Democracy, confirmation that Linkola and Evola are two of the supreme Orwellian thought-criminals of our era.

One can only wonder, however, who this terrorist could have imagined he was rebelling against, for this idea that "all lives are the same" is precisely the official ideology of the System of Modern Technology anyway. His "heroic devotion to the cause" is therefore all the more ironic, since he himself likely absorbed this ideology simply as a result of oversocialization under the influence of Modern Technology rather than through any spontaneous recognition of the "objective difference between good and evil" he claimed to take so seriously. One certainly would never arrive at such a strange conclusion that "all lives are the same" simply from empirically comparing the worst serial child molester in prison with a selfless doctor risking his or her own life working in a war zone. In fact, one might wonder how his own act of violence could be justified if all lives are exactly the same, since he certainly didn't appear to have trouble harming some of them in the process of "fighting for peace," a blatant example of Orwellian double-think in itself.

Unlike virtually any other mainstream thinker, Linkola has the guts to admit the supremely politically incorrect fact that the vast majority of human lives today are either irrelevant or directly harmful; only a shockingly small fraction of them can be considered to have anything like the "high worth" we are expected to automatically confer on every life. He does not, however, frame this judgment through the elitist dismissal of the "ignorant masses" who lack sufficient wealth, education, or political correctness to be considered worthy of esteem. Rather, Linkola frames this judgment strictly in ecological terms. The truth is that the majority of humans alive today, especially among the pampered well-to-do classes of First World nations, are whole-heartedly devoted to only one thing: maximizing environmental destruction through a single-minded attachment to insatiable economic consumption; mindless electronic entertainment; and selfish, hedonistic pleasure-seeking. It is no exaggeration to say that for many of them, their very existence represents an ongoing eco-crime against the biosphere. Yet somehow, they have managed to combine the traits of being both the most materially wasteful organisms in the history of the Earth and the most discontent of them all as well, since exactly *no one* among the well-to-do would answer "yes" if asked whether they currently have enough money and enough consumer goods.

Of course, unless one is speaking from somewhere way out on the fringes, in a competition between politically correct appeals to the intrinsic worth of all human life whatsoever and the hard scientific facts regarding human overpopulation's burden on the ecosystem, it is clear that the humanistic chimera of "democratic equality" will always win the battle for representation. Yet Linkola warns that "man's values [(even the supposed value of all human life)] are irrelevant" to the ongoing ecological catastrophes, since these humanistic phantoms will lose their sole foundation for manifestation if human extinction makes it impossible for anyone to value them in the first place. It will be one of the supreme ironies of World History if human life disappears precisely as a result of an irrational overemphasis on human life.

Needless to say, most leftist academics would react to Linkola's calls for a strong centralized authority to forcefully regulate population and economic growth by dismissing such ambitions as examples of "eco-fascism." It is supremely ironic, however, that the same social justice leftists also favored suspending democratic political procedures in order to force the

System to do "the right thing" after Trump's electoral college victory in 2016. Any user of social media that year surely saw a petition calling for signatures to bully the Electoral College members into giving the election to Hillary Clinton against their own states' voters' wishes, simply because she was "objectively the right choice." In other words, the same people who ridiculed Trump's accusations of election rigging just a few months earlier *literally promoted election rigging* after the voters had made "the wrong choice" and required correction from their "more educated" peers in the academic industry.

We must be careful to distinguish this from a similar call to overturn "the official results" in the 2000 presidential election. As Zizek mentioned in his 2008 book *In Defense of Lost Causes*, there is something of an ambiguity in the term "Democracy."[289] On one hand, Democracy refers to the impersonal electoral procedure which must be respected even when it flatly contradicts the will of the people. In this sense of the term, Bush's fraudulent victory in Florida in 2000 was not a contradiction of Democracy; it *was* Democracy, reduced to a stupid formal process which must be upheld if one hopes to avoid slipping into anarchy or totalitarianism. On the other hand, Democracy refers to the will of the people itself, as a powerful and monstrous presence which is only ever imperfectly reflected by the formal procedure; Zizek designates contemporary populism as an example of this phenomenon.[290] The great political challenge of Democracy is finding a proper reconciliation between these two forces.[291]

Whereas in 2000, liberals called for the official results to be overturned out of outrage that Democracy as a formal procedure had cheated Democracy as the will of the people, in 2016 the exact opposite was the case: liberals insisted that the will of the people itself was wrong and angrily demanded that the formal procedure be artificially manipulated through bullying electoral college members into giving the election to Clinton for no reason except that a handful of whining college professors and graduate students had

---

[289] Slavoj Zizek, *In Defense of Lost Causes* (London: Verso, 2008), p. 264.
[290] Ibid., p. 266.
[291] Ibid., p. 268.

done the "hard work" of devoting 20 seconds of their time to signing a petition that had circulated on their social media newsfeeds. It is therefore intellectually dishonest to claim that Linkola's calls for strong authoritarian responses to prevent eco-crimes represents a style of governing which they categorically reject, for they have already proven themselves to have no trouble suspending democratic political procedures in order to force the "objectively right" choice to go through when it serves the interests of the Democrat Party or when it builds up their own public profiles as "professional political activists," yet they somehow find this objectionable when applied to the cause of saving the Earth.

We shall also consider John Michael Greer's critique of environmentalism, specifically within the first few years of his *Archdruid Report* posts. In February, 2009, Greer responded to readers' requests that he recommend a set of essential texts to help understand his idiosyncratic views on Peak Oil and the impending decline of Industrial Civilization. Surprisingly, Greer chose not to open the list with a text on Peak Oil or Industrial Civilization at all. Instead, he opened with the request that the reader find a "general textbook of scientific ecology."[292] As one might expect, his list also included more-familiar classics about economic collapse, such as *The Limits to Growth* and *Overshoot*; texts on the life cycles of great civilizations, such as Oswald Spengler's *Decline of the West;* and even "a practical introduction to intensive organic gardening." Still, he emphasized that the texts "should be read, if you can manage that, in the order I've listed them."[293] We can assume that if one has failed to grasp basic ecological principles, even the most sincere efforts to understand the topics of economic collapse, civilizational decline, and organic gardening will always remain incomplete at best. Ecology is therefore something like a universal skeleton key which will allow one to unlock the secrets of numerous other seemingly-unrelated fields.

In fact, Greer has gone as far as to argue that the laws of ecology are useful for understanding more than just physical

---

[292] John Michael Greer, "A Deindustrial Reading List", in *Archdruid Report*, Vol. 3 (Chicago: Founders House, 2018), p. 25.
[293] Ibid.

phenomena. He has claimed that ecology even holds the key to understanding magic and the realm of spirits. More specifically, he has suggested that in both areas (physical and spiritual), ecology provides a reliable means for solving the mystery of why something went wrong. This claim is not at all controversial when applied to entities with physical bodies, such as in the explanation for how the Ebola virus came to infiltrate human populations in Africa as a result of a disruption to a local ecosystem's balance:

> [Ecological models are not at all controversial when] used to explain outbreaks of lethal tropical diseases such as Ebola fever. According to that theory, the Ebola virus is a natural part of the ecosystem of the central African tropical forest, an ecosystem that also includes human beings, chimpanzees, okapis, and many other creatures. When human beings disrupt the balance of the ecosystem—usually because their traditional cultures, which tend to hold the ecosystem in balance, have broken down—the ecosystem shifts and people begin to die.[294]

Ecological explanations are every bit as reasonable when applied to spiritual problems. The example of the Old Hag and the Hmong demonstrated that when people find themselves unable to perform the traditional magical rituals to seek out friendly spirits' protection against malicious spirits, not only did the evil spirits "really come" afterwards, they even proved capable of seriously harming the people as a result. It is not unreasonable, therefore, to say that "what went wrong" was that the delicate balance in the ecosystem of spiritual forces had been suddenly disrupted, in a way not unlike what happened with the Ebola crises in Africa. The solution, in both cases, might be to restore that ecological balance rather than try to work against it. The only reason why this explanation seems perfectly reasonable and "scientific" when applied to physical entities but drops down to the status of "baseless superstition" when applied to spirits is that the horizon of Pneumatic Hermeneutics has

---

[294] John Michael Greer, *Monsters: An Investigator's Guide to Magical Beings* (Woodbury: Llewellyn, 2001), p. 19.

been deformed beyond recognition in our era. We are effectively hermeneutically blind as a result of technological domination and empty linguistification.

Even in the realm of historical phenomena with no overtly-spiritual dimension, Greer has found the laws of ecology to be a widely-neglected set of tools. Yet it would be a mistake to think that Greer believes that history, for example, is merely similar to ecology on a metaphorical level. Rather, in an October, 2007 post titled "Climbing Down the Ladder," he went as far as to say that "history is simply human ecology mapped onto the dimension of time."[295] Put briefly, history is not just *like* ecology; history quite literally *is* ecology, mapped into the dimension of time rather than the dimension of space. The context for this bold claim lay in his warning against the tendency to think that major historical changes occur simply as a result of conscious human decisions; specifically, Greer warned against fantasies that anyone has the power to control what kind of society will fill the power vacuum left by the collapse of Industrial Civilization. In addition to being disagreeable at the level of ideology, such an ambition would be impossible to fulfill on ecological grounds alone.

Interestingly, Ted Kaczynski also sought to downplay the role of human decision-making as the cause behind major historical shifts. In fact, this subject interested him even as early as his 1971 essay "Progress Versus Wilderness."[296] In this essay, Kaczynski largely relied on the resources of Complexity Theory to explain why historical shifts are emergent properties which are impossible to predict in advance, even from the most bulletproof analysis of the individuals' intentions within the population. Decades later, he expanded this argument to encompass the first chapter of his fragmentary magnum opus *Anti-Tech Revolution: Why and How;* in it, he discussed the impossibility for a society to predict its own behavior, let alone consciously steer it in a particular direction,

---

[295] John Michael Greer, "Climbing Down the Ladder", in *Archdruid Report*, Vol. 1 (Chicago: Founders House, 2017), p. 295.

[296] Ted Kaczynski, "Progress Versus Wilderness," Ted Kaczynski Papers, Labadie Collection at the University of Michigan's Special Collections Library, Ann Arbor, p. 6.

because the very concept of a self-predicting society was riddled with logical impasses reminiscent of Russell's Paradox.[297] In short, a society would have to have full knowledge of itself to make an accurate prediction; however, the prediction itself would preclude any attempt at full self-knowledge because the prediction would in turn modify the system as a whole.

Greer's explanation for the same problem differed in that he emphasized the ecological problems with such an ambition rather than focus exclusively on its logical problems. In a November, 2007 post titled "Waiting for the Other Shoe," Greer clarified his stance on the matter by emphasizing that all historical changes are really ecological shifts in disguise:

> One of the reasons I find ecology a useful guide to history is that the natural world and the human world relate to time and change in similar ways. Most of the time in an ecosystem or a human society, change happens gradually, cycling through predictable patterns or bridging the space between one set of conditions and another.[298]

The Industrial Revolution, for example, did not succeed just because some group of humans, however powerful, "agreed to make it happen"; rather, it was only the ecological context of tapping into abundant fossil fuel reserves that allowed it to outcompete other economic arrangements which relied on less concentrated sources of energy, such as human labor or horses.[299] For precisely this reason, however, Industrial Civilization is impossible to sustain into the indefinite future, since the fossil fuel reserves which once made it wildly successful have already entered the downward slope of permanent decline.

Ironically, this basic ecological truth is literally unthinkable for most people alive today, but is quite easy to understand when

---

[297] Ted Kaczynski, *Anti-Tech Revolution: Why and How* (Scottsdale: Fitch & Madison, 2016), p. 16.
[298] John Michael Greer, "Waiting for the Other Shoe," in *Archdruid Report*, Vol. 1 (Chicago: Founders House, 2017), pp. 316-7.
[299] Ibid.

applied to field mice rather than humans. Greer opened his 2009 classic *The Ecotechnic Future* by asking the reader to consider what would happen if a truckload of grain were accidentally deposited into the habitat of a group of field mice one day. Initially, the surplus of resources would cause the mice population to grow rapidly to previously unimaginable levels; however, once the extra grain ran out, the mice population would quickly shrink back down to the more modest size which that particular ecosystem was able to sustain without the artificial inputs it temporarily received from afar.[300]

Once again, even the feeblest human mind could understand this ecological truth when applied to field mice, yet the highest IQ's in our era are all too often incapable of accepting these conclusions in the context of human civilization. Greer has warned that this difficulty cannot be attributed to intellectual shortcomings alone. The true cause is, rather, spiritual in nature. More specifically, the problem is mythological.

In a 2009 interview with Peak Moment titled "The Twilight of an Age," Greer noted that efforts to "solve Peak Oil" miss the entire point that Peak Oil is "not a technical problem" at all:

> One of the problems we face in dealing with the phenomenon of Peak Oil and trying to cope with the future of industrial society is that people think of it as a technical problem. It's not. The technical aspects could have been solved a long time ago. It's a cultural problem, it's a mental problem, and a problem woven into the stories that we tell and that we use to define the world of our experience. That's where the core of the problem lies and those are the things that need to be understood and changed if we're going to achieve anything constructive.[301]

---

[300] John Michael Greer, *The Ecotechnic Future* (Gabriola Island: New Society, 2009), p. 6.
[301] This interview is available on YouTube at the following link: https://www.youtube.com/watch?v=ceRP8rSwIMc

No matter how much progress one might make in efforts to find rationally-plausible solutions for the engineering challenges presented by fossil fuel decline, one will still never reach the core of the problem if such efforts leave the underlying mythological narrative of progress untouched. Humans have accomplished Herculean leaps in technical efficiency yet all too often remain incapable of doing something as basic as imagining that a different story might explain the future. Once again, the problem with our dysfunctional relation to ecology is not a lack of scientific data or a lack of complicated theoretical models; it is ultimately a problem of motivation.

In fact, Greer noted in a February, 2009 post titled "Toward Ecosophy" that even self-proclaimed environmentalists all too often fail to understand ecology precisely because they are incapable of abandoning the narrative of progress. This occurs despite the fact that many have a fairly good formal education in ecological principles:

> [T]he great flaw in most of today's schemes for social change is their failure to grasp the ecological dimensions of human society. That flaw has been almost impossible to avoid, because it is not simply a matter of consciously held beliefs; many of the people drafting plans for social change these days [actually] have learned quite a bit about ecology. It's the unexamined and often unconscious presuppositions underlying most such plans that blind them to ecological reality.[302]

More specifically, even self-proclaimed environmentalists often remain blind to the ecological dimensions of problems affecting human civilization because their thought process is primarily structured by an unconscious mythology, a mythology which distorts even their reception of what are supposed to be "objective scientific data." That myth is the myth of humans' "conquest of nature."[303]

---

[302] John Michael Greer, "Toward Ecosophy", in *Archdruid Report*, Vol. 3 (Chicago: Founders House, 2018), p. 29.

Even when mainstream environmentalists lament humans' conquest of nature, they fail to see that it is an inherently questionable thing to believe in in the first place: "Even the narratives of modern environmentalism, far from rejecting this [myth], reinforce it; most of them glorify human power . . . by embracing the claim that humanity has become so almighty that it can destroy the Earth and itself in the bargain."[304] In 2019, Congresswoman Alexandria Ocasio-Cortez publicly begged humans to be nice enough to choose not to destroy the Earth when she warned them that "the world is going to end in 12 years if we don't address climate change."[305] Simply from an ecological perspective, however, this viewpoint gets the problem exactly backwards. It is not at all the case that humans are so powerful that the fate of the world hinges upon whether they choose not to destroy it. In fact, Greer noted that references to "human power" only demonstrate that one has completely misunderstood the ecological dimensions of the problem:

> Human limits, not human power, define the situation we face today, because the technological revolutions and economic boom times that most modern people take for granted resulted from a brief period of extravagance in which we squandered half a billion years of stored sunlight. The power we claimed was never really ours, and we never conquered nature; instead, we stole as many of her carbon assets as we could reach, and [wasted] most of them. Now the bills are coming due, the balance left in the account won't meet them, and the only question left is how much of what we bought with all that carbon will be ours when nature's foreclosure proceedings finish with us.[306]

---

303 Ibid., p. 30.

304 Ibid., p. 31.

305 William Cummings, "'The world is going to end in 12 years if we don't address climate change,' Ocasio-Cortez says." *USA Today*, 22, January, 2019.

306 John Michael Greer, "Toward Ecosophy", in *Archdruid Report*, Vol. 3 (Chicago: Founders House, 2018), p. 29.

One might even argue for the following rule of thumb: if someone thinks that the primary ecological challenge of our era is to find some way to convince humans to use their immense power for good rather than evil by choosing not to destroy the Earth even though they could, that person has definitively proven that he or she has little grasp on ecology as such. Shockingly, ecological understanding is missing precisely among the self-proclaimed environmentalists who claim to be guided by it. Yet Greer's claim that the ultimate source of the problem lies in a flawed interpretation of mythology implies that the only solution to this deadlock of fundamental misunderstanding will be hermeneutical in nature rather than scientific. We shall only be able to end our currently dysfunctional relation to ecological problems if we abandon fantasies of human power and instead realize that the key to grasping our situation lies in our ability to hermeneutically interpret limitation. Even our ability to pollute and damage the environment is simply a limitation in disguise, since it is only through the ever more limited fossil fuel energy sources that any of this is possible. There is still time to make this change, but it will require that we adjust our deepest expectations about ecology by realizing that it is above all the hermeneutical horizon of limitation.

Finally, we shall consider how John Zerzan's scepticism regarding theoretical systems of knowledge leads to a quite different political stance than Kaczynski, Linkola, or Greer favoured. In Zerzan's early collection of essays *Elements of Refusal*, he suggested that there could never be any hope of using one of the symbolic systems of knowledge as a means for learning to stop the catastrophe of Modern Industrial Civilization, because every one of these symbolic systems is merely a sign of technological alienation in disguise. One can't use science to rebel against civilization, for science simply *is* civilization. Far from being an objective set of truths with no anthropological bias, scientific knowledge is indigenous to only one mode of life: agricultural civilization. Prehistoric hunter gatherers did not lack science simply because they were "too primitive" or "too stupid" to do it; science was absent from their worldview because it was not even possible in such a context. Likewise, there could never be any question of using it to stop the runaway train of technological development, for that would require science to somehow to break out of its own native territory while still retaining its identity.

Zerzan's scepticism towards a "scientific awakening against civilization" should not be dismissed as mere anti-intellectualism, because he exposed the extent to which science itself relies upon more fundamental structures than itself in order to be carried out. These structures, in turn, are all forms of technological alienation which were unheard of in the prehistoric hunter gatherer past.

For example, the scientific method requires language.[307] It is all too often forgotten by the boot-licking worshippers of progress that science is not Nature itself; science is simply Man's attempt to understand Nature. This can only occur through a set of descriptive statements which are formulated in a language of some kind. Zerzan claims that language as we know it today is actually a new thing which the primordial hunter gatherers did not know, simply because there was no need for it. One of Zerzan's most controversial claims was that the primordial hunter gatherers of the past were able to communicate without language, though it remains somewhat unclear what he meant by this. Even Ted Kaczynski dismissed this as a far-fetched claim that humans once had telepathic mind-reading abilities. At the very least, we must admire Zerzan for his consistency as a thinker.

Science also requires mathematical formalization.[308] As we saw in the previous chapter, Zerzan has argued that mathematics is not a counter example to language but is rather the ultimate example of it, since number is only the emptiest of all linguistic constructs. One should note that scientific progress is measured precisely by its level of mathematical formalization. Graduate students in Physics routinely joke about having to read papers written exclusively in symbolic notation, a trend which is mimicked by economists, analytic philosophers, and other pseudo-scientists who desperately crave to get a piece of this prestige (and funding) for their own

---

[307] John Zerzan, "Language: Origin and Meaning," in *Elements of Refusal* (Kindle Edition).
[308] John Zerzan, "Number: Its Origin and Evolution," in *Elements of Refusal* (Kindle Edition).

academic departments. From Zerzan's viewpoint, it would therefore be absurd to expect scientific progress to ever lead away from mathematical alienation, for that would contradict its very essence.

The scientific method also requires time.[309] Progress is an inherently temporal phenomenon, since one can only evaluate how far progress has succeeded through maintaining strict records which devalue past accomplishments as mere stepping stones on the path towards some idealized future state. Even relics from earlier eras which would still be useful in our time are discarded as worthless simply because they originated in a "more primitive" time. At a micro level, time is also necessary for science because the procedures of hypothesis-formation, experimentation, and evaluation of results occur within a rigid structure of temporal organization which Zerzan claims would be unthinkable within the prehistoric hunter gatherer worldview.

Far more controversial than dismissing language, number, and time was Zerzan's claim that art is also a sign of technological alienation rather than a means to overcome it. Although he admitted in his "Case Against Art" that art might gesture towards transcendent spiritual themes, it can't actually succeed in establishing the bridge to access them. Art is therefore just one more example of technological alienation, since it can never accomplish the leap to access the ineffable "big ideas":

> Art is always about "something hidden." But does it help us connect with that hidden something? I think it moves us away from it.[310]

Zerzan has dismissed even the idea that art provides an ideal pathway for Man to develop his creative potential, because he has noted that humans had equally impressive accomplishments in tool-making long before the historical anomaly of cave art appeared some 30,000 years ago. Zerzan argues therefore that art is simply an alienated form of tool making. The same impulses towards

---

[309] John Zerzan, "Beginning of Time, End of Time," in *Elements of Refusal* (Kindle Edition).
[310] John Zerzan, "The Case against Art," in *Elements of Refusal* (Kindle Edition).

craftsmanship which had occurred without alienation for countless millennia suddenly took the form of art when the earliest stirrings of civilization had begun to emerge. Expecting art to provide the pathway to break free from civilization is as baseless as seeking out the revolution in the realm of mathematics.

Zerzan's decision to devalue all of these systems naturally left only one pathway for the revolution against civilization to occur. It could only happen through abruptly suspending the project of agricultural civilization and accomplishing a leap of faith back into our hunter gather origins. It is not only science that would lose its foundation if this occurred. Our sprawling artificial political structures would also find their fundamental presuppositions disappear if the shift from agriculture back to hunting and gathering were to occur. Zerzan therefore openly identifies himself as an anarchist but he does not suggest that the anarchist non-state would require a violent revolution. There would be no need to forcefully overthrow institutions if a simple change in the anthropological mode of survival were sufficient in itself to deprive them of their foundations of existence. Nor would the result be a Hobbesian war of all against all. There would be no need to fight for the scraps that remain amidst the smouldering ruins of a fallen civilization, for the very concept of war is indigenous to agricultural civilization.[311] Zerzan speculates that peace would flow without effort, since the automatic shape through which the world is viewed would change from agricultural domination back to hunter gatherer egalitarianism.[312]

It is quite interesting that the greatest thinkers of the movement reach such different conclusions regarding which political response should follow from the theoretical problem regarding the impossibility of changing behaviour simply after learning information. Kaczynski favoured revolution as the only means to stop a System with no stop button of its own. Linkola proposed a strong, centralized eco-authoritarian force to implement unpopular regulations even amidst widespread public resistance.

---

[311] John Zerzan, "On the Origin of War," in *Twilight of the Machines* (Port Townsend: Feral House, 2008), p. 25.

[312] John Zerzan, "The Iron Grip: the Axial Age," in *Twilight of the Machines* (Port Townsend: Feral House, 2008), p. 31.

Greer noted that the political solution must begin at the spiritual level if any real change is to be made. Zerzan claimed that anarchy could be achieved without violence simply through returning to hunting and gathering. The following table synopsizes these results.

[1]

Thinker	Political Stance
Ted Kaczynski	Revolution
Pentti Linkola	Eco-Authoritarianism
John Michael Greer	Spiritual Adjustment
John Zerzan	Anarcho-Primitivism

Chapter Four
Nature and Technology:
The End of Ecology

Greta Thunberg: The Woman Who Found Out

From a political perspective, the term "non-environmentalist ecophilosophy" may very well sound like a contradiction to a reader who has been accustomed by the media to believe that any concern for ecological problems is automatically "environmentalist" in nature. Those who lack even the most basic training in logical fallacies will then quickly conclude that "guilt by association" would force such concern to be intrinsically leftist in nature. In turn, we are told that one can only "really love Nature" if one first publicly proves one's loyalty to the Democrat Party by linearly listing out statements which reflect perfect dogmatic conformity with dozens of other unrelated issues, then signing the oath in blood.

This hostage situation in which the social justice leftists have put a metaphorical gun to the environmentalist movement's head and forced it to drive to ever more liberal pastures is nothing new. In Ted Kaczynski's fragmentary magnum opus *Anti-Tech Revolution: Why and How*, he found Earth First!'s failure to enact meaningful change as a result of leftist infiltration to be so exemplary that he included their story in the third postulate for his purified rules for major social change.

> *Postulate 3.* Probably every radical movement tends to some extent to attract persons who join it from motives that are only loosely related to the goals of the movement. When Earth First! was founded in the 1980s, its goal was simply the defense of wilderness, but it attracted individuals of leftist type who were less interested in wilderness than in activism for its own sake. A good example was Judi Bari, who was a radical feminist, demonstrated against U.S. involvement in Central America, and participated in pro-choice and anti-nuclear movements. Eventually, she added

212

environmentalism to her list of causes and became an Earth First!er. The influx of numerous individuals of this type did lead to the blurring of Earth First!'s original mission, which became contaminated with "social justice" issues.[313]

As Kaczynski noted, Earth First! Was originally supposed to be a movement in which concern for the Earth was the only criterion to join. Over time, however, one might argue that an unspoken rule was that one could only "really care about the Earth" if one also expressed at least equal concern for the issues of abortion, U.S. involvement in Central America, and nuclear weapons. Of course, in this context, "concern" for these issues could only be acceptable if it was also definitively situated within a leftist viewpoint.

It is all the more ironic, therefore, that a movement whose name was quite literally "Earth *First!*" quickly found that a large number of other issues should also come first and that some of them should be "more first" even than concern for the Earth. In typical Orwellian fashion, "all these issues are first, but some are more first than others."[314] Similarly, the Environmentalist Movement's current absorption into the Social Justice Movement would suggest that we have literally reached the point at which only people who know that there are 68 genders are allowed to express concern over the pollution of drinking water sources which everyone, social justice purist or not, depends upon for survival.

Needless to say, even those few leftists with sufficient ideological perfection to be included in this ever-shrinking reserve of the "good guys" have proven themselves to be utterly incompetent at doing anything beyond the meaningless gesture of standing on street corners once or twice per year and angrily demanding that someone else find a solution to the problem for them. John Michael Greer noted in an early 2007 *Archdruid Report* post titled "The View from the Grassy Knoll" that there is nothing original about this fantasy that "someone else" will wake up after hearing the protesters' message and make the right adjustments so

---

[313] Ted Kaczynski, *Anti-Tech Revolution: Why and How* (Scottsdale: Fitch & Madison, 2016), pp. 96-7.
[314] George Orwell, *Animal Farm* (New Delhi: Penguin, 2011).

that we as individuals don't have to change anything ourselves. Each repetition of this idea is simply another variation on the same myth which he called the "The Man who Found Out."[315] In this myth, an ordinary person identifies an impending disaster which will affect the whole System and spends the majority of the story ignored by the clueless masses; near the end, this person somehow manages to get the attention of the authorities, who make the proper adjustments to prevent catastrophe just in time. Greer has claimed that this story is so deeply-ingrained in our collective imagination that he betted that if one made a trip to the local movie theatre today, one could probably find some variation of it playing right now.

As compelling as this fantasy might be on narratological grounds, it bears mentioning that this "someone else" who makes the adjustments to save the day just in time is, of course, just a euphemism for the System itself. Ted Kaczynski noted in his short essay "The System's Neatest Trick" that the System is incapable of challenging Modern Technology because it quite literally *is* Modern Technology.[316] Expecting Modern Technology to shut itself down to save the Earth (the only realistic option to halt ecological devastation) is therefore an *a priori* impossibility.

One might argue that Swedish teen activist Greta Thunberg's campaign against Climate Change has caught fire within the public imagination simply because it is faithfully replaying a familiar story called "The Woman who Found Out." Few have noticed, though, that her current media spotlight shows without any question that even if one does accomplish the ultimate dream of reaching out to the authorities in person, this will already be doomed to be a futile exercise for generating serious change. The only thing the current Greta Thunberg media circus proves is that even if someone short circuits the frustrating process of street corner-protesting and penetrates into the heart of the beast by speaking directly to the U.N. in person, effectively *nothing* will

---

[315] John Michael Greer, "The View from the Grassy Knoll" in The Archdruid Report, Vol. 1 (Chicago: Founders House, 2017), p. 212.
[316] Ted Kaczynski, "The System's Neatest Trick", in *Technological Slavery* (Scottsdale: Fitch & Madison, 2019).

actually result from this gesture except a flood of millions upon millions of partisan tweets and internet flame wars. Few have dared to mention that even the social media activity filled with praise for her message still carries a devastating ecological cost. The local daily newspapers in the author's region of India, for example, have measured her success by how many retweets, likes, and responses her social media profile has generated, without realizing the grand irony that this is literally a euphemism for admitting that Greta Thunberg's U.N. appearance likely succeeded more at generating data center-based carbon dioxide pollution than any change to our currently dysfunctional relation to the environment. This is not at all to suggest that she maliciously intended these effects or that her concern for the environment is not genuine. This episode just conclusively demonstrates that seizing the System's attention, even with unanimous approval from the politically correct pseudo-environmentalist media, is a hopeless project for accomplishing any real change. This should not come as a great surprise, since expecting the System to stop fossil fuel-based pollution is to miss the point that the System *is* fossil fuels. One might argue that David Icke's supremely politically incorrect words are a more likely projection for our future than anything the media is currently willing to allow onto the airwaves. As he noted near the end of his 1994 classic *Robots' Rebellion:*

The System has to collapse if real change is to be realized.[317]

We shall now consider a few more of the most notable thinkers who have attempted to understand the properly political dimension of ecological hermeneutics. Often, these thinkers agree that ecology is, if nothing else, something to be contrasted with Modern Technology. The author shall ultimately argue that Modern Technology can never become the Soma of an ecological context or a memological worldview. There is no deep meme of Modern Technology, for it simply destroys the very possibility of ecology. A full discussion of this topic must be deferred to the book-length

---

[317] David Icke, *Robots' Rebellion: The Story of the Spiritual Renaissance* (Bath, Gateway: 1994).

text *Hermeneutical Death: The Technological Destruction of Subjectivity*, as that book shall be the second volume in the broader study of ecology and technology which the present text opens up.

At any rate, an examination of the greatest ecological thinkers' political ideologies will prove surprising. It is peculiar that the responses of the very best thinkers have varied drastically. We have already seen that whereas some propose strong authoritarian structures which disregard democratic procedures in order to enact necessary changes (Linkola), others have argued that organized political institutions are themselves merely parasitic upon technology and that anarchy is therefore the natural stance which must follow from restoring our proper ecological balance (Zerzan, pre-arrest Kaczynski). The author's own view shall be considered afterwards. At any rate, we shall begin by examining the failures of mainstream environmentalists to consider any political solutions which can be taken seriously on ecological or philosophical grounds, a failure which can largely be attributed to their having missed the point that technology and ecology are fundamentally incompatible. Modern Technology can never become the Soma, for it is inherently anti-hermeneutical. Its "progress" will end in the death of each of us as mentatic subjects capable of hermeneutical interpretation.

The Philosophy of David Klass

Although virtually nothing is easier than to find self-proclaimed environmentalists among the intellectual and political elites of the West, virtually nothing is harder than to find one whose thought contains enduring substance worthy of serious consideration. Rather than waste time examining the countless celebrities, CEO's, politicians, and media talking heads who easily pass the former test but completely fail at the latter, we shall simply cut to the chase and examine the thought process of one of the very best mainstream environmentalist thinkers. Even the cream of the crop shall be found to embody very troubling shortcomings founded on philosophical flaws.

216

David Klass, for example, is most widely-known not as an environmentalist per se but as an author within the genre of Young Adult Fiction. His books appear to have been marketed more often to educational institutions and public libraries (usually, to provide reading material to middle school students) than to individual customers for personal reading purposes. The author of the present text, for example, first encountered Klass's work by finding a copy of *California Blue* within his eighth grade Language Arts classroom; he read it as part of the obligatory "quiet reading time" which, at least in the year 2003, was still a part of the daily routine for middle school students in the United States. Although this is also merely anecdotal, nearly every used copy of David Klass's novels which the author has later purchased were discarded library copies, often from educational institutions.

Typically, Klass's books focus on a teenager in crisis, often framed within an exciting sports-based plotline with no shortage of High School drama. However, he was not content to merely entertain his readers; over time, he expressed an ever-greater desire to also awaken them to pursue meaningful changes in their own communities, and perhaps even to change the course of World History itself. It appears that David Klass eventually realized that this particular economic arrangement of selling his books to libraries and schools provided an ideal opportunity to influence the next generation of thinkers; this was because his books could potentially reach every kid in the nation without having to convince a single one of them to purchase the novel by choice. Above all, the issue David Klass hoped to inform young readers about was the ongoing destruction of the environment; particularly, the problem of mass extinction.

Klass's 1994 *California Blue* was one of his earliest attempts to dedicate an entire book to these two issues.[318] The novel tells the story of a teenage boy from a small town in Northern California whose conflicted relationship with his father suddenly becomes even more complicated when he finds out that his father has been diagnosed with blood cancer and has less than one more

---

[318] David Klass, *California Blue* (New York: Scholastic, 1994).

year to live. At just the same time, the boy discovers an unfamiliar type of blue butterfly while jogging in the local Redwood Forest and captures the specimen for examination. His biology teacher admits even she has no idea what it is and consults the help of her best professor from her alma mater at Berkeley. The world-renowned expert concludes that it is indeed a previously undiscovered species and that it is critically endangered. Worse still, the boy happened to discover it while illegally trespassing on company land owned by the same sawmill which employs his father and much of the town. The boy therefore must make a choice whether to save the butterfly and put his father and the whole town out of work, or to maintain their respect but allow a unique species to go extinct forever.

Like all of the other sawmill workers within the town, the boy's father hates environmentalists because he perceives their calls to halt deforestation as a direct threat to his livelihood. Worse still, the townspeople often find environmentalists' campaigns to be laughably trivial. The stereotypical image of a group of college students being bussed in from a distant Bay Area campus in order to protest and call to shut down the local people's workplace in order to save an obscure species of mouse which "no one cares about" is arguably outdone when the townspeople learn that it is none other than a tiny insect which threatens their jobs:

> "What'd this hotshot find that's so important, anyway?"
> "Get ready for this. A bug."
> "A bug? You're kidding, right? You sure he didn't pull it out of his own long hair?"
> "This is a special bug. Some kind of mutant butterfly."
> "Give me another beer . . . You sure he wants to close down the mill for a butterfly? Why the hell are they even letting him speak?"[319]

The townspeople are therefore portrayed as holding roughly the same attitude towards the species as the individual; if one would

---

[319] Ibid., pp. 106-7.

squash a little bug to death without a second thought if one caught it in one's house, why would one care any more about allowing an entire species to disappear if it happened to get in the way of one's work?

Above all, Klass portrays this attitude as one which demonstrates a lack of education, since no one who has actually studied ecology at a scientific level could hold such careless views on a matter as important as mass extinction. In direct contrast with the naïve view of the townspeople, the Berkeley professor embodies a viewpoint which is both better informed by empirical science and is also ethically more sophisticated, since it does not presume that humans hold a privileged position relative to any other animals within the ecosystem. This viewpoint is articulated most clearly during the town hall scene in which the professor faces down an angry crowd of hecklers but keeps his cool and appeals to reason over emotion. In his lengthy speech about the decline of sockeye salmon populations, we can assume that the professor is something of a mouthpiece for Klass himself:

> "When I was a boy, growing up in Oregon, we used to watch the wild salmon runs every year, and I can tell you there was nothing like it . . . When I was a teenager, which wasn't so long ago, thousands upon thousands of them used to churn up the water. Things have changed since then. We haven't only been over-fishing them and polluting their rivers; we've also been building dams. More than seventy of them — deadly obstacles to the salmon runs. In 1989, there were only two sockeye nests, sighted at the sprawling grounds. Year after that, I was part of a team of scientists and naturalists who went to monitor the crisis in wild salmon runs. Only one sockeye salmon — one . . . made the nine hundred-mile journey to its ancestral spawning grounds. Watching that one solitary, noble fish swim up the river, jumping, fighting the falls, maybe the last of its species . . . trying to breed but truly swimming towards extinction, well . . . I know people and jobs are important but there are things that are more important."[320]

It is interesting that even in a novel about a butterfly and Redwood Forests, Klass mentioned the topic of overfishing. This issue proved to be so important to him that it became the central environmental problem portrayed in his later 2006 novel *Firestorm*. *Firestorm* differs from *California Blue* by adopting an even more explicitly apocalyptic tone regarding environmental issues, in that it tells the story of a boy sent from a thousand years in the future back to our era to warn us about the apocalyptic scale of ecological damage which will effectively turn the Earth of the far future into a nearly-uninhabitable eco-dystopia. Interestingly, the boy is teleported by time machine back to the early 21st Century because this era represented the "Turning Point" at which the Earth crossed over into irredeemable environmental degradation.[321] The boy has a severely limited amount of time to prevent this crisis and save the last chance for life on Earth to survive into the far future. Of course, the boy himself is something of a metaphor for each middle school reader who happened to find this book in his or her school library or classroom; each of them bears the same mission of preventing the Turning Point from being reached and preventing the Earth from suffering permanent ecological damage.

Although the Turning Point remains ambiguous for much of the novel, we eventually learn that it amounts to the destruction of the possibility of life within the oceans. In fact, the novel notes that the term "Earth" is something of a misnomer, since it would be far closer to the truth to call our planet one of oceans rather than one of land:

> The "earth" is a misnomer— seen from space, we live on a blue planet of oceans. The Turning Point hinged on the emptying of those oceans.[322]

---

[320] Ibid., pp. 120-1.

[321] It is ironic that Klass references a major Turning Point in a novel presumably written in 2005, the same year that the globe hit Peak Oil. Needless to say, this is not at all the Turning Point he had in mind.

[322] David Klass, *Firestorm* (New York: SquareFish, 2009), p. 203.

It is undeniable that current industrial fishing operations (particularly, those practiced in the West) are unsustainable; in fact, in his 2016 book *Dark Age America,* John Michael Greer warned that seafood will eventually become a fond memory from the past which no one, however wealthy, will ever eat again after current depletion rates lead to their inevitable ecological conclusion.[323] However, David Klass's particular explanation for why this might occur is unsatisfactory and reflects a central flaw within his environmentalist philosophy as a whole. In a conversation between the boy from the future and his telepathic dog Gisco, Klass uses the dog as a mouthpiece to explain his own belief that blaming "human ingenuity" is a sufficient explanation for our current dysfunctional relation to the environment:

> So what happened to the cod? I ask Gisco.
> *Human ingenuity is what happened. Great factory ships set out from Europe that could catch a hundred tons of cod in an hour. In the blink of an eye the schools were gone for good and tens of thousands of Newfoundland fisherman like the grandfather of this boozing blowhard were out of work.*[324]

The dog goes on to explicitly reduce the problem to one of improper methodology. The problem, he claims, is that humans have simply decided to use more harmful methods rather than safer methods of fishing:

> I admit [that seeing the industrial fishing operation] today wasn't pleasant. But people need to eat. You seem to think that all fishing is evil.
> *No. Wrong. The problem lies in the methods.*[325]

Klass's belief that mass extinction is merely a problem of "human ingenuity" implies that the solution is for humans to rationally choose to abandon ecologically-harmful methods and

---

[323] John Michael Greer, *Dark Age America* (Gabriola Island: New Society, 2016).
[324] David Klass, *Firestorm* (New York: SquareFish, 2009), p. 198.
[325] Ibid., p. 202.

adopt sensible methods instead. Above all, therefore, the problem lies in a dysfunctional attitude towards the Earth fuelled by illusions of dominance and by ignorance of the ecological consequences which will follow from these actions. Or rather, in John Michael Greer's words, Klass believes that humans are so powerful that the fate of the Earth hinges upon whether they will decide to destroy it or decide *not* to destroy it. In a conversation between the boy and his martial arts trainer, a shape-shifting girl named Eko, Klass uses her as a mouthpiece for his own beliefs regarding these matters:

> "We changed [the Earth]?" I ask softly. "That's why you say we're an appalling species? We damaged the world?"
> "Permanently." She nods. "Irreparably."
> "Pollution?" I guess. "The ozone layer?"
> "Sure . . . And do you know why we did it?"
> "No." I admit softly. "Why?"
> "Because we're human," Eko tells me, and there's a ring of disdain and self-loathing in her voice. "That's the reason. That's what humans do. That's what sets us apart from the rest of the animals. We think. We create. We try to control."[326]

As an entertainer, Klass is nothing short of a genius. As an environmentalist, there is no doubt that his intentions are good. However, from a philosophical standpoint, his explanation for our current crises is very problematic. To claim that "human thinking" is the source of the problem and the one thing that definitively "sets us apart from the rest of the animals" naturally implies that environmental destruction is the result of wrong thinking and wrong thinking alone. The solution, of course, would therefore just be to replace the wrong thoughts in people's minds with right thoughts, thoughts better informed by environmental science and ecological ethics. This process of getting rid of wrong opinions and acquiring scientific truths is better known as "education." Of course, Ted Kaczynski, Pentti Linkola, and John Michael Greer have conclusively demonstrated that "learning to stop economic growth"

---

[326] Ibid., p. 127.

on a purely theoretical level is both impossible for the System to learn and impossible for humans to learn. Klass's optimism that education alone will be enough to avert ecological crisis is therefore fundamentally problematic.

It is not at all hyperbole to say that Klass believes that better education will be a sufficient solution to the problem. Even in *California Blue*, education is implicitly cited as the chief factor separating the "ignorant" sawmill workers from the Berkeley professor who realizes the dangers of mass extinction and unbridled deforestation. Further, education is cited as the chief factor which separates the boy himself from his father and his father's co-workers, as the boy is portrayed as a top science student in his class and is even implicitly promised admission to attend college at Berkeley. Clearly, getting an education really is portrayed in this novel as the key to avoid the fate of being trapped working for a sawmill in a small town.

In a certain sense, the fishing boat crew in *Firestorm* directly parallels the sawmill workers in *California Blue*. In both cases, we do not get the sense that these are uniquely evil beings who are motivated by any conscious or malicious intent to destroy the environment; rather, we cannot help but feel pity for people who are forced to do the dirty work for industrial interests simply out of a need to remain employed, fed, and housed:

> [Gisco was] watching the men . . . doing the work of lowering the nets. Crew members of every race and colour, stripped to the waist and sweating in the hot sun. Their muscles, straining. Their serious faces. Eyes intent on their tasks. None of them look like bad or evil men. *As they scraped the floor of the oceans bare reef by reef and acre by acre, they were just too busy to care. It was a hard job on a sunny day. They were just going fishing.*[327]

It is troublingly easy to take the next logical step and propose that universal college attendance will be sufficient both to save the

---

[327] David Klass, *Firestorm* (New York: SquareFish, 2009), p. 187.

environment and to set each person on a promising career path which would remove the very need to participate in work that harms the environment and provides little opportunity for personal advancement anyway.

This is not merely hypothetical, as one of the most famous of all so-called environmentalists, Democrat Party presidential candidate Bernie Sanders himself, proposed universal free college education as the solution to both the ecological and the economic woes afflicting our nation. Presumably, diverting more tax dollars to universities will kill two birds with one stone, in that the students will be empowered to pursue "better careers" just as the university research departments will get more money to discover "clean energy" alternatives which supposedly create millions of high-paying jobs while generating no pollution.

An obscure 2016 book written for the sole purpose of condensing Sanders' policies into a short, easy-to-reference pamphlet (literally called *Bernie Sanders: The Essential Guide*) devoted a great deal of time to praising universal free college education but offered almost no specific information on Bernie Sanders' environmental policies. In this book, the chapter titled "Environmental Policy" is little more than a single page long. The author of the pamphlet himself somehow admits that environmental issues are among the most important concerns yet feels that Sanders' having received approval from environmentalist groups excuses the Sanders Campaign from needing to provide any specific details over how they will handle the situation better than previous administrations:

> Despite the environment being one of the major concerns facing voters today, we can keep this section incredibly brief, given the level of clarity regarding Sanders's positions and record on the environment and climate change. Bernie Sanders has an impeccable record on the environment, receiving high marks from environmentalist groups and leading the charge on many key issues.[328]

---

[328] Elliott, Okla. *Bernie Sanders: The Essential Guide.* Squint Books, Eyewear Publishing LTD. Kindle Edition.

Shockingly, one of the only solutions which is explicitly mentioned in this short chapter is Sanders' plan to divert government funds into research for "new technologies" which will somehow accomplish the impossible task of saving the environment and growing the economy at the same time:

> If the United States wants to be a leader on climate change—and a leader in new technologies that will bring in billions of dollars over the coming decades—we need a president who understands the magnitude of the issue and is willing to put it front and centre in our nation's political discourse.[329]

We are never told what these mystery technologies are which will somehow bring in billions of dollars in profits while simultaneously cutting greenhouse gas emissions and reversing Global Warming, but it is troublingly easy to suspect that this is simply another advertising gimmick to divert government funds to so-called alternative energy companies. One would be wise to apply Michael Ruppert's warning regarding similar promises about shale gas to any mystery energy source which makes similarly suspect claims but relies on the blaring noise of media fanfare to shield it from any questions related to inconvenient little things like the Laws of Thermodynamics:

> Surprisingly, there was not a lot of serious detail [from the media] on how shale gas is produced or what environmental risks might be involved. Nobody seemed inclined to disclose what kinds of chemicals were involved exactly. I remember the old adage, "If it sounds too good to be true, it probably is."[330]

---

[329] Ibid.
[330] Ruppert, Michael C.. *Confronting Collapse* . Chelsea Green Publishing. Kindle Edition.

Anyone with even a passing familiarity with the so-called "green" sources which are implicitly promoted by Sanders will know that all of them require fossil fuels for their construction and maintenance and even with this hidden subsidy from fossil fuel resources, not even one of them can provide a respectable EROEI (Energy Returned on Energy Invested). Appealing to "clean energy" to bail us out of the ecological problems generated by fossil fuels is embarrassingly naïve; anyone who makes such a claim is actually just furthering the media's attempts to inflate speculative bubbles which are only intended to benefit wealthy shareholders who have no serious commitment to solving any environmental issues.

At any rate, it is shocking that Sanders would claim that new technologies are the solution to the very problems which were generated by Modern Technology in the first place. David Klass's stance is equally unacceptable due to a similarly problematic relation to technology. Klass never suggests that Modern Technology is intrinsically problematic on ecological grounds; rather, he implies that specific technologies can be used for evil or for good, solely depending upon the rational intentions of the humans who use them. Worse still, Klass implies that technological improvements will continue into the indefinite future, even in a future so ravaged by poverty and violence that a boy must be sent back in time to prevent it from materializing:

> You say you are from here yet not from here. You speak of my generation not being telepathic. The technologies you use— laser guns, paralysis darts, and plasma nets — are beyond anything I think the government is working on, even in the present.[331]

Even more bizarre are Klass's claims that the people from the dystopian future would look down upon the citizens of our era, simply because of the mismatch between their level of technological sophistication and ours. This could hardly be taken seriously as a description of people who had traded Hell on Earth in the future for

---

[331] David Klass, *Firestorm* (New York: SquareFish, 2009), p. 80.

a world in the early 21st Century which is actually characterized by comfort, peace, and an abundance of material goods:

> Yet they have come back here [from a thousand years in the future] and are battling over something in this world. How they must look down upon it, and all the ignorant, backward people who populate it![332]

In fact, Klass's faith in infinite technological progress is so unshakable that he even claims that the time travel technology had vastly improved between the time the boy had been teleported back to our era and the time his would-be killers had been.[333] One might legitimately wonder why anyone would fight so hard to prevent such a future from arriving if it is defined by such unimaginable leaps in technical efficiency. Arguably, Klass's dystopia is even better at embodying progress than our world is now.

Contrary to his claim to challenge human arrogance, Klass is so much an Anthropocene thinker that he argues that the Earth might someday be destroyed because humans will have re-invented themselves into magical beings through cracking the scientific code to access mystical powers:

> They created cyborgs.
> *And they experimented wildly with genetic material. A chimera in Greek mythology had a lion's head, a goat's body, and a serpent's tail. But in genetics, a chimera is a creature with DNA from more than one source.*
> You're saying Dargon may not be human?
> *He may be more than human.*[334]

He literally portrays technological innovation as an unstoppable force which eventually "gets bored" with conquering every physical challenge it encounters. At that point, it simply crosses over from

---

332 Ibid., p. 84.
333 Ibid., p. 164.
334 Ibid., p. 235.

the realm of physical manipulations into the realm of supernatural powers such as shape-shifting, mind-reading, curses, and prophecy:

> *But over hundreds of years, as life on earth changed and darkened, the powers of the mind deepened. You yourself as a descendent of Dann have some of these abilities. You mastered telepathy. You've seen shape-changing. There are other powers that to you might seem magical, but that I fully accept [such as] curses and spells. And by far the rarest power is prophecy.*[335]

Suffice it to say that the term "technology" has effectively become meaningless if it can leap out of the realm of physical materialism and encompass *"other powers that to you might seem magical,"* as the novel literally says.

Just as Klass's definition of technology is so loose that it is effectively meaningless, his definition of Nature is equally problematic. At one point in the novel, he embodies outright self-contradiction when he has Eko claim that the sole philosophical difference between her side and the Dark Army which seeks to kill the boy in order to solidify their control of the future is that her side "believe[s] in what is natural" while the Dark Army thrive on what is "unnatural":

> "We want to save the earth. They [the Dark Army] thrive as conditions worsen. We believe in what is natural. They were created by the unnatural. It's a battle to the death, Jack. It has been for centuries. And it's nearing a conclusion."[336]

Literally just two pages after claiming to be only in favour of what is natural, she trains the boy to use a jetpack; ironically enough, she introduces it precisely by claiming it overturns Newton's Law of Gravity:

---

[335] Ibid., p. 219.
[336] Ibid., p. 137.

"Do you remember the apple that fell on Newton's head? This shirt would make Newton's apple jump back onto the tree."[337]

The very term "natural" is effectively meaningless if one can claim to be strictly committed to natural ways of life while simultaneously valuing jetpack-shirts for their ability to suspend natural laws. Clearly, the same ambiguity towards Nature from which the entire Environmentalist Movement suffers is glaringly present even in the best of its thinkers.

Modern Technology poses an easily-overlooked challenge to Klass's emphasis on "human ingenuity" as the chief factor to be changed, since Modern Technology has progressively made human activity of any kind more and more irrelevant. Klass's claim that changing human thoughts is the only thing necessary to save the Earth doesn't even begin to address the true source of the ecological problems afflicting our era because most of the environmental damage today is being done by electronic brains running on autopilot, a troubling factor to which only a few Orwellian thought criminals such as Jacques Ellul and Ted Kaczynski have given due attention. Human thinking has actually become one of the least important factors in the entire operation, as human minds are becoming ever more unnecessary to automated processes which find less and less need for fallible human brains.[338] Klass misses this point entirely by claiming that the fate of the Earth hinges upon inspiring a superhuman boy to use his massive power to choose to personally "save the whole future."[339] One can hardly imagine a more inappropriate description of our ecological situation, since there is no understanding here that ecology is primarily a matter of limitation rather than a matter of human ingenuity. David Klass might be one of the best mainstream environmentalist thinkers alive today, but he still ultimately fails the test of Somatic Hermeneutics

---

[337] Ibid., p. 139.
[338] See the second chapter of Chad Haag's *The Philosophy of Ted Kaczynski: Why the Unabomber was Right about Modern Technology*.
[339] Ibid., p. 236.

and cannot be considered to embody the kind of ecological awareness which is required to make a difference for our future.

David Klass's approach as a mainstream environmentalist utterly fails the test of political viability because of his failure to take the distinction between Nature and Modern Technology seriously, despite paying lip-service to "favouring only what is natural." We shall now consider a thinker who developed a much more viable ecological philosophy precisely through respecting this distinction more.

The Philosophy of Varg Vikernes

Varg Vikernes, best known as the frontman for the Norwegian Black Metal project Burzum, is one of the most neglected philosophical thinkers of our era; not coincidentally, this is because he is arguably the single most controversial intellectual alive today. In fact, even before the present text was written some viewers openly objected to my decision to include Vikernes in a discussion of non-leftist ecological thinkers, on grounds that I was providing a platform for "reprehensible racists" to air their views. Apparently, even mentioning the man's name has become one of the most forbidden Orwellian thought crimes.

It is arguable that Vikernes has dropped to an even lower layer of Internet Hell than David Icke, Paul Joseph Watson, or Laura Loomer occupy, since all three of these figures were banned by Facebook but remain, at least for the moment, available on YouTube. Like Alex Jones's accounts, Vikernes's *Thulean Perspective* channel was banned from the video streaming service, despite having a committed popular following and some of the more amusing comment sections on the site. Banning him outright is, however, an unfortunate way to deal with someone who legitimately has very interesting things to say on the topic of ecology. However controversial he may be, it would be intellectually dishonest to exclude him from this discussion and still claim to have provided an exhaustive analysis of relevant contemporary thinkers. The present text shall therefore break the silence by treating him as an ecophilosopher with a viewpoint worthy of serious examination.

In case this is not crystal clear: my decision to discuss Vikernes's views on ecology does not mean that I endorse any of Vikernes's comments, whether they originated from *Vargsmål* or any other literature which he has authored. However, one must still acknowledge that Vikernes is especially relevant to any serious discussion of ecological thinkers who do not fit neatly into leftist and mainstream environmentalist frameworks. Above all, Vikernes's perspective as an ecological thinker who actively resists the philosophy of materialism is worthy of examination in an era where figures such as Jane Bennett threaten to subsume ecology under the banner of post-modernist materialism, effectively ruling out any attempts at ecophilosophy which contradict this base, stereotypical, academic viewpoint. Will the results prove surprising even to Vikernes's fans? Let's find out.

While it is true that Vikernes has made numerous controversial statements on the issue of race, it is far too simplistic to claim that his understanding of the topic fits neatly into the identity categories currently popular among social justice leftists. One problem with the media caricature of monolithic "white supremacy" is that in *Vargsmål*, a rare text he authored while in prison in 1994, he appears not to have been interested in "race" in this sense of the word at all. Rather, one of his more memorable discussions of the topic lay in his claim to have identified certain notable distinctions even among the three peoples of Scandinavia. For example, in the 42nd section of *Vargsmål*, Vikernes contemplated whether Scandinavians are a single ethnic group, or whether Swedes, Norwegians, and Danes embody different tendencies which persist even to the present day, despite ideological calls to pretend they don't exist. Although such a question would deeply offend the politically correct sensibilities within the academic industry today, a thinker no less widely read than Nietzsche himself essentially asked the same thing in his classic *Beyond Good and Evil*, since he found no problem asking why the so-called "industrious races" exhibit certain "instincts" which are lacking in other "races":

Industrious races find it a great hardship to be idle: it was a master stroke of English instinct to hallow and begloom Sunday to such an extent that the Englishman unconsciously hankers for his week – and workday again – as a kind of cleverly devised, cleverly intercalated fast, such as is also found in the ancient world (although, as is appropriate in southern nations, not precisely with respect to work.) [340]

Interestingly, Vikernes claims that such differences are largely the effects of the unique environmental conditions which characterize each nation.[341] Likewise, his discussion actually focused on the different ecological conditions which each people evolved under, differences generated by each nation's natural geographical features. He notes, for example, that Danes have tended to live on relatively warm and flat islands, while Sweden is made up of mountains, rivers, and forests. In contrast with both, Norwegians have tended to live in locations spread out over the coastline. He suggests that some geographical conditions are intrinsically more difficult to live under than others. For example, he claims that while Swedish forests provided abundant protection against enemies and allowed people to live in relatively dense populations, Norwegians lacked the luxury of natural barriers of defence, since they had to live in sparsely-populated farming communities over a coastline which bore an intrinsically higher risk of attack by invaders. He claims that these ecological conditions forced Norwegians to become strong individuals, since they had to be capable of both defending themselves against seafaring attackers and of maintaining their own farms in the absence of a dense population of labourers to shoulder the burden for them.

Even though virtually everyone in the West lives under the same artificial technologized conditions today, Vikernes claims that these long-established traits are still subtly visible within these

---

[340] Friedrich Nietzsche, *Beyond Good and Evil* (New Delhi: Fingerprint Classics, 2017), p. 103.
[341] Varg Vikernes, *Vargsmål* (unpublished, unofficial 1997 English translation from Norwegian manuscript).

nations' populations today, due to many generations of evolution. In fact, he repeatedly claims that Norwegians' natural tendency to embody strength and power is only difficult to perceive in our era because the System has exerted considerable effort to suppress it through utilizing the massive power of its political,[342] economic/financial,[343] media,[344] and educational[345] apparatuses of control to indoctrinate them into accepting subordinate positions of weakness, fear, and obedience. One of his main interests within the text, therefore, is to call his fellow Norwegians to break this spell of forced amnesia imposed by the System and to reawaken their natural tendencies toward strength and greatness which, he claims, have been suppressed for far too long.

It is shocking, however, that he suggests that the path to do so lies in having his fellow Norwegians reject, of all things, *materialism*.[346] On one hand, his call to reject materialism takes the more predictable form of urging them to abandon needless economic consumption and to instead favour simple living, self-sufficiency (farming, homesteading etc.), and the development of practical skills which would remove the very need to depend upon the System for survival.[347]

More surprisingly, though, he urges them to reject the philosophy of materialism itself. Vikernes's understanding of philosophical materialism is quite unconventional, in that he claims that it is a foreign ideology with no organic connection to Norway and that it ultimately originated in the monotheistic religions which were imported into Scandinavia from the Middle East centuries ago.[348] Vikernes claims, quite controversially, that the System of Judeo-

---

[342] Section 28
[343] Section 38
[344] Section 12
[345] Sections 16 and 51.
[346] Vikernes rejects materialism particularly vehemently in the 8th and 13th sections of Vargsmål. These are his critique of pornography and his critique of materialist non-pagan religion, respectively.
[347] In the 51st section of the text he critiques institutional education and instead favours learning skills at home from one's own family.
[348] Varg Vikernes, *Vargsmål* (unpublished, unofficial 1997 English translation from Norwegian manuscript).

Christian values provides the true epistemological foundation for the philosophy of materialism because even the supposedly spiritual constructs of these religions are actually materialistic motifs in disguise. In the eighth section of *Vargsmål,* for example, he claims that acts of extreme Christian asceticism are not the courageous rejections of worldly comforts they appear to be but are motivated only by the most vulgar desire to obtain the material pleasures of this world, only at a later time. He claims, for example, that (Catholic) monks who trap themselves in monasteries and submit their bodies to physical torture only do so because of the promise that they will receive a reward in heaven in the future. Interestingly, he claims that even this reward is just a materialist construct in disguise rather than any genuinely spiritual essence. He argues, in fact, that Christianity's concept of heaven is a "material paradise," sustained by the promise of granting the same bodily pleasures which it forbids the monks from pursuing in this life. We might argue that Vikernes implies that the Christian heaven fails the test of Pneumatic Hermeneutics, in that it fails to transcend the same vulgar framework which the decadent modern culture already embodies.

More shocking still is the fact that this dismissal of Christian pleasure as thoroughly materialistic occurs within a section of the text dedicated to his critique of, of all things, *pornography.* The eighth section of the text, in which this discussion occurs, provides a useful window to reveal why Vikernes cannot be reduced to any of the mainstream clichés of thought available in our era. On one hand, Vikernes of course does not buy the argument that pornography should be rejected for no reason except that the Pope forbids it. However, this section reveals that blind, fearful obedience to the Vatican is far from the only reason a person might have for raising serious questions about a product which even in the early 1990s was coming to be more and more thoughtlessly accepted in the mainstream, despite its negative consequences. On the other hand, even before the term "sex positive" had become a ubiquitous ideological staple on college campuses, Vikernes noticed that the secularist materialist attitude of mindless acceptance was paradoxically creating inhibitions which affected one's

234

performance; ironically, the attitude of "anything goes" risks eventually shrinking down to "almost nothing goes anymore." In addition, Vikernes rejects the views of anti-porn feminists, perhaps the largest group of people who were critical of the industry without having religious motivations to do so. Vikernes's stance is therefore genuinely impossible to locate within the regions of accepted thought, for there is literally no ideological space for the media and academic intelligentsia to conceptualize a pagan who rejects sex positive materialism, Christian morality, and feminism. Above all, we shall find that Vikernes's criticism of pornography can only be understood on ecological grounds.

Vikernes opens the section by noting that, even in the era before high speed internet, pornography was coming to be so widely-accepted that one could even see advertisements for it in the newspaper. We were told, however, that this was not merely driven by the financial motivation for these companies to make a profit; rather, there was a politically correct ideological justification as well, since after far too many years of needless cultural taboos we were finally being allowed to feel no shame about our own naked bodies. Vikernes was one of the few thinkers with the courage to acknowledge the inconvenient fact that consumption of artificial material over a television screen or within the pages of a dirty book does not exactly transfer over to improving one's performance in "the real thing," let alone strengthening intimacy with one's human partner.

One reason for this mismatch is simply the natural element of time. Vikernes notes himself that it takes a lot of time to really learn what one's partner values. Pornography, however, circumvents that entire natural process by trivializing even the most bizarre stuff into something "daily" to be taken for granted as commonplace and to be instantly available at any time. In fact, quite literally the only barriers the industry respects are those put forward by the law.[349] Short of illegal content, virtually *anything* is accepted within this medium and relentlessly marketed as normal. Contrary to expectation, Vikernes claims that this ruins the excitement of

---

[349] Even these, by the way, are not always respected, as in cases of lying about a performer's age or producing material involving human feces.

doing something forbidden oneself. In fact, the pleasure of feeling that one is doing something no one else is doing becomes effectively impossible to achieve, except by resorting to extreme measures. Vikernes states that many people will not be satisfied with just giving this up; instead, they will seek out opportunities in more unconventional areas, even if they are illegal. Controversial as it might be, he reports the fact that some children are raped as a result, an uncomfortable fact which continues to be empirically confirmed in our era. In addition, some turn to necrophilia, sado-masochism, and even Satanist sex rituals in order to find some unconventional avenue to satisfy the need for novelty and the need to feel that one is doing something which no one else is doing. On a purely historical level, one should bear in mind that these sexual needs were, until quite recently, fulfilled in perfectly ordinary, legal circumstances but suddenly require literally criminal situations.

Interestingly, Vikernes claims that those who turn to Satanist rituals are not really worshipping the "devil" they claim to but are rather worshipping the "sickness and deformities in themselves." This claim is worthy of serious examination. What is all too easy to miss in a casual reading of Vikernes's work is the fact that, above all, his critique of pornography might be considered a critique of Modern Technology and its incompatibility with Man on ecological grounds alone. What Vikernes is really referring to in this context are ecological deformities and ecological sicknesses with a technological origin.

Even without any appeal to traditional morality, one must acknowledge that the historically-unprecedented technological disruption of pornography has damaged many people, even on physical grounds alone. Although virtually no one wants to discuss the topic, more and more young men in our era have found themselves forced to seek medical help for erectile dysfunction before the age of 30, and in some cases, before the age of 20. Professional sex addiction therapists have reported that their worst clients have found themselves incapable of getting aroused without seeing gore. It is frightening to think that some addicts' erectile dysfunction has gotten so bad that literally the most beautiful women on Earth would still remain incapable of exciting them unless hard-core violence or some other illegal taboo were added in. Worse still, in Japan the term "herbivore" has come to refer to a man who has lost all interest in human partners, presumably because cartoon pornography has rewired his brain to hold expectations which are literally impossible to fulfil outside the artificial realm of animation.

Nor has this suffering been limited to the viewers. Pornography's hard-wired need to continually break new barriers has created an industry in which many performers admit to needing a cocktail of illegal drugs, pain killers, or alcohol to endure the physical abuse required to meet the viewer's demand for constant novelty, taboo situations, and violent shock value. In some cases, life-altering injuries sustained while filming have created a far more serious problem than the temporary fix of drugs could solve. There is at least one case where a female performer allegedly had a piece of the muscle in her anus fall out on the set while filming a brutal anal scene,[350] while another female performer was allegedly killed while filming a bondage scene gone wrong in Southern California in the early 2000s.

Without any reference to moral concerns, one must acknowledge that a delicate ecological balance has been disrupted by the possibilities opened up by Modern Technology. A typical young man today has already seen more naked women than any of his male ancestors going all the way back to the Stone Age, even if for some of these men all of the women were just virtual pixels on a laptop screen. Further, the images are so artificially manipulated by technology (i.e., camera angles, lighting, video editing, plastic surgery etc.) that even the women themselves bear little resemblance to their own "professional personas" when spotted in some other context, such as when their "normal face" appears in an arrest mug shot on the news or in an interview with some podcast after retiring from the industry.

No matter how "sex positive" someone might claim to be, it would be hard to argue that all of this would have no effect on one's physical and psychological functioning. The reasons why, though,

---

[350] See Matt Fradd's *The Porn Myth*.

are not quite as mysterious as they might seem. What is all too easily forgotten is that Man is an ecological being who will be sickened, and eventually destroyed, by Modern Technology. One might be reminded that *all* technological innovations (whatever their content might be) categorically expose humans to conditions which contradict hundreds of thousands of years of evolutionary adaptation, as Kaczynski noted in the 178th paragraph of *Industrial Society and Its Future*:

> Whatever else may be the case, it is certain that technology is creating for human beings a new physical and social environment radically different from the spectrum of environments to which natural selection has adapted the human race physically and psychologically. If man is not adjusted to this new environment by being artificially re-engineered, then he will be adapted to it through a long and painful process of natural selection. The former is far more likely than the latter.[351]

Vikernes concludes the section by warning that the philosophy of materialism is the reason why Christian and feminist responses are inadequate, since both of the latter philosophies are just forms of materialism in disguise. Like much of the overall text, this section holds challenges of readability. One reason for this difficulty is that the text was written under the unusual circumstances of Vikernes's solitary confinement at a time when the prison authorities were closely monitoring his work, even confiscating some of his research materials in the process, as he mentioned in the ninth section of the book. Vikernes's own commentary on the text from his official Burzum website also reveals that he was not even allowed the luxury of proofreading the manuscript and was forced to leave it in a fragmentary, unfinished state:

---

[351] Ted Kaczynski, *Industrial Society and Its Future*, in *Technological Slavery* (Scottsdale: Fitch & Madison, 2019), para. 178.

I wrote [the book] when I was 21 years old, in late 1994. When I wrote it I had just received a 21-year conviction and I was isolated in a security block in Bergen prison for about a year. I wrote the book because I felt a strong need to defend myself against all the media lies and lie-propaganda. All my correspondence was stopped, I was allowed to talk on the phone for only 10 minutes a week and receive one (one hour) visit every week, so writing a book was basically my only way to disclose the lies of the media and talk back. "Vargsmål" was written in anger, while I was young and on isolation, and the book is marked by this. What made it even worse was the fact that the prison authorities confiscated the manuscript, and for several years I wasn't allowed to even proof-read it. It was an unfinished manuscript, consisting of many separate articles, and ideally I would have been able to make some changes before it was published, but I wasn't. Eventually I gave up and just published it as it was - with all the errors and not-so-balanced articles. I figured that it was better to live with the embarrassing errors, than not to publish it at all. [352]

Also, because of the text's supremely controversial content and its author's notorious status as the "Black Metal murderer," the unofficial translations from Norwegian to English have been criticized even by Vikernes himself as quite inadequate.[353]

Despite these difficulties, a perceptive reader can identify the following trends in his conclusion of the discussion of porn. Above all, he claims that the current "talk about sex" and the philosophy of materialism are "two sides of the same" coin, because all three mainstream views (sex positive, Christian, feminist)

---

[352]https://www.burzum.org/eng/library/a_comment_to_vargsmal_and_other_books_by_varg_vikernes.shtml

[353] "I know of at least two English translations. The one I saw, in 1999, was sent to me by the guys at www.burzum.com, and it was so bad I didn't know if I should laugh or weep or what . . . The whole translation was so horrible that I didn't even manage to read through all of it . . . My fear is that when people think of "Vargsmål" they think of this horrible attempt at an English translation"

"cannot see anything other than material pleasure in today's sex." He claims that this stems from reducing the human body to a "pleasure object" and nothing more. Interestingly, these flawed ideologies misunderstand the body precisely by obsessing over tearing away the curtain of mystery and reducing it to a naked object with no remaining social barriers inhibiting its public exposure. The mainstream critics of porn (whether Christian or feminist) who focus exclusively on religious morality or gender identity politics therefore miss the ecological point precisely through an overemphasis on materialistic concerns. Vikernes's originality as a thinker lies in his ability to recognize that ecology is not reducible to its materialistic elements; one can only really grasp the ecological dimension of a problem if one is open to its spiritual dimension as well.

The human body, ultimately, can only be understood if one grasps its spiritual content in addition to its materiality. In the author's own terminology, Vikernes claims that ecology can only occur within the mythological horizon of Pneumatic Hermeneutics. Because Vikernes rejects Christianity as just another form of materialism, he urges his fellow Norwegians to return to the pagan traditions of the Old Norse era to accomplish this spiritual shift and to escape the doomed trajectory of Modernity. Paradoxically, he implies that they can only overcome alienation from their own physically-embodied Norwegian nature if they restore the lost spiritual connection with the pagan religious traditions first. The philosophical difficulty of understanding Vikernes's thought is therefore that he appeals to the ecological evolution of a people without falling into Darwinist materialist reductivism or any other readily-available cliché. Vikernes's thought similarly contradicts the Post-Modernist cliché that "everything is language" because he insists that the embodied nature of a people cannot simply be deconstructed away because it involves ecological rather than purely ideological origins.

Vikernes argues that Norse Mythology is simultaneously a window into spiritual truth and natural truth, yet he is careful to insist that one dimension is not reducible to the other. That is to say, although the mythological account does not contradict the scientific explanation, contemporary science has not at all rendered the archaic mythologies worthless. In fact, no matter how much progress the scientists might make in their understanding of Nature, Vikernes claims that the wealth of knowledge contained in the Old Norse myths will always remain a "bottomless well" in comparison.[354]

For example, in the opening section of the text he claims that one has only really understood the mythological motif of the giant if one has understood that it is a personification of an uncontrollable force of nature, a force which only comes under control through the godly strength of Odin and his brothers.[355] The world itself was created through such an act of divine battle, in which they transformed the unruly giant Ylmir into the natural order of the world as we know it. When Odin and his two brothers killed Ylmir, the giant's skull became the heavens, his blood became the oceans, his flesh became the earth, his hair became the trees, and so on.

It is important to note, however, that this myth does not at all reduce the Earth to a dead lump of matter which lost its spiritual significance sometime in the vastly distant past; it is not just another example of John Zerzan's "will to dominate Nature." A principle of giant's life remains discernible within natural phenomena even to the present day, provided one still has the mythological resources to grasp it. For example, Norse Mythology tells us that the wind emerges when the giant Hrsvaelgr, clad in an eagle's skin, beats his wings. The waves of the ocean similarly result from the giant Egir's activity. One only retains this ability to "see the giants" behind the natural forces, however, if one retains the mythological framework of the traditional worldview. Opting for the crass materialist reductivism of contemporary scientism will never allow the natural phenomena to appear in quite the same way; at best, one will be left with an empty shell which is somehow untrue without being incorrect. Removing the pneuma leaves only linguisitification.

Vikernes's idiosyncratic views on the connection between natural truth and spiritual truth has led him to venture into

---

[354] Section One.
[355] Varg Vikernes, Vargsmål (unpublished, unofficial 1997 English translation from Norwegian manuscript).

controversial territory few would imagine entering. Like Linkola, Vikernes has distinguished himself through his willingness to shock readers by challenging technological distortions of modern life with no regard for how widely accepted they might be. In addition to the topic of pornography, few ecological thinkers, for example, would dream of challenging toothpaste. In the seventh section of the text, though, Vikernes argues that if one is really serious about criticising modern medicine as something which unexpectedly harms rather than heals the human body, one must include the historical anomaly of daily toothbrushing. One should bear in mind that although it seems absolutely necessary today, modern toothpaste is an artificial product which only became widely-used within the general population after the start of the industrial era. According to Vikernes, excessive use of a toothbrush actually makes the body *more* susceptible to cavities in the long run.

Vikernes does not single out toothpaste as uniquely evil, since he argues that any form of medicine which makes the body dependent upon the System is harmful because it directly negates the body's own natural ability to fulfil the same function. Just as toothpaste weakens the tooth's enamel, moisturizing creams negate the skin's ability to produce its own moisture. It is not only one's own body that suffers as a result; one's ecological relation to other humans is also disrupted. The human body naturally emits certain scents to attract the opposite sex, but we have willingly replaced these with artificial perfumes. He claims that if this goes on long enough, the natural scent will disappear altogether, and along with it, the very notion of humankind as a natural or ecological entity.

Vikernes does not consider any of this to be accidental. The technological destruction of Man's natural functions is not the result of some tragic miscalculation on the part of beneficent institutions which can be trusted to have Man's best interest in mind. Rather, Vikernes identifies these eco-crimes as smaller parts of a vast conspiracy by the System to enslave the population through intentionally weakening them to the point of helplessness. Vikernes differs from other so-called conspiracy theorists, however, in that he identifies that the System's crimes against the human population are ultimately eco-crimes in disguise. This means that Man's ecological dimension is the main battlefield for this competition to try to salvage human freedom. If one loses the ecological battle by allowing the System to destroy one's natural functions and one's ability to exist within one's ecosystem, any other victories will prove futile.

The early Vikernes appears to have understood the relation between ecology and politics to be built upon this opposition between Nature and the System. The return to ecological normality and the rejection of the System's artificial and anti-natural technological controls is inherently political, since the strength to rebel can only be restored through ecological means in the first place. At the same time, political engagement is inherently ecological, since the rebellion is teleologically oriented towards affirming Nature, even including the supremely politically incorrect notion of an objectively-embodied "Norwegian nature."

One can only have the power and the courage to stand against the System if one provides an ecological foundation for this strength. In the 14th section of the text, Vikernes urges his readers to reject drugs but, surprisingly, he includes coffee and coca cola in a list that includes more conventional drugs like meth and cannabis. What they all have in common, he argues, is that they are all artificial stimulants which damage the body's ability to function independently in the long term.[356] Any drug that gives the user a status he or she would not have without it is just another means for the System to control the user politically through degrading him or her ecologically. In contrast, in the 34th section of the text he recommends rigorous physical exercises, such as jogging in the forest, to build up one's strength both physically and psychologically.

In conclusion, one might argue that political action is always founded on an ecological context. No matter how hard one fights on a political level, if one loses the battle on ecological grounds through surrendering to junk food, drugs, porn, and other artificial slow-killers engineered by the System for nefarious purposes, one's best efforts will always remain insufficient. Although Vikernes does

---

[356] Section 14.

not seem to go as far as to identify these ecological contexts as somatic contexts dominated by a particular crucial resource, his insight is nonetheless far closer to the truth than any of the mainstream leftist environmentalists active today, since for them "going green" all too often simply means shopping at overpriced "organic" foods markets or protesting on street corners to bully politicians into dumping more government funds into solar panels and self-driving electric cars. Any rebellion against the System that takes the form of fighting for the "right kinds of technology" is inherently contradictory, for technology is itself the problem.

The Philosophies of Jacques Ellul and Ted Kaczynski

One might argue that for Vikernes, the primary political struggle of our era can be defined as a battle between Nature and the System. On one hand, he certainly does include artificial technologies among the means the System uses to control the population and, in this sense, he contrasts technology with Nature and, more broadly, with ecology. One might argue, though, that at least in this early text, Vikernes does not go quite far enough, since he largely considers technology to be a tool which is used by the System to accomplish goals which a handful of privileged elites consciously intend. In this sense, he understands technology to be something which has only escaped control of *some* of the human population due to an unjust political situation but remains fundamentally capable of remaining under the control of humans.

In contrast, Jacques Ellul and Ted Kaczynski have distinguished themselves through radicalizing the emphasis on Modern Technology itself. One justification lay in demonstrating that any appeal to humans "steering the machine" is illusory at best, for that would imply that there are still some humans left who are powerful enough to control the runaway train of Modern Technology. Ellul warned in *The Technological Society* that even if man continues to appear to "steer the machine, [he will do so] only at the price of his [genuinely human] individuality."[357] In other

---

[357] Jacques Ellul, *The Technological Society* (New York: Vintage Books, 1964), p. 397.

words, he will only do so at the cost of becoming something other than human in the process.

In Kaczynski's 1971 essay "Progress Versus Wilderness," he went even further by claiming that the very metaphor of trying to steer a car is a misleading way to describe the attempt to control a society steeped in Modern Technology. Because one is dealing with complex systems with emergent properties and complicated feedback loops, it would be closer to the truth to compare it to trying to divert the course of a charging elephant.[358] Even the nominal political figureheads of the System are just as incapable of determining the course which the beast of Modern Technology will take in the long run. Kaczynski noted in the first chapter of his fragmentary 2016 magnum opus *Anti-Tech Revolution: Why and How* that even before the rise of Modern Technology, figures who seemed to have absolute power such as Medieval Chinese Emperors were just as incapable of controlling major social changes against the entrenched interests within the System.[359] Of course, as Technique advanced, seemingly-supreme political leaders have become even more incapable of determining the course which their society shall take.

One need not appeal to any uniquely human conspiracy to explain this, as there is a strictly technical reason for this loss of power. As Technique progressed, the decisions themselves have grown so complicated that it is literally outside the reach of any natural brain to interfere with decision-making processes reserved for electronic brains running on autopilot. Ellul noted in *The Technological Society:*

> [O]n very advanced technical levels, unchallengeable decisions have already been made by "electronic brains" in the service of the National Bureau of Standards . . . little by

---

[358] Ted Kaczynski, "Progress Versus Wilderness," Ted Kaczynski Papers, Labadie Collection at the University of Michigan's Special Collections Library, Ann Arbor, p. 6.
[359] Ted Kaczynski, *Anti-Tech Revolution: Why and How* (Scottsdale: Fitch & Madison, 2016), p. 21.

little he [the politician] is being stripped of any real power and reduced to the role of a figurehead.[360]

For Ellul and Kaczynski, Modern Technology is not one instrument among many within the System's arsenal. Modern Technology simply *is* the System. There can be no conspiracy to use technology to advance one group's interests, for the very idea of some human agent occupying a position of superiority above the machine is progressively being ruled out as ever more farfetched. In fact, the most certain outcome of allowing Modern Technology to continue its development is nothing short of human extinction.[361] This may occur either through damaging the ecosystem so badly that it is no longer able to support complex life of any kind, though it is equally certain to follow from allowing artificially intelligent machines to progress to the point that *no human* will be deemed worthy of survival, no matter how intelligent, wealthy, or politically powerful he or she might appear to be by human standards. In either case, Kaczynski has insisted that the revolution against technology is the *only* pathway to prevent the supreme violent catastrophe.

Slavoj Zizek vs. Pentti Linkola

Not everyone shares this pessimistic view on the incompatibility of technology and human survival. Even among the great thinkers alive today, there are some who claim that technology, not Nature, provides the medium for human subjectivity to perform the leap of faith to realize its freedom the most fully.

The final chapter of Zizek's *In Defense of Lost Causes*, titled "Unbehagen in der Natur," is dedicated to addressing the problem of ecological crisis and its relation to global capitalism. Zizek included a whole chapter on ecology within this particular book because it fit into his broader theme of trying to redeem the totalitarian spirit of "big changes" in an era when such an attitude

---

[360] Jacques Ellul, *The Technological Society* (New York: Vintage Books, 1964), p. 259.
[361] Ted Kaczynski, *Anti-Tech Revolution: Why and How* (Scottsdale: Fitch & Madison, 2016), p. 70.

has become unfashionable even among so-called "radical" thinkers. Zizek argues, however, that this aversion to totalitarian terror has merely made us all into Fukuyamans in disguise. The Social Justice Movement, for example, has basically accepted that global capitalism is here to stay, so the only task that remains is to optimize it by making it "more tolerant."[362]

In contrast with this spirit of defeatism, Zizek argues that it is reasonable to seriously challenge global capitalism. This, however, can only be done through taking the leap of faith into the abyss of radical negativity by dabbling in projects which will inevitably offend modern politically correct sensibilities as "totalitarian." This broader attack on global capitalism provides the context in which even ecological threats must be situated. The irony of the situation, in other words, is that even threats against the Earth itself must be redefined in terms of their role within the all too human system of global capitalism.

Zizek's rationale for demoting ecology to this secondary position within the hierarchy of concerns was justified through arguing that ecological crises must not be fetishized into substantial problems "in themselves" but must instead be understood as only one of several different antagonisms of global capitalism. Ecological threats, along with Third World slums, are excesses generated by the "substantial base" of the global capitalist system rather than independent entities which could be analysed in abstraction from that foundation.[363]

Zizek admits, however, that the classical Marxist belief that the revolution will materialize simply as a result of inevitable historical processes has become somewhat out of date. Ecological threats in particular force us to reevaluate the old standard clichés about how waiting around for the System to self-destruct through its own contradictions and flaws will be "good enough." On the contrary, for the first time in history, we are living in an era where one subjective intervention has the potential to "directly intervene in the historical substance" through a single catastrophic disturbance. For example, it is not impossible for some bio-warfare specimen to

---

[362] Slavoj Zizek, *In Defense of Lost Causes* (London: Verso, 2008), p. 421.
[363] Ibid., p. 420.

escape a lab and bring about human extinction as a result of one subjective miscalculation. Zizek argues therefore the old Hegelian phrase "not only as substance but also as subject" is more relevant now than ever before.[364]

Although ecological thinkers stereotypically tend to call for renouncing human "instrumental reason" in favor of Adorno's mimesis or some other mystical stance of reverence for the Other, Zizek argues that this attitude actually gets the problem exactly backwards: what we need now is to seize subjective agency rather than surrender any claim to it. This claim is far from speculative, as the historical record confirms that Hugo Chavez, for example, succeeded in rebellion precisely by "going legit" within the state system rather than remaining an outsider.[365] Similarly, it is now actually the big industrial polluters and CEO's who continue to "resist the state" by circumventing its environmental regulations. Zizek asserts that we must instead grab power by the state if we hope to achieve any real change, despite the fact that such a demand will no doubt be dismissed as "totalitarian" by the liberal intelligentsia.

Zizek warns that no ecological stance can be legitimate if it disregards the class struggle criteria of a Marxist rebellion against capitalism. For example, any deep ecologist who uses the objective standard of eco-crimes to legitimize the oppression of the "polluting poor" will lose his or her credibility, because Zizek identifies ecology as a smaller part of the broader critique of global capitalism rather than the "objective factor" of our historical situation.

It will be useful to consider Zizek in direct contrast with Linkola, because for Linkola ecology is the fundamental issue, far beyond capitalism and even technology. Linkola arguably provides the most purified example of a thinker defined by a strict adherence to ecological principles without regard for the distortion of human bias, since even the dimension of empathy would have to be suspended in order to implement reductions in economic growth and human population without "giving in" to human sob stories. For this reason, he would see no reason to obey Zizek's Marxist

---

[364] Ibid., p. 421.
[365] Ibid., p. 427.

demands to subordinate ecology to capitalism, since this would only amount to giving the Third World poor a "get out of jail free card" out of owning up to their own admittedly-vast contribution to global pollution. Linkola would insist one should not elevate political criteria above ecological ones, since economic and political policies are simply a means to an end to enforcing the same set of ecological restrictions regardless of personal bias. In this sense, Linkola's hypothetical "green police" would provide a direct short circuit between the impersonal laws of Nature and the all too human institution of a regulatory force. Unclouded by social distractions, the green police would simply execute the will of Nature without personal preference for any one group, even the genuinely exploited proletariat of global capitalism.

Zizek finds this approach short-sighted because, for him, ecology is only one of four major issues confronting us today, along with the problems of intellectual property rights, unprecedented scientific developments, and new forms of apartheid/walls. Any attempt to address ecology without respecting this broader context is therefore bound for failure. This warning is not merely hypothetical, as Zizek notes that without the proper context, ecology devolves into the engineering problem of how to maintain "sustainable development" through finding some way to achieve a "green" form of capitalism. He claims that Whole Foods and Starbucks have already done just that, since they have merged consumption and political activism into a single act. We are told that there is no need to feel bad about spending $5 on a cup of coffee distributed by a major corporate organization, since a fraction of the total bill goes towards building schools in Guatemala etc.

Zizek finds this approach of "ethical consumerism" to be unsatisfactory because ecology is a problem situated within the context of the very antagonisms of global capitalism. For this reason, it is impossible to address this broader context *without* a certain amount of terror being involved. Interestingly, he borrows Kierkegaard's reference to "fear and trembling" to argue that the difference between attitudes of "fear" and the willingness to confront the "trembling" of terror provide the true standard to determine how authentic one's response to all of these problems will be. Whereas fear attempts to maintain stability against threats, only terror openly confronts the "shattering experience of negativity" necessary for any real change.[366] Zizek dismisses the majority of deep ecologists as being stuck in the mode of fear, since for them preventing disturbances and clinging to some semblance of order is the unspoken requirement which shapes their strategies in confronting ecological dangers.[367] Insofar as deep ecology is just one more space for institutionalized distrust in big changes, it only reinforces the hegemonic ideology of global capitalism.

These desperate attempts to "not rock the boat too much" are ironic, since our current trajectory is actively paving the way for the ultimate change to occur, as nothing short of Nature itself is disappearing as we speak. Shockingly, however, this is occurring precisely through having Man lose his status as a natural entity.[368] As scientists work to crack the codes to unearth how organisms function, they transform these creatures from naturalistic mysteries into fully replicable electronic appliances. Current legal frameworks provide the green light for corporations to literally come in afterwards and patent their DNA as their own "intellectual property."

Paradoxically, this is *not* the ultimate anthropocentric conquest of Nature, because it is precisely when Nature vanishes as an impenetrable mystery that Man himself also ceases to exist.[369] John Zerzan's critique of "Man's domination over the Earth" is actually somewhat out of date. Far from merely seeking to control Nature or clone it faithfully, contemporary scientific projects are actually oriented towards producing something radically new.[370] Zizek notes, both in this work and in his 2014 *Absolute Recoil*, that current efforts to advance A.I. are not at all defined by a desire to replicate the human brain; the point has shifted to generating something altogether different and unquestionably superior. Nor is

---

[366] Ibid., p. 433.
[367] Ibid., p. 438, 440.
[368] Ibid., p. 435.
[369] Ibid.
[370] Ibid., p. 436.

this attitude limited to the artificial realm of machines. Fantasies of a new biological monster that can nearly-infinitely reproduce itself asexually are bringing the psychoanalytic motif of the "undead life" one step closer to becoming an empirical object which literally exists within the world.[371]

Zizek warns, however, that the response from mainstream ecologists is fundamentally misguided, since all too often they seek to prevent these nightmarish scenarios by turning Nature into the object of a new religion. This attitude of pious devotion and fearful submission simply transforms Nature into another "unquestionable authority" which is free to impose arbitrary limits on human subjects, out of the belief that such regulations are necessary evils to curb humans' dangerous activity.[372] Under this view, Linkola's vision of a green police which directly embodies the "will of Nature" without human bias is almost like an eco-pope whose infallibility is guaranteed through a direct channel of communication to the God of Nature. Zizek warns that this is merely an unconscious reversion to religious escapism. Linkola's eco-authoritarians would therefore seem to merely substitute the Will of God for the Will of Nature and employ a new eco-priesthood to defend the sacred dogmas and punish the heretics.

Zizek finds this religious submission to Nature to be the greatest delusion of all, since it negates the Cartesian dimension of radically negative subjectivity by elevating Nature to a new sacred mystery which must never be unlocked, only bowed down to in pious reverence. He warns that this retreat into ecological context is the very antithesis of Cartesian subjectivity: "[Within this religion of deep ecology,] we are not Cartesian subjects extracted from reality, we are finite beings embedded in a biosphere which vastly transcends our horizon."[373] Zizek claims that this provides the missing link to explain why despite all of their calls for people to "radically change their behavior" to prevent collapse, the big changes never actually arrive, not even within the environmentalists' own personal lives. He argues that this failure to

---

[371] Ibid., p. 437.
[372] Ibid., p. 439.
[373] Ibid., p. 439.

enact even the most modest changes is no coincidence, since deep ecology is actually all about shying away from revolutionary disruptions in order to maintain some semblance of a functioning status quo.

Although environmentalism is often associated with the political Left, Zizek finds that it is actually an inherently conservative movement, since it assumes that "any change can only be a change for the worse."[374] This resistance to change is, however, a misunderstanding of how Nature works. Anyone who cites Darwin as a secular prophet to justify this renunciation has only missed Darwin's real point, which was precisely that Nature is not a static whole which must be maintained but is something which constantly improves itself through adaptations.[375]

In various other conference talks, Zizek has mentioned that it's peculiar to try to defend Nature against catastrophe, because Nature actually *is* the catastrophe. The fact that some 90% of human DNA is "junk" is evidence that evolution did not occur through some perfectly-engineered plan; it was in itself something of an accident and contradiction.[376] In this text as well, Zizek repeats his famous quote that it's misguided to try to save Nature because "Nature doesn't exist." Human activity is not some extrinsic obstacle which must be eliminated to allow Nature to function properly. At this point, there is quite literally no such thing as "Nature without human activity." If we disappeared tomorrow, Nature itself would collapse because it has fully adapted itself to all of our intrusions.[377]

Contrary to expectation, this realization that Nature doesn't exist is not the madness of solipsistic idealism, for Zizek assures us that it is the only stance possible for someone who is really a materialist. The true materialist accepts that Nature in itself is an idealist fiction.[378] Zizek even goes as far as to openly promote the seemingly-contradictory stance of an "ecology without Nature" as

---

[374] Ibid., p. 441.
[375] Ibid.
[376] Ibid., p. 442.
[377] Ibid., p. 442.
[378] Ibid., p. 444.

the only viable path forward. Although he does not use the term "eco-fascism" in the text, we can assume that this is exactly what he warns the reader will result if one does not accept Nature's dissolution as a substantial entity. It is reasonable to suspect that Zizek would find Linkola's ambitions for a "green police" to be fundamentally misguided because any attempt to directly embody "the will of Nature" into a human institution which would impose equally strict limits on economic growth, overpopulation, and pollution regardless of a person's status within the political context of global capitalism misses the point that there is no such thing as "the will of Nature" as such. Nature cannot have a firm, consistent message for humans to obey if it does not exist in the first place.

According to Zizek, the irony, in other words, is that the main obstacle to ecological progress is our belief that Nature exists as a whole.[379] Deep ecology calls for humans to abandon their delusions of grandeur and incorporate themselves back into the lifeworld miss the point entirely, since it is precisely the horizon of the common sense lifeworld that inhibits us from actually taking ecological threats seriously. If one gazes at the sky in its immediacy, for example, one won't see any hole in the ozone layer, only a clear blue sky. This retreat into natural beauty therefore gets the problem exactly backwards, for it is only by suspending our common sense immersion in the horizon of Nature that we can take the problem of ecological damage seriously.

Strangely, Zizek also argues that subjectivity itself can only be salvaged if we take the plunge into "materialism without Nature" and abandon the religion of deep ecology. He justifies this bizarre idea by noting the more materialized the objective body becomes, the emptier the cogito is revealed to be. Yet this void of empty subjectivity is exactly the confrontation with radical negativity which totalitarian "big picture" revolutions entail.[380]

One might be reminded that Heidegger warned the biggest danger is not that some unexpected catastrophe will occur which will reveal all the hopes of unbridled technologization to be false; on the contrary, the real danger is that the catastrophe *won't* arrive,

---

[379] Ibid., p. 445.
[380] Ibid., pp. 446-7.

and that the machine will function smoothly until the very horizon of hermeneutical openness is silently closed off forever.[381] Zizek warns that ecology has already fallen prey to this smooth incorporation into the System. After all, isn't recycling simply a technological project to maximize the usefulness of resources and prevent waste?[382] Unexpectedly, however, for this very reason, Zizek condemns any attempts to dismiss the coming post-human universe as inherently "meaningless," as though meaning could only be possible against the backdrop of traditional human nature. He argues that this is actually a very conservative way to view it, since it ignores the real point that post-humanism is all about the possibility of a multitude of possible meanings.[383]

In fact, any aversion to post-humanism which promotes a decelerationist withdrawal back into the natural life-world will fail to solve the problem of Modern Technology. It is only through seizing the radical abyss of negativity that we can find that technological post-humanism provides an outlet to liberate humans. Rather than remain stuck at the level of being "symbolic plants" rooted in a certain ecological milieu, technology actually allows us to embrace the subjective position of radical negativity, the true meaning of the Cartesian cogito.[384] The book ends with the following memorable quote: "Against the background of this acceptance, we should mobilize ourselves to perform the act which will change destiny itself and thereby insert a new possibility into the past."[385]

The Death Context

Zizek's trust that Modern Technology will allow human subjectivity to realize itself as radical negativity is based on his belief that it will allow us to definitively break the illusion that Man is bound to any one ecological milieu, even the milieu of Nature itself, which he

---

381 Ibid., pp. 447-8.
382 Ibid., p. 448.
383 Ibid., p. 449.
384 Ibid., p. 452.
385 Ibid., p. 460.

claims does not really exist. This suggests, though, that the "lost cause" he wrote this book to "defend" is none other than linguistification itself. Such a stance could only be held through devaluing ecological hermeneutics to the status of a fundamental misunderstanding. Far from being the purest form of understanding, as we have argued earlier, somatic hermeneutics would devolve into an obstacle inhibiting Man from seizing the opportunity to transcend outdated frameworks and explode into the post-human universe of new possibilities.

Isn't Zizek's dream of a post-ecological and post-humanist subjectivity simply the idea of an entity for whom the Soma is Modern Technology itself? It is inherently questionable, though, to posit this as the crucial resource for survival, because given its hard-wired orientation to bring about human extinction, Modern Technology is not just one more Soma alongside all the others. It can never disclose an ecological context that grounds the worldview and life of a people, for its true meaning is simply the death of humans and all complex life forms.

It is similarly suspect to claim that leaping into the "death context" of Modern Technology would provide the most hospitable milieu for human subjectivity to realize itself. If we consider the Techno-Industrial System as an impersonal self-propagating system oriented towards incorporating exterior influences into some mechanistic ordering or eliminating them outright if they refuse to submit, we shall find that this System has no intrinsic need for humans, especially not ones with any level of freedom. In fact, the System actively treats any manifestation of spontaneous human agency as a technical problem which it is hard-wired to remove. It is inherently contradictory to say that any ecological context could be opened up by it, let alone the ideal one. It is simply the antithesis of ecology, and the destruction of subjectivity. Robots have no deep memes, for they lack the very ability for hermeneutical interpretation. They can only reduplicate the structures generated by the System. We are all quickly becoming robots in this sense as well.

Yet even beyond the political problem of the loss of freedom under technology, one can consider the epistemological problem of what kind of knowledge the robots are forced to mindlessly reduplicate under the System's influence. The very need to capture a transcendent essence such as the number 3, π, the logical relation of implication, or the grammatical universal of the locality principle has eroded away altogether. Under Modern Technology, there is no need for a system to provide a hermeneutical space for them to "appear" because all of the constructs one works with are generated imminently through ad hoc designs and artificial engineering. In the contrived systems of Modern Technology, "3" cannot mean anything except some binary signature defined by some combination of electronic states. Even language itself devolves into a set of ones and zeros which are nothing more than high voltage and low voltage combinations. Somewhere in the process, the subject loses his or her ability to penetrate beyond the realm of the self and grasp the universal essences. Instead, the machine provides a set of closed pathways which are merely redundancies of flows of electricity.

There is no need for any ecological context to determine how a system can manifest itself according to the logic of a crucial resource, such as woolly mammoth, herd of camels, or even fossil fuels, for the pseudo-mathematical constructs have no need to appear to any conscious subject at all. Execution within hardware components actively replaces contemplation within consciousness.

These systems do not fulfill the historical trajectory which other systems have established so much as they destroy the foundation for such an inquiry to take place at all.

In archaic eras, Man largely worked with Metaphysical Systems. In Thomas Aquinas' Middle Ages, for example, every object has a meaningful essence defined by its part within the whole of the universe as designed by God, the ultimate conscious knower.

With the closing of the 18th Century and the mature stage of the Enlightenment, Man shifted to transcendental systems. With Kant, objects were revealed to have meaning only insofar as they accorded with the transcendental structures of the subject, such as the *a priori* categories, the regulative Idea, and even space and time themselves.

From Frege onwards, systems became formal. Rather than be grounded in a transcendental subject who originates the structures of meaning through some spontaneous act of synthesis, formal systems became fully autonomous while still remaining abstract. Frege and Russell held that all of the constructs of mathematics can be derived on analytic *a priori* grounds alone because they are actually just logical constructs in disguise. While the subject can access them, it is only because humans have a mysterious "power to think" these results. The results themselves would remain objectively valid even in the absence of any human minds since, according to Frege, they are located in the third realm beyond both subjective minds and objective things.

The rise of Modern Technology does not represent just one more stage in this series of phases, any more than it opens up one more Soma alongside all the others. Systems have suffered a tragic deterioration which threatens to erase the very possibility for their existence. In our era, they have become executable systems. Unlike the formal systems of Analytic Philosophy, they are fully autonomous but have lost all abstraction. Language, number, logic, and image have literally devolved to euphemisms for expenditures of fossil fuel energy. The system only "exists" as long as hardware is in a state of execution.

This discussion, important as it may be, shall have to end here, as such concerns can only be treated properly in a whole text of their own. The author's next book *Hermeneutical Death: The Technological Destruction of Subjectivity* shall resume this discussion by providing a sequel to the present text. Together, the two make up the interlude between the two volumes of *Being and Oil*.

Among the technophile worshippers of progress, the subject has already vanished entirely. The struggle to prevent this aforementioned hermeneutical death by technology from extending to the rest of the population, effectively blotting out the final remaining islands of mentatic light by driving them irreversibly into non-hermeneutical darkness, is the single most important battle of our era. Above all, this is the fight to salvage ecology through saving the very horizon of interpretation while the dimming candle of subjectivity still flickers. It remains to be seen whether it will be enough.

Made in the USA
Las Vegas, NV
18 June 2023

73603110R00152